MOHAMMAD

The Prophet and Messenger of Allah

DR. TAREK ZAYED

©journeytoparadise.org
journeytoparadise2020@gmail.com

Published by Journey to Paradise, Org., 2021
www.journeytoparadise.org
journeytoparadise2020@gmail.com
© Copyright 2021 by Tarek Zayed. All rights reserved.

First Edition

1442 / 2021
All rights reserved for
Journey to Paradise

For charitable printing and distribution of the book,
Please, contact:
journeytoparadise2020@gmail.com

TABLE OF CONTENTS

Chapter	PAGE
Preface	1
Chapter I: Exceptional Morals of our Beloved Prophet	6
Chapter II: Remarkable Social Intelligence of our Beloved Prophet	23
Chapter III: The Prophet as a Role Model for Husbands	36
Chapter IV: The Prophet as a Role Model for Fathers	42
Chapter V: The Prophet as a Role Model for Teachers	53
Chapter VI: The Prophet as a Role Model for Leaders	65
Chapter VII: Concluded Remarks and Recommendations	76
References	82

Preface

O Allah Guide them... They Do Not Know our Beloved Prophet

One cannot neglect what is happening these days in France and the reflection of Muslims across the globe. Every now and then, few people try to insult our beloved Prophet by publishing few inappropriate drawings that reflect their ignorance about him (SAS). Such people think, by this action, that they are able to dilute the image or reduce the respect of our Prophet in the minds and hearts of others. However, they are not able to achieve their objectives because the characters of our Prophet (SAS) are unbeatable and his position in the hearts of people is higher than their reach. The reputation of the Prophet (SAS) in the minds of people is unshakable. No one, whether he/she is a believer or not, read the biography of the Prophet (SAS) without standing out of respect to him. His characters (SAS) are great and amazing, which oblige his followers and enemies to admire and regard him. These characters position him (SAS) in the best creation of Allah (SWT). Therefore, let me teach those who are ignorant of the Prophet (SAS): Who is he? What are his characters? How can we support him (SAS)?

The Prophet (SAS) has great personal characters and always recommends his followers to attain such type of characters. This is central to the core values of believers wherever they are. He (SAS) knows that good characters lead to success in life. For example, a scientist will not have a great success in his/her career without a strong code of ethics and conduct. A husband will not succeed in building a strong family without high standard of ethics, morals, and characters. Similarly, success in all life matters cannot be accomplished without good characters. Scholars, therefore, said that religion is but a set of good characters. The Prophet (SAS) practiced and recommended all his followers to practice good characters with all human beings whether they are followers or opponents. Let us walk through several verses and narrations that support the above argument. He (SAS) emphasizes the essence of good character in the following narration:

وعن أبى الدرداء رضي الله عنه: أن النبى ﷺ قال: "ما من شئ أثقل في ميزان المؤمن يوم القيامة من حسن الخلق، وإن الله يبغض الفاحش البذي" رواه الترمذي وقال: حديث حسن صحيح.

Abud-Darda (May Allah be pleased with him) reported: The Prophet (ﷺ) said, "Nothing will be heavier on the Day of Resurrection in the Scale of the believer than good manners. Allah hates one who utters foul or coarse language." [At-Tirmidhi, who classified it as Hadith Hasan Sahih]. https://sunnah.com/riyadussalihin/introduction/625

In the following narration, he (SAS) stresses on the fact that good character is heavier in our scale of deeds than anything else, in the day of Judgement.

عَنْ أَبِي الدَّرْدَاءِ، قَالَ سَمِعْتُ النَّبِيَّ ﷺ يَقُولُ "مَا مِنْ شَيْءٍ يُوضَعُ فِي الْمِيزَانِ أَثْقَلُ مِنْ حُسْنِ الْخُلُقِ وَإِنَّ صَاحِبَ حُسْنِ الْخُلُقِ لَيَبْلُغُ بِهِ دَرَجَةَ صَاحِبِ الصَّوْمِ وَالصَّلاَةِ" . قَالَ أَبُو عِيسَى هَذَا حَدِيثٌ غَرِيبٌ مِنْ هَذَا الْوَجْهِ . رواه الترمذي

Abu Ad-Dardh narrated that the Messenger of Allah said: "Nothing is placed on the Scale that is heavier than good character. Indeed the person with good character will have attained the rank of the person of fasting and prayer." Jami` at-Tirmidhi 2003. https://sunnah.com/tirmidhi/27/109

He (SAS) was the first one to practice such good characters and requested from his followers to act upon his teachings. His characters (SAS) were well known to and appreciated by everyone as shown in the following narration:

وعن أنس رضي الله عنه قال: كان رسول الله ﷺ أحسن الناس خلقاً (متفق عليه).

Anas (May Allah be pleased with him) reported: The Messenger of Allah (ﷺ) was the best of all the people in behaviour. [Al- Bukhari and Muslim]. https://sunnah.com/riyadussalihin/introduction/620

I am really amazed of the Prophet's (SAS) great characters and how the creator of this universe (Allah (SWT)) describes him in the Quran. Let us walk through few verses of the Quran and how he (SAS) is highly regarded in them:

1- Allah (SWT) describes the Prophet (SAS) as the person of great morals and characters as shown in the following verse:

وَإِنَّكَ لَعَلَىٰ خُلُقٍ عَظِيمٍ(4) القلم (https://quran.com/68/4/)

Chapter Al-Qalam **(4) And indeed, you are of a great moral character.**

2- He (SAS) is also described as the great example and role model for all human beings in all matters, in this life, as follows:

لَقَدْ كَانَ لَكُمْ فِي رَسُولِ اللَّهِ أُسْوَةٌ حَسَنَةٌ لِمَن كَانَ يَرْجُو اللَّهَ وَالْيَوْمَ الْآخِرَ وَذَكَرَ اللَّهَ كَثِيرًا(21) الأحزاب

Chapter Al-Ahzab **(21) There has certainly been for you in the Messenger of Allah an excellent pattern for anyone whose hope is in Allah and the Last Day and [who] remembers Allah often.** (https://quran.com/33/21/)

3- In the following verse, Allah (SWT) is explaining the rationale of sending his Messenger, Muhammad (SAS), to humanity.

هُوَ الَّذِي بَعَثَ فِي الْأُمِّيِّينَ رَسُولًا مِنْهُمْ يَتْلُو عَلَيْهِمْ آيَاتِهِ وَيُزَكِّيهِمْ وَيُعَلِّمُهُمُ الْكِتَابَ وَالْحِكْمَةَ وَإِن كَانُوا مِن قَبْلُ لَفِي ضَلَالٍ مُبِينٍ(2) الجمعة (https://quran.com/62/2/)

Chapter Al-Jumaah **(2) It is He who has sent among the unlettered a Messenger from themselves reciting to them His verses and purifying them and teaching them the Book and wisdom - although they were before in clear error –**

Purifying people is the main reason behind the Prophet's message. Purification includes the body, the spirit, the soul, and the intention from any unlawful thoughts, actions, and characters. Such purification cannot be accomplished by someone who is not purified. On the contrary, in order to purify others, you should be at the maximum level of purification. He (SAS) is the role model of pure heart, spirit, soul, and thoughts.

4- Allah (SWT) continues describing the Prophet (SAS) of being lenient towards and merciful with people around him, otherwise, he would have lost all of them. This character distinguishes him (SAS) from all his peers who are rude and harsh as they live in a tough environment. Having such a great character in this place, i.e., Makkah, at this era is a great deal because of the tough nature in the desert life. This nature impacted the character of people and all aspects of their social life. It is quite clear that the character of Prophet's lenience helped much in opening the hearts of people to him, in getting people closer to him, and in taking him as a great model as follows:

فَبِمَا رَحْمَةٍ مِنَ اللَّهِ لِنْتَ لَهُمْ ۖ وَلَوْ كُنْتَ فَظًّا غَلِيظَ الْقَلْبِ لَانْفَضُّوا مِنْ حَوْلِكَ ۖ فَاعْفُ عَنْهُمْ وَاسْتَغْفِرْ لَهُمْ وَشَاوِرْهُمْ فِي الْأَمْرِ ۖ فَإِذَا عَزَمْتَ فَتَوَكَّلْ عَلَى اللَّهِ ۚ إِنَّ اللَّهَ يُحِبُّ الْمُتَوَكِّلِينَ(159) آل عمران (https://quran.com/3/159/)

Chapter Al-Imran **(159) So by mercy from Allah, [O Muhammad], you were lenient with them. And if you had been rude [in speech] and harsh in heart, they would have disbanded from about you. So pardon them and ask forgiveness for them and consult them in the matter. And when you have decided, then rely upon Allah. Indeed, Allah loves those who rely [upon Him].**

5- The described Prophet's characters in the following verse are fascinating. The Prophet (SAS), who was one of the people living in Arabia, was sent to his people with the great message of good character. His message was to save them from the miserable life and the distracted Hereafter. He (SAS) had a great heart to be very keen about saving his people and consequently, the humanity. He did not like for his people to pass through hardships in both lives, i.e., this life and the Hereafter. He cared much of them with his heart broken when they did not listen to him (SAS). He was also blessed with the utmost kindness and mercy to all people as shown in the following verse:

لَقَدْ جَاءَكُمْ رَسُولٌ مِنْ أَنْفُسِكُمْ عَزِيزٌ عَلَيْهِ مَا عَنِتُّمْ حَرِيصٌ عَلَيْكُم بِالْمُؤْمِنِينَ رَءُوفٌ رَّحِيمٌ(128) التوبة

Chapter Al-Tawbah **(128) There has certainly come to you a Messenger from among yourselves. Grievous to him is what you suffer; [he is] concerned over you and to the believers is kind and merciful.** (https://quran.com/9/128/)

6- The description of Allah (SWT) to the Prophet (SAS) in the following verse is comprehensive. He (SAS) was sent as a mercy to all mankind until the day of Judgement. Imam Al-Qurtubi said: "Whoever believes in the Prophet and his message will be the winner in all lives with full of pleasure. And whoever disbelieves in him and his message will be given the opportunity to return back until death. They would not be collectively punished in this life due to their disbelief compared to the disbelievers in the old times." This is why he (SAS) was a mercy to all human beings, i.e., believers and disbelievers.

وَمَا أَرْسَلْنَاكَ إِلَّا رَحْمَةً لِلْعَالَمِينَ(107) الأنبياء (https://quran.com/21/107/)

Chapter Al-Anbiyaa **(107) And We have not sent you, [O Muhammad], except as a mercy to the worlds.**

The Prophet (SAS) was once asked to pray to Allah to curse the disbelievers. His answer was exceptional. He rejected to accept the request and explained that he was sent as a mercy to all humanity not as a means of harm to them as shown in the following narration:

عَنْ أَبِي هُرَيْرَةَ، قَالَ قِيلَ يَا رَسُولَ اللَّهِ ادْعُ عَلَى الْمُشْرِكِينَ قَالَ " إِنِّي لَمْ أُبْعَثْ لَعَّانًا وَإِنَّمَا بُعِثْتُ رَحْمَةً " . مسلم

Abu Huraira reported it was said to Allah's Messenger (ﷺ): Invoke curse upon the polytheists, whereupon he said: I have not been sent as the invoker of curse, but I have been sent as mercy." Sahih Muslim 2599, https://sunnah.com/muslim/45/111

7- The Prophet (SAS) was very sad for and sympathized with the disbelievers because they did not know what would happen to them in the Hereafter. He had a broken heart for them to the extent that Allah (SWT) mentioned such emotional moments of the Prophet (SAS) in many verses. An example is shown in the following verse:

........فَلَا تَذْهَبْ نَفْسُكَ عَلَيْهِمْ حَسَرَاتٍ ۚ إِنَّ اللَّهَ عَلِيمٌ بِمَا يَصْنَعُونَ(8) فاطر (https://quran.com/35/8)

Chapter Fatir **(8) Then is one to whom the evil of his deed has been made attractive so he considers it good [like one rightly guided]? For indeed, Allah sends astray whom He wills and guides whom He wills. So do not let yourself perish over them in regret. Indeed, Allah is Knowing of what they do.**

Isn't that a great heart to be broken for the people who were torturing him and his companions? This example is exactly similar to the mother who has broken heart for her kids who have bad character(s)/behavior(s). Although she knows they are hurting themselves by their actions, but still she loves for them to come back and practice good characters. Her heart is always with them, praying for them, and hoping for their return to be good. This is how the Prophet (SAS) looks after all human beings, believers and disbelievers. His mercy (SAS) exceeded that of the parents to their kids.

It is really amazing when Allah (SWT) describes a human being by such extraordinary descriptions. Try to think about it on the scale of Allah (SWT) not on our scale. How amazing this person whom Allah (SWT) describes as of great character. Look at the answer of the mother of believers, Aishah, may Allah be pleased with her, to a question about the character of the Prophet (SAS) as shown in the following narration:

عَنْ سَعْدِ بْنِ هِشَامٍ، ..... . قَالَ يَا أُمَّ الْمُؤْمِنِينَ أَنْبِئِينِي عَنْ خُلُقِ رَسُولِ اللَّهِ ﷺ . قَالَتْ أَلَيْسَ تَقْرَأُ الْقُرْآنَ قَالَ قُلْتُ بَلَى . قَالَتْ فَإِنَّ خُلُقَ نَبِيِّ اللَّهِ ﷺ الْقُرْآنُ . ..... .سنن النسائي

It was narrated from Sa'd bin Hisham that: ....I asked Aishah: "O Mother of the Believers, tell me about the character of the Messenger of Allah." She said: "Don't you read the Qur'an?" I said: "Yes." She said "The character of the Messenger of Allah (ﷺ) was the Qur'an." ...." Sunan an-Nasa'i 1601. https://sunnah.com/nasai/20/4

Let us contemplate the character of the Prophet (SAS) that is described as the practical implementation of the Quran. Since Quran is the word of Allah (SWT), therefore, the characters of the Prophet (SAS) are considered the true realization of Quran in the human being's life and practice. They are considered the real hands-on training of Quran implementation in our daily life as humans. As explained by Anas Ibn Malik, may Allah be pleased with him, that he served the Prophet (SAS) for 10 years during which he (SAS) never talked harshly to him:

عَنْ أَنَسِ بْنِ مَالِكٍ قال: ما مسست ديباجاً ولاحريراً ألين من كف رسول الله ﷺ ، ولا شممت رائحة قط أطيب من رائحة رسول الله ﷺ ولقد خدمت رسول الله ﷺ عشر سنين، فما قال لي قط :أف، ولا قال لشئ فعلته: لم فعلته؟ ولا لشئ لم أفعله: ألا فعلت كذا؟ (متفق عليه).

Anas (May Allah be pleased with him) reported: I never felt any piece of velvet or silk softer than the palm of the Messenger of Allah (ﷺ), nor did I smell any fragrance more pleasant than the smell of Messenger of Allah (ﷺ). I served him for ten years, and he never said 'Uff' (an expression of disgust) to me. He never said 'why did you do that?' for something I had done, nor did he ever say 'why did you not do such and such' for something I had not done. [Al- Bukhari and Muslim]. https://sunnah.com/riyadussalihin/introduction/621

Imagine yourself living and working with another person for 10 years without any issues and concerns that make this person mad at you. Can we imagine something like that to happen or even just to dream of it? It is unbelievable to have such amazing characters and morals. Such type of people is very exceptional in this life. In another narration, Abu Sa'id described the Prophet (SAS) as follows:

عَنْ عَبْدِ اللَّهِ بْنِ عُبَيْدِ اللَّهِ مَوْلَى أَنَسٍ قَالَ: سَمِعْتُ أَبَا سَعِيدٍ قَالَ: كَانَ النَّبِيُّ ﷺ أَشَدَّ حَيَاءً مِنَ الْعَذْرَاءِ فِي خِدْرِهَا، وَكَانَ إِذَا كَرِهَ شَيْئًا عَرَفْنَاهُ فِي وَجْهِهِ. , صححه الألباني

Abu Sa'id said, "The Prophet, may Allah bless him and grant him peace, had more modesty than a virgin in her tent. When he disliked something, that could be seen in his face." Sahih (Al-Albani). https://sunnah.com/adab/30/62

In conclusion, the person, whom some ignorant people are trying to insult, i.e., the Prophet (SAS), is an incredible person based on the description of his character by the creator, Allah (SWT), and the Prophet's companions. If the Prophet (SAS) is living in our era, the world would have been totally different. The above description in this chapter is too little to what he (SAS) deserves. In the coming chapters, I will continue discussing his characters (SAS) in more depth.

Recommendations:

Based upon the above discussion, I think the Prophet (SAS) deserve our continuous remembrance and prayers/supplications. Therefore, I am recommending to pray or supplicate for the Prophet (SAS) many times daily according to his recommendation as shown below:

وعن عبد الله بن عمرو بن العاص، رضي الله عنهما أنه سمع رسول الله ﷺ يقول: "من صلى علي صلاة، صلى الله عليه بها عشرًا" (رواه مسلم).

1- 'Abdullah bin 'Amr bin Al-'As (May Allah be pleased with them) reported: I heard the Messenger of Allah (ﷺ) saying: "Whoever supplicates Allah to exalt my mention, Allah will exalt his mention ten times." [Muslim]. https://sunnah.com/riyadussalihin/14/1

وعن أبي محمد كعب بن عجرة رضي الله عنه قال: خرج علينا النبي ﷺ فقلنا: يا رسول الله، قد علمنا كيف نسلم عليك، فكيف نصلي عليك؟ قال: "قولوا: اللهم صلِ على محمد، وعلى آل محمد، كما صليت على آل إبراهيم، إنك حميد مجيد. اللهم بارك على محمد وعلى آل محمد، كما باركت على آل إبراهيم، إنك حميد مجيد" (متفق عليه).

2- Abu Muhammad Ka'b bin 'Ujrah (May Allah be pleased with him) reported: The Prophet (ﷺ) came to us and we asked him, "O Messenger of Allah, we already know how to greet you (i.e., say As-salamu 'alaikum), but how should we supplicate for you?" He (ﷺ) said, "Say: [O Allah, exalt the mention of Muhammad and the family of Muhammad as you exalted the family of Ibrahim. You are Praised and Glorious. O Allah, bless Muhammad and the family of Muhammad as You blessed the family of Ibrahim. You are Praised and Glorious.'" [Al-Bukhari and Muslim]. https://sunnah.com/riyadussalihin/14/9

Chapter I

Exceptional Morals of our Beloved Prophet

In the preface, I have walked you through the main characters of our beloved Prophet (SAS) that have been described by Allah (SWT) and his companions. We have concluded that the Prophet (SAS) has been an incredible person with high standards of ethics and morale. If the Prophet (SAS) is alive right now, the world would have changed and the truth would have been better spread worldwide. Unfortunately, we are in an era of disrespect to and undermining of good characters. In this chapter, I will go deeply in various types of characters that are attained and practiced by our beloved Prophet (SAS). Looking at these characters and values, I feel ashamed of partially practicing such incredible morale. Allah (SWT) sends the Prophet (SAS) to be a human role model for all of us to follow. If we do not, we are losers in this life and in the Hereafter. If you look for the authentic narrations that show the great character of the prophet (SAS), you will find tens of them that need books to cover all. However, due to size limitation, I will only present a selected sample of narrations. Before I classify different narrations to different characters of the Prophet (SAS), let me introduce the comprehensive description of Khadejah, mother of believers, May Allah be pleased with her, in the following narration (highlighted in blue).

عَنْ عَائِشَةَ أُمِّ الْمُؤْمِنِينَ، أَنَّهَا قَالَتْ أَوَّلُ مَا بُدِئَ بِهِ رَسُولُ اللَّهِ ﷺ مِنَ الْوَحْىِ الرُّؤْيَا الصَّالِحَةُ فِي النَّوْمِ، فَكَانَ لاَ يَرَى رُؤْيَا إِلاَّ جَاءَتْ مِثْلَ فَلَقِ الصُّبْحِ، ثُمَّ حُبِّبَ إِلَيْهِ الْخَلاَءُ، وَكَانَ يَخْلُو بِغَارِ حِرَاءٍ فَيَتَحَنَّثُ فِيهِ ـ وَهُوَ التَّعَبُّدُ ـ اللَّيَالِيَ ذَوَاتِ الْعَدَدِ قَبْلَ أَنْ يَنْزِعَ إِلَى أَهْلِهِ، وَيَتَزَوَّدُ لِذَلِكَ، ثُمَّ يَرْجِعُ إِلَى خَدِيجَةَ، فَيَتَزَوَّدُ لِمِثْلِهَا، حَتَّى جَاءَهُ الْحَقُّ وَهُوَ فِي غَارِ حِرَاءٍ، فَجَاءَهُ الْمَلَكُ فَقَالَ اقْرَأْ. قَالَ " مَا أَنَا بِقَارِئٍ ". قَالَ " فَأَخَذَنِي فَغَطَّنِي حَتَّى بَلَغَ مِنِّي الْجَهْدَ، ثُمَّ أَرْسَلَنِي فَقَالَ اقْرَأْ. قُلْتُ مَا أَنَا بِقَارِئٍ. فَأَخَذَنِي فَغَطَّنِي الثَّانِيَةَ حَتَّى بَلَغَ مِنِّي الْجَهْدَ، ثُمَّ أَرْسَلَنِي فَقَالَ اقْرَأْ. فَقُلْتُ مَا أَنَا بِقَارِئٍ. فَأَخَذَنِي فَغَطَّنِي الثَّالِثَةَ، ثُمَّ أَرْسَلَنِي فَقَالَ ﴿اقْرَأْ بِاسْمِ رَبِّكَ الَّذِي خَلَقَ * خَلَقَ الإِنْسَانَ مِنْ عَلَقٍ * اقْرَأْ وَرَبُّكَ الأَكْرَمُ﴾ ". فَرَجَعَ بِهَا رَسُولُ اللَّهِ ﷺ يَرْجُفُ فُؤَادُهُ، فَدَخَلَ عَلَى خَدِيجَةَ بِنْتِ خُوَيْلِدٍ رضى الله عنها فَقَالَ " زَمِّلُونِي زَمِّلُونِي ". فَزَمَّلُوهُ حَتَّى ذَهَبَ عَنْهُ الرَّوْعُ، فَقَالَ لِخَدِيجَةَ وَأَخْبَرَهَا الْخَبَرَ " لَقَدْ خَشِيتُ عَلَى نَفْسِي ". فَقَالَتْ خَدِيجَةُ كَلاَّ وَاللَّهِ مَا يُخْزِيكَ اللَّهُ أَبَدًا، إِنَّكَ لَتَصِلُ الرَّحِمَ، وَتَحْمِلُ الْكَلَّ، وَتَكْسِبُ الْمَعْدُومَ، وَتَقْرِي الضَّيْفَ، وَتُعِينُ عَلَى نَوَائِبِ الْحَقِّ. فَانْطَلَقَتْ بِهِ خَدِيجَةُ حَتَّى أَتَتْ بِهِ وَرَقَةَ بْنَ نَوْفَلِ بْنِ أَسَدِ بْنِ عَبْدِ الْعُزَّى ابْنَ عَمِّ خَدِيجَةَ ـ وَكَانَ امْرَأً تَنَصَّرَ فِي الْجَاهِلِيَّةِ، وَكَانَ يَكْتُبُ الْكِتَابَ الْعِبْرَانِيَّ، فَيَكْتُبُ مِنَ الإِنْجِيلِ بِالْعِبْرَانِيَّةِ مَا شَاءَ اللَّهُ أَنْ يَكْتُبَ، وَكَانَ شَيْخًا كَبِيرًا قَدْ عَمِيَ ـ فَقَالَتْ لَهُ خَدِيجَةُ يَا ابْنَ عَمِّ اسْمَعْ مِنَ ابْنِ أَخِيكَ. فَقَالَ لَهُ وَرَقَةُ يَا ابْنَ أَخِي مَاذَا تَرَى فَأَخْبَرَهُ رَسُولُ اللَّهِ ﷺ خَبَرَ مَا رَأَى. فَقَالَ لَهُ وَرَقَةُ هَذَا النَّامُوسُ الَّذِي نَزَّلَ اللَّهُ عَلَى مُوسَى ﷺ يَا لَيْتَنِي فِيهَا جَذَعًا، لَيْتَنِي أَكُونُ حَيًّا إِذْ يُخْرِجُكَ قَوْمُكَ. فَقَالَ رَسُولُ اللَّهِ ﷺ " أَوَمُخْرِجِيَّ هُمْ ". قَالَ نَعَمْ، لَمْ يَأْتِ رَجُلٌ قَطُّ بِمِثْلِ مَا جِئْتَ بِهِ إِلاَّ عُودِيَ، وَإِنْ يُدْرِكْنِي يَوْمُكَ أَنْصُرْكَ نَصْرًا مُؤَزَّرًا. ثُمَّ لَمْ يَنْشَبْ وَرَقَةُ أَنْ تُوُفِّيَ وَفَتَرَ الْوَحْىُ.

رواه البخارى

Narrated 'Aisha: (the mother of the faithful believers) The commencement of the Divine Inspiration to Allah's Messenger (ﷺ) was in the form of good dreams which came true like bright daylight, and then the love of seclusion was bestowed upon him. He used to go in seclusion in the cave of Hira where he used to worship (Allah alone) continuously for many days before his desire to see his family. He used to take with him the journey food for the stay and then come back to (his wife) Khadija to take his food likewise again till suddenly the Truth descended upon him while he was in the cave of Hira. The angel came to him and asked him to read. The Prophet (ﷺ) replied, "I do not know how to read." The Prophet (ﷺ) added, "The angel caught me (forcefully) and pressed me so hard that I could not bear it any more. He then released me and again asked me to read and I replied, 'I do not know how to read.' Thereupon he caught me again and pressed me a second time till I could not bear it any more. He then released me and again asked me to read but again I replied, 'I do not know how to read (or what shall I read)?' Thereupon he caught me for the third time and pressed me, and then released me and said, 'Read in the name of your Lord, who has created (all that exists), created man from a clot. Read! And your Lord is the Most Generous." (96.1, 96.2, 96.3) Then Allah's Messenger (ﷺ) returned with the Inspiration and with his heart beating severely. Then he went to Khadija bint Khuwailid and said, "Cover me! Cover me!" They covered him till his fear was over and after that he told her everything that had happened and said, "I fear that something may happen to me." **Khadija replied, "Never! By Allah, Allah will never disgrace you. You keep good relations with your kith and kin, help the poor and the destitute, serve your guests generously and assist the deserving calamity-afflicted ones."** Khadija then accompanied him to her cousin Waraqa bin Naufal bin Asad bin 'Abdul 'Uzza, who, during the pre-Islamic Period became a Christian and used to write the writing with Hebrew letters. He would write from the Gospel in Hebrew as much as Allah wished him to write. He was an old man and had lost his eyesight. Khadija said to Waraqa, "Listen to the story of your nephew, O my cousin!" Waraqa asked, "O my nephew! What have you seen?" Allah's Messenger (ﷺ) described whatever he had seen. Waraqa said, "This is the same one who keeps the secrets (angel Gabriel) whom Allah had sent to Moses. I wish I were young and could live up to the time when your people would turn you out." Allah's Messenger (ﷺ) asked, "Will they drive me out?" Waraqa replied in the affirmative and said, "Anyone (man) who came with something similar to what you have brought was treated with hostility; and if I should remain alive till the day when you will be turned out then I would support you strongly." But after a few days Waraqa died and the Divine Inspiration was also paused for a while. Sahih al-Bukhari. https://sunnah.com/bukhari/1/3

The Prophet (SAS) has always helped the needy, being fair, and never demoralize anyone. He has always been approachable and available for those who need support. These are the main Prophet's characters that will never let him down and guarantee the support of Allah (SWT) to him. In the following sections of this chapter, let us start looking deeply at the Prophet's specific characters and deduce lessons learned.

Character of Truthfulness and Honesty
The characters of truthfulness and honesty have made the Prophet (SAS) unique and pioneer in his generation. No one, whether a friend or an enemy, has been able to deny these characters as they were obvious in him (SAS) even before knowing that he is selected to be a Messenger of Allah (SWT). He has been distinct among his peers and within Makkah as the trustful and honest. There are many incidents that prove the trustfulness and honesty of the Prophet (SAS), however, no space to mention all of them here. I will just show few examples to highlight the essence of these two characters in him (SAS). For example, when the Prophet has been ordered to go in public with his message, he asked Makkah residence to gather in an open space and listen to him (SAS). They have been gathered where he (SAS) asked them a question as follows:

عَنِ ابْنِ عَبَّاسٍ ـ رضى الله عنهما ـ قَالَ لَمَّا نَزَلَتْ {وَأَنْذِرْ عَشِيرَتَكَ الأَقْرَبِينَ} صَعِدَ النَّبِيُّ ﷺ عَلَى الصَّفَا فَجَعَلَ يُنَادِي " يَا بَنِي فِهْرٍ، يَا بَنِي عَدِيٍّ ". لِبُطُونِ قُرَيْشٍ حَتَّى اجْتَمَعُوا، فَجَعَلَ الرَّجُلُ إِذَا لَمْ يَسْتَطِعْ أَنْ يَخْرُجَ أَرْسَلَ رَسُولاً لِيَنْظُرَ مَا هُوَ، فَجَاءَ أَبُو لَهَبٍ وَقُرَيْشٌ فَقَالَ " أَرَأَيْتَكُمْ لَوْ أَخْبَرْتُكُمْ أَنَّ خَيْلاً بِالْوَادِي تُرِيدُ أَنْ تُغِيرَ عَلَيْكُمْ، أَكُنْتُمْ مُصَدِّقِيَّ ". قَالُوا نَعَمْ، مَا جَرَّبْنَا عَلَيْكَ إِلاَّ صِدْقًا. قَالَ " فَإِنِّي نَذِيرٌ لَكُمْ بَيْنَ يَدَىْ عَذَابٍ شَدِيدٍ ". ..... رواه البخارى

Narrated Ibn `Abbas: When the Verse:--'And warn your tribe of near-kindred, was revealed, the Prophet (ﷺ) ascended the Safa (mountain) and started calling, "O Bani Fihr! O Bani `Adi!" addressing various tribes of Quraish till they were assembled. Those who could not come themselves, sent their messengers to see what was there. Abu Lahab and other people from Quraish came and the Prophet (ﷺ) then said, "Suppose I told you that there is an (enemy) cavalry in the valley intending to attack you, would you believe me?" They said, "Yes, for we have not found you telling anything other than the truth." He then said, "I am a warner to you in face of a terrific punishment." ...." (111.1-5), Sahih al-Bukhari 4770. https://sunnah.com/bukhari/65/292

This was evident of his great characters based on the impression of his enemies. Let us look at another incident that has occurred despite the huge conflict with the disbelievers in Makkah. Abu Suffyan was the leader of Makkah and a disbeliever at the time of this incident. When he visited Al-Sham, i.e., Syria, Lebanon, Palestine, and Jordan, he was called by Hercules, the ruler of Roman at this time. Hercules asked Abu-Suffyan about the Prophet (SAS) where he answered as follows:

عَنِ ابْنِ عَبَّاسٍ، أَنَّ أَبَا سُفْيَانَ، أَخْبَرَهُ مِنْ، فِيهِ إِلَى فِيهِ قَالَ انْطَلَقْتُ فِي الْمُدَّةِ الَّتِي كَانَتْ بَيْنِي وَبَيْنَ رَسُولِ اللَّهِ ﷺ قَالَ فَبَيْنَا أَنَا بِالشَّأْمِ إِذْ جِيءَ بِكِتَابٍ مِنْ رَسُولِ اللَّهِ ﷺ إِلَى هِرَقْلَ يَعْنِي عَظِيمَ الرُّومِ ـ قَالَ ـ وَكَانَ دِحْيَةُ الْكَلْبِيُّ جَاءَ بِهِ فَدَفَعَهُ إِلَى عَظِيمِ بُصْرَى فَدَفَعَهُ عَظِيمُ بُصْرَى إِلَى هِرَقْلَ فَقَالَ هِرَقْلُ هَلْ هَا هُنَا أَحَدٌ مِنْ قَوْمِ هَذَا الرَّجُلِ الَّذِي يَزْعُمُ أَنَّهُ نَبِيٌّ قَالُوا نَعَمْ ـ قَالَ ـ فَدُعِيتُ فِي نَفَرٍ مِنْ قُرَيْشٍ فَدَخَلْنَا عَلَى هِرَقْلَ فَأَجْلَسَنَا بَيْنَ يَدَيْهِ فَقَالَ أَيُّكُمْ أَقْرَبُ نَسَبًا مِنْ هَذَا الرَّجُلِ الَّذِي يَزْعُمُ أَنَّهُ نَبِيٌّ فَقَالَ أَبُو سُفْيَانَ فَقُلْتُ أَنَا فَأَجْلَسُونِي بَيْنَ يَدَيْهِ وَأَجْلَسُوا أَصْحَابِي خَلْفِي ثُمَّ دَعَا بِتَرْجُمَانِهِ فَقَالَ لَهُ قُلْ لَهُمْ إِنِّي سَائِلٌ هَذَا عَنِ الرَّجُلِ الَّذِي يَزْعُمُ أَنَّهُ نَبِيٌّ فَإِنْ كَذَبَنِي فَكَذِّبُوهُ . قَالَ فَقَالَ أَبُو سُفْيَانَ وَايْمُ اللَّهِ لَوْلاَ مَخَافَةُ أَنْ يُؤْثَرَ عَلَىَّ الْكَذِبُ لَكَذَبْتُ . ثُمَّ قَالَ لِتَرْجُمَانِهِ سَلْهُ كَيْفَ حَسَبُهُ فِيكُمْ قَالَ قُلْتُ هُوَ فِينَا ذُو حَسَبٍ قَالَ فَهَلْ كَانَ مِنْ آبَائِهِ مَلِكٌ قَالَ قُلْتُ لاَ . قَالَ فَهَلْ كُنْتُمْ تَتَّهِمُونَهُ بِالْكَذِبِ قَبْلَ أَنْ يَقُولَ مَا قَالَ قُلْتُ لاَ . قَالَ وَمَنْ يَتَّبِعُهُ أَشْرَافُ النَّاسِ أَمْ ضُعَفَاؤُهُمْ قَالَ قُلْتُ بَلْ ضُعَفَاؤُهُمْ . قَالَ أَيَزِيدُونَ أَمْ يَنْقُصُونَ قَالَ قُلْتُ لاَ بَلْ يَزِيدُونَ . قَالَ هَلْ يَرْتَدُّ أَحَدٌ مِنْهُمْ عَنْ دِينِهِ بَعْدَ أَنْ يَدْخُلَ فِيهِ سَخْطَةً لَهُ قَالَ قُلْتُ لاَ . قَالَ فَهَلْ قَاتَلْتُمُوهُ قُلْتُ نَعَمْ . قَالَ فَكَيْفَ كَانَ قِتَالُكُمْ إِيَّاهُ قَالَ قُلْتُ تَكُونُ الْحَرْبُ بَيْنَنَا وَبَيْنَهُ سِجَالاً يُصِيبُ مِنَّا وَنُصِيبُ مِنْهُ . قَالَ فَهَلْ يَغْدِرُ قُلْتُ لاَ . قَالَ وَنَحْنُ مِنْهُ فِي مُدَّةٍ لاَ نَدْرِي مَا هُوَ صَانِعٌ فِيهَا . قَالَ فَوَاللَّهِ مَا أَمْكَنَنِي مِنْ كَلِمَةٍ أُدْخِلُ فِيهَا شَيْئًا غَيْرَ هَذِهِ . قَالَ فَهَلْ قَالَ هَذَا الْقَوْلَ أَحَدٌ قَبْلَهُ قَالَ قُلْتُ لاَ . قَالَ لِتَرْجُمَانِهِ قُلْ لَهُ إِنِّي سَأَلْتُكَ عَنْ حَسَبِهِ فَزَعَمْتَ أَنَّهُ فِيكُمْ ذُو حَسَبٍ وَكَذَلِكَ الرُّسُلُ تُبْعَثُ فِي أَحْسَابِ قَوْمِهَا . وَسَأَلْتُكَ هَلْ كَانَ فِي آبَائِهِ مَلِكٌ فَزَعَمْتَ أَنْ لاَ . فَقُلْتُ لَوْ كَانَ مِنْ آبَائِهِ مَلِكٌ قُلْتُ رَجُلٌ يَطْلُبُ مُلْكَ آبَائِهِ . وَسَأَلْتُكَ عَنْ أَتْبَاعِهِ أَضُعَفَاؤُهُمْ أَمْ أَشْرَافُهُمْ فَقُلْتَ بَلْ ضُعَفَاؤُهُمْ وَهُمْ أَتْبَاعُ الرُّسُلِ . وَسَأَلْتُكَ هَلْ كُنْتُمْ تَتَّهِمُونَهُ بِالْكَذِبِ قَبْلَ أَنْ يَقُولَ مَا قَالَ فَزَعَمْتَ أَنْ لاَ . فَقَدْ عَرَفْتُ أَنَّهُ لَمْ يَكُنْ لِيَدَعَ الْكَذِبَ عَلَى النَّاسِ ثُمَّ يَذْهَبَ فَيَكْذِبَ عَلَى اللَّهِ . وَسَأَلْتُكَ هَلْ يَرْتَدُّ أَحَدٌ مِنْهُمْ عَنْ دِينِهِ بَعْدَ أَنْ يَدْخُلَهُ سَخْطَةً لَهُ فَزَعَمْتَ أَنْ لاَ . وَكَذَلِكَ الإِيمَانُ إِذَا خَالَطَ بَشَاشَةَ الْقُلُوبِ . وَسَأَلْتُكَ هَلْ يَزِيدُونَ أَوْ يَنْقُصُونَ فَزَعَمْتَ أَنَّهُمْ يَزِيدُونَ وَكَذَلِكَ الإِيمَانُ حَتَّى يَتِمَّ . وَسَأَلْتُكَ هَلْ قَاتَلْتُمُوهُ فَزَعَمْتَ أَنَّكُمْ قَدْ قَاتَلْتُمُوهُ فَتَكُونُ الْحَرْبُ بَيْنَكُمْ وَبَيْنَهُ سِجَالاً يَنَالُ مِنْكُمْ وَتَنَالُونَ مِنْهُ . وَكَذَلِكَ الرُّسُلُ تُبْتَلَى ثُمَّ تَكُونُ لَهُمُ الْعَاقِبَةُ . وَسَأَلْتُكَ هَلْ يَغْدِرُ فَزَعَمْتَ أَنَّهُ لاَ يَغْدِرُ . وَكَذَلِكَ الرُّسُلُ لاَ تَغْدِرُ . وَسَأَلْتُكَ هَلْ قَالَ هَذَا الْقَوْلَ أَحَدٌ قَبْلَهُ فَزَعَمْتَ أَنْ لاَ . فَقُلْتُ لَوْ قَالَ هَذَا الْقَوْلَ أَحَدٌ قَبْلَهُ قُلْتُ رَجُلٌ ائْتَمَّ بِقَوْلٍ قِيلَ قَبْلَهُ . قَالَ ثُمَّ قَالَ بِمَ يَأْمُرُكُمْ قُلْتُ يَأْمُرُنَا بِالصَّلاَةِ وَالزَّكَاةِ وَالصِّلَةِ وَالْعَفَافِ قَالَ إِنْ يَكُنْ مَا تَقُولُ فِيهِ حَقًّا فَإِنَّهُ نَبِيٌّ وَقَدْ كُنْتُ أَعْلَمُ أَنَّهُ خَارِجٌ وَلَمْ أَكُنْ أَظُنُّهُ مِنْكُمْ وَلَوْ أَنِّي أَعْلَمُ أَنِّي أَخْلُصُ إِلَيْهِ لأَحْبَبْتُ لِقَاءَهُ وَلَوْ كُنْتُ عِنْدَهُ لَغَسَلْتُ عَنْ قَدَمَيْهِ وَلَيَبْلُغَنَّ مُلْكُهُ مَا تَحْتَ قَدَمَىَّ . قَالَ ثُمَّ دَعَا بِكِتَابِ رَسُولِ اللَّهِ ﷺ فَقَرَأَهُ فَإِذَا فِيهِ " بِسْمِ اللَّهِ الرَّحْمَنِ الرَّحِيمِ مِنْ مُحَمَّدٍ رَسُولِ اللَّهِ إِلَى هِرَقْلَ عَظِيمِ الرُّومِ سَلاَمٌ عَلَى مَنِ اتَّبَعَ الْهُدَى أَمَّا بَعْدُ فَإِنِّي أَدْعُوكَ بِدِعَايَةِ الإِسْلاَمِ أَسْلِمْ تَسْلَمْ وَيُؤْتِكَ اللَّهُ أَجْرَكَ مَرَّتَيْنِ وَإِنْ تَوَلَّيْتَ فَإِنَّ عَلَيْكَ إِثْمَ الأَرِيسِيِّينَ وَ { يَا أَهْلَ الْكِتَابِ تَعَالَوْا إِلَى كَلِمَةٍ سَوَاءٍ بَيْنَنَا وَبَيْنَكُمْ أَنْ لاَ نَعْبُدَ إِلاَّ اللَّهَ وَلاَ نُشْرِكَ بِهِ شَيْئًا وَلاَ يَتَّخِذَ بَعْضُنَا بَعْضًا أَرْبَابًا مِنْ دُونِ اللَّهِ فَإِنْ تَوَلَّوْا فَقُولُوا اشْهَدُوا بِأَنَّا مُسْلِمُونَ} فَلَمَّا فَرَغَ مِنْ قِرَاءَةِ الْكِتَابِ ارْتَفَعَتِ الأَصْوَاتُ عِنْدَهُ وَكَثُرَ اللَّغْطُ وَأَمَرَ بِنَا فَأُخْرِجْنَا . قَالَ فَقُلْتُ لأَصْحَابِي حِينَ خَرَجْنَا لَقَدْ أَمِرَ أَمْرُ ابْنِ أَبِي كَبْشَةَ إِنَّهُ لَيَخَافُهُ مَلِكُ بَنِي الأَصْفَرِ ـ قَالَ ـ فَمَا زِلْتُ مُوقِنًا بِأَمْرِ رَسُولِ اللَّهِ ﷺ أَنَّهُ سَيَظْهَرُ حَتَّى أَدْخَلَ اللَّهُ عَلَىَّ الإِسْلاَمَ . رواه مسلم

It has been narrated on the authority of Ibn Abbas who learnt the tradition personally from Abu Suffyan. The latter said: I went out (on a mercantile venture) during the period (of truce) between me and the Messenger of Allah (ﷺ). While I was in Syria, the letter of the Messenger of Allah (ﷺ) was handed over to Hiraql (Ceasar), the Emperor of Rome (who was on a visit to Jerusalem at that time). The letter was brought by Dihya Kalbi who delivered it to the governor of Busra The governor passed it on to Hiraql, (On receiving the letter), he said: Is there anyone from the people of this man who thinks that he is a prophet. People said: Yes. So, I was called along with a few others from the Quraish. We were admitted to Hiraql and he seated us before him. He asked: Which of you has closer kinship with the man who thinks that he is a prophet? Abu Suffyan said: I. So they seated me in front of him and stated my companions behind me. Then, he called his interpreter and said to him: Tell them that I am going to ask this fellow (i. e. Abu Suffyan) about the man who thinks that he is a prophet. If he tells me a lie, then refute him. Abu Suffyan told (the narrator): By God, if there was not the fear that falsehood would be imputed to me I would have lied. (Then) Hiraql said to his interpreter: Inquire from him about his ancestry, I said: He is of good ancestry among us. He asked: Has there been a king among his ancestors? I said: No. He asked: **Did you accuse him of falsehood before he proclaimed his prophethood? I said: No**. He asked: Who are his follower people of high status or low status? I said: (They are) of low status. He asked: Are they increasing in number or decreasing? I said. No. they are rather increasing. He asked: Does anyone give up his religion, being dissatisfied with it, after having embraced it? I said: No. He asked: Have you been at war with him? I said: Yes. He asked: How did you fare in that war? I said: The war between us and him has been wavering like a bucket, up at one turn and down at the other (i. e. the victory has been shared between us and him by turns). Sometimes he suffered loss at our hands and sometimes we suffered loss at his (hand). He asked: **Has he (ever) violated his covenant? I said: No**. but we have recently concluded a peace treaty with him for a period and we do not know what he is going to do about it. (Abu Suffyan said on oath that he could not interpolate in this dialogue anything from himself more than these words) He asked: Did anyone make the proclamation (Of prophethood) before him? I said: No. He (now) said to his interpreter: Tell him, I asked him about his ancestry and he had replied that he had the best ancestry. This is the case with Prophets; they are the descendants of the noblest among their people (Addressing Abu Suffyan), he continued: I asked you if there had been a king among his ancestors. You said that there had been none. If there had been a king among his ancestors, I would have said that he was a man demanding his ancestral kingdom. I asked you about his followers whether they were people of high or low status, and you said that they were of rather low status. Such are the followers of the Prophets. **I asked you whether you used to accuse him of falsehood before he proclaimed his prophethood, and you said that you did not. So I have understood that when he did not allow himself to tell a lie about the people, he would never go to the length of forging a falsehood about Allah.** I asked you whether anyone renounced his religion being dissatisfied with it after he had embraced it, and you replied in the negative. Faith is like this when it enters the depth of the heart (it perpetuates them). I asked you whether his followers were increasing or decreasing. You said they were increasing. Faith is like this until it reaches its consummation. I asked you whether you had been at war with him, and you replied that you had been and that the victory between you and him had been shared by turns, sometimes he suffering loss at your hand and sometimes you suffering lost at his. This is how the Prophets are tried before their final victory. **I asked you whether he (ever) violated his covenant, and you said that he did not. This is how the Prophets behave. They never violate (their covenants).** I asked you whether anyone before him had proclaimed the same thing, and you replied in the negative. I said: If anyone had made the same proclamation before, I would have thought that he was a man following what had been proclaimed before. **(Then) he asked: What does he enjoin upon you? I said: He exhorts us to offer Salat, to pay Zakat, to show due regard to kinship and to practice chastity. He said: If what you have told about him is true, he is certainly a Prophet.** I knew that he was to appear but I did not think that he would be from among you. If I knew that I would be able to reach him. I would love to meet him; and it I had been with him. I would have washed his feet (out of reverence). His dominion would certainly extend to this place which is under my feet. Then he called for the letter of the Messenger of Allah (may peace be upon him) and read it. The letter ran as follows:" In the name of Allah, Most Gracious and Most Merciful. From Muhammad, the Messenger of Allah, to Hiraql, the Emperor of the Romans. Peace be upon him who follows the guidance. After this, I extend to you the invitation to accept Islam. Embrace Islam and you will be safe. Accept Islam, God will give you double the reward. And if you turn away, upon you will be the sin of your subjects." O People of the Book, come to the word that is common between us that we should worship none other than Allah, should not ascribe any partner to Him and some of us should not take their fellows as Lords other than Allah. If they turn away, you should say that we testify to our being Muslims [iii. 64]." When he hid finished the reading of the letter, noise and confused clamour was raise around him, and he ordered us to leave. Accordingly, we left. (Addressing my companions) while we were coming out (of the place). I said: Ibn Abu Kabsha (referring sarcastically to the Holy Prophet) has come to wield a great power. Lo! (even) the king of the Romans is afraid of him. I continued to believe that the authority of the Messenger of Allah (ﷺ) would triumph until God imbued me with (the spirit of) Islam. Sahih Muslim 1773 a. https://sunnah.com/muslim/32/89.

It is obvious from the response of Abu Suffyan, the opponent of the Prophet (SAS), that he never lies nor betrays anyone in his life. This is fascinating when his enemies witness such characters in him (SAS).

In another incident, when the Prophet (SAS) migrated to Al-Madeenah, the Jews are eager to check and test him to ensure he is a messenger from Allah (SWT). The incident has occurred as follows:

عَنْ عَبْدِ اللَّهِ بْنِ سَلَامٍ، قَالَ لَمَّا قَدِمَ رَسُولُ اللَّهِ ـ ﷺ ـ الْمَدِينَةَ انْجَفَلَ النَّاسُ إِلَيْهِ . وَقِيلَ قَدِمَ رَسُولُ اللَّهِ ـ ﷺ ـ . فَجِئْتُ فِي النَّاسِ لأَنْظُرَ إِلَيْهِ فَلَمَّا اسْتَثْبَتُّ وَجْهَ رَسُولِ اللَّهِ ـ ﷺ ـ عَرَفْتُ أَنَّ وَجْهَهُ لَيْسَ بِوَجْهِ كَذَّابٍ فَكَانَ أَوَّلَ شَىْءٍ تَكَلَّمَ بِهِ أَنْ قَالَ " يَا أَيُّهَا النَّاسُ أَفْشُوا السَّلاَمَ وَأَطْعِمُوا الطَّعَامَ وَصَلُّوا بِاللَّيْلِ وَالنَّاسُ نِيَامٌ تَدْخُلُوا الْجَنَّةَ بِسَلاَمٍ " . رواه ابن ماجه

It was narrated that 'Abdullah bin Salam said: "When the Messenger of Allah (ﷺ) came to Al-Madinah, the people rushed towards him and it was said: 'The Messenger of Allah (ﷺ) has come!' I came along with the people to see him, and when I looked at the face of the Messenger of Allah (ﷺ), I realized that his face was not the face of a liar. The first thing he said was: "O people, spread (the greeting of) Salam, offer food to people and pray at night when people are sleeping, you will enter Paradise in peace." Ibn Majeh, https://sunnah.com/ibnmajah/5/532

Abdullah Ibn Salam was able to recognize his truthfulness from his face (SAS) and his talk. Look at the concepts that he (SAS) first talked about when he has met the people in

Al-Madeenah; spread peace for all. This is the root of Islam as a religion, i.e., peace everywhere. The Prophet (SAS) also has ordered his companions and followers in many occasions to be truthful no matter what situation they are in. Let us look at his teachings in the following narration:

عَنْ عَبْدِ اللهِ، عَنِ النَّبِيِّ ﷺ قَالَ: عَلَيْكُمْ بِالصِّدْقِ، فَإِنَّ الصِّدْقَ يَهْدِي إِلَى الْبِرِّ، وَإِنَّ الْبِرَّ يَهْدِي إِلَى الْجَنَّةِ، وَإِنَّ الرَّجُلَ يَصْدُقُ حَتَّى يُكْتَبَ عِنْدَ اللهِ صِدِّيقًا، وَإِيَّاكُمْ وَالْكَذِبَ، فَإِنَّ الْكَذِبَ يَهْدِي إِلَى الْفُجُورِ، وَالْفُجُورَ يَهْدِي إِلَى النَّارِ، وَإِنَّ الرَّجُلَ لَيَكْذِبُ حَتَّى يُكْتَبَ عِنْدَ اللهِ كَذَّابًا. صحيح الألباني

'Abdullah reported that the Prophet, may Allah bless him and grant him peace, said, "You must be truthful. Truthfulness leads to dutifulness and dutifulness leads to the Garden. A man continues to tell the truth until he is written as a siddiq with Allah. Beware of lying. Lying leads to deviance and deviance leads to the Fire. A man continues to lie until he is written as a liar with Allah." Sahih (Al-Albani). https://sunnah.com/adab/21/2

If you are looking for Paradise in the Hereafter and great living in this life, the only solution is truthfulness in all matters. Do you think a person with these characters, who has taught his companions and followers to be truthful, is a liar? If he is always telling the truth, do you think he might lie to Allah (SWT)? The answer is no. He (SAS) brought to us the belief that will save us in the Day of Judgement. Does he deserve to be insulted because he brings the lifebuoy to save us from devil in this life? I think the people, who are doing so, lost their way. They are astray and would like from all of us to be similarly astray. May Allah guide them all to the best?

Character of Mercy
This character is one of the most important acquired characters by the Prophet (SAS). There are tens of narrations discussing such character in him (SAS). For example, in the following narration, a man once urinated in the mosque, i.e., the place of prayer that should be always clean. It is an unusual act that might be due to ignorance, negligence, or hatred. In a situation like that, a human being will be very angry, irritated and bothered. However, the response of the Prophet (SAS) has been totally different, which shows how merciful he is as shown in the following narration:

أَنَّ أَبَا هُرَيْرَةَ، أَخْبَرَهُ أَنَّ أَعْرَابِيًّا بَالَ فِي الْمَسْجِدِ، فَثَارَ إِلَيْهِ النَّاسُ لِيَقَعُوا بِهِ فَقَالَ لَهُمْ رَسُولُ اللَّهِ ﷺ " دَعُوهُ، وَأَهْرِيقُوا عَلَى بَوْلِهِ ذَنُوبًا مِنْ مَاءٍ ـ أَوْ سَجْلاً مِنْ مَاءٍ ـ فَإِنَّمَا بُعِثْتُمْ مُيَسِّرِينَ، وَلَمْ تُبْعَثُوا مُعَسِّرِينَ ". (رواه البخارى).

Narrated Abu Huraira: A bedouin urinated in the mosque, and the people rushed to beat him. Allah's Messenger (ﷺ) ordered them to leave him and pour a bucket or a tumbler (full) of water over the place where he has passed urine. The Prophet then said, "You have been sent to make things easy (for the people) and you have not been sent to make things difficult for them." Sahih al-Bukhari 6128. https://sunnah.com/bukhari/78/155

The Prophet (SAS) and his companions have been tortured by the disbelievers in Makkah. The only solution in his hand (SAS) is to supplicate to Allah (SWT) to punish these disbelievers and get rid of them. Any human being in his place will do that. However, he (SAS) has a different aspect. He thinks in a different domain of ethics and good characters. He (SAS) react with high level of morals that we are not used to them. Let us look at his response in the following narration:

عَنْ أَبِي هُرَيْرَةَ، قَالَ قِيلَ يَا رَسُولَ اللهِ ادْعُ عَلَى الْمُشْرِكِينَ قَالَ " إِنِّي لَمْ أُبْعَثْ لَعَّانًا وَإِنَّمَا بُعِثْتُ رَحْمَةً " . رواه مسلم

Abu Huraira reported it was said to Allah's Messenger (ﷺ): Invoke curse upon the polytheists, whereupon he said: I have not been sent as the invoker of curse, but I have been sent as mercy." Sahih Muslim 2599. https://sunnah.com/muslim/45/111

He (SAS) has been sent by Allah (SWT) to achieve a different function than that of cursing his opponents. On the contrary, he was sent to supplicate for them to be guided. How much positive energy the Prophet has in order to be merciful to his enemies like that. This is unimaginable acts, particularly in our era. Look at his teachings to all his followers in the following two narrations:

عَنْ عَبْدِ اللَّهِ بْنِ عَمْرٍو، قَالَ قَالَ رَسُولُ اللَّهِ ﷺ " الرَّاحِمُونَ يَرْحَمُهُمُ الرَّحْمَنُ ارْحَمُوا مَنْ فِي الأَرْضِ يَرْحَمْكُمْ مَنْ فِي السَّمَاءِ الرَّحِمُ شُجْنَةٌ مِنَ الرَّحْمَنِ فَمَنْ وَصَلَهَا وَصَلَهُ اللَّهُ وَمَنْ قَطَعَهَا قَطَعَهُ اللَّهُ " . قَالَ أَبُو عِيسَى هَذَا حَدِيثٌ حَسَنٌ صَحِيحٌ . الترمذى

Abdullah bin 'Amr narrated that the Messenger of Allah said: "The merciful are shown mercy by Ar-Rahman. Be merciful on the earth, and you will be shown mercy from Who is above the heavens. The womb is named after Ar-Rahman, so whoever connects it, Allah connects him, and whoever severs it, Allah severs him." Jami` at-Tirmidhi 1924 (Hasan). https://sunnah.com/tirmidhi/27/30

عَنْ عِيَاضِ بْنِ حِمَارٍ الْمُجَاشِعِيِّ، أَنَّ رَسُولَ اللَّهِ ﷺ قَالَ ذَاتَ يَوْمٍ فِي خُطْبَتِهِ "...." قَالَ وَأَهْلُ الْجَنَّةِ ثَلاَثَةٌ ذُو سُلْطَانٍ مُقْسِطٌ مُتَصَدِّقٌ مُوَفَّقٌ وَرَجُلٌ رَحِيمٌ رَقِيقُ الْقَلْبِ لِكُلِّ ذِي قُرْبَى وَمُسْلِمٍ وَعَفِيفٌ مُتَعَفِّفٌ ذُو عِيَالٍ - قَالَ - وَأَهْلُ النَّارِ خَمْسَةٌ الضَّعِيفُ الَّذِي لاَ زَبْرَ لَهُ الَّذِينَ هُمْ فِيكُمْ تَبَعًا لاَ يَتْبَعُونَ أَهْلاً وَلاَ مَالاً وَالْخَائِنُ الَّذِي لاَ يَخْفَى لَهُ طَمَعٌ وَإِنْ دَقَّ إِلاَّ خَانَهُ وَرَجُلٌ لاَ يُصْبِحُ وَلاَ يُمْسِي إِلاَّ وَهُوَ يُخَادِعُكَ عَنْ أَهْلِكَ وَمَالِكَ " . وَذَكَرَ الْبُخْلَ أَوِ الْكَذِبَ " وَالشِّنْظِيرُ الْفَحَّاشُ " . وَلَمْ يَذْكُرْ أَبُو غَسَّانَ فِي حَدِيثِهِ " وَأَنْفِقْ فَسَنُنْفِقَ عَلَيْكَ " . رواه مسلم

'Iyad Ibn Himar reported that Allah's Messenger (ﷺ), while delivering a sermon one day, said: ……… The inmates of Paradise are three: One who wields authority and is just and fair, one who is truthful and has been endowed with power to do good deeds. And the person who is merciful and kind hearted towards his relatives and to every pious Muslim, and one who does not stretch his hand in spite of having a large family to support. And He said: The inmates of Hell are five: the weak who lack power to (avoid evil), the (carefree) who pursue (everything irrespective of the fact that it is good or evil) and who do not have any care for their family or for their wealth. And those dishonest whose greed cannot be concealed even in the case of minor things. And the third. who betray you morning and evening, in regard to your family and your property. He also made a mention of the miser and the liar and those who are in the habit of abusing people and using obscene and foul language. Abu Ghassan in his narration did not make mention of" Spend and there would be spent for you." Sahih Muslim 2865 a https://sunnah.com/muslim/53/76

This is what the Prophet (SAS) asked us to practice in this life if we are looking for success in the Hereafter. We should be merciful to others in all maters and deal with everyone in a kind and merciful way. He (SAS) has a great heart and asked us all to have similar type of heart, which is hard to find nowadays. He (SAS) did not harm anyone and asked us to act in a similar manner towards all human beings. Do we have in this world right now a leader like that? This becomes scarce in our era of oppression and ruthless. I supplicate to Allah (SWT) to put mercy in the hearts of mankind towards each other and remove all hatred from their hearts. Ameen.

Character of Justice
The Prophet (SAS) has been always just with his companions and opponents. He dealt

with all alike in terms of rights. He has been different from all rulers in his era and in the world until the Day of Judgement. The following narrations show his justice (SAS) with his companions:

عَنْ أَبِي هُرَيْرَةَ، قَالَ قَالَ رَسُولُ اللَّهِ ﷺ " اللَّهُمَّ إِنَّمَا أَنَا بَشَرٌ فَأَيُّمَا رَجُلٍ مِنَ الْمُسْلِمِينَ سَبَبْتُهُ أَوْ لَعَنْتُهُ أَوْ جَلَدْتُهُ فَاجْعَلْهَا لَهُ زَكَاةً وَرَحْمَةً " . رواه مسلم

Abu Huraira reported Allah's Messenger (ﷺ) as saying: O Allah, I am a human being and for any person amongst Muslims upon whom I hurl malediction or invoke curse or give him whipping make it a source of purity and mercy. Sahih Muslim 2601 a. https://sunnah.com/muslim/45/114.

عَنْ عَمْرِو بْنِ أَبِي قُرَّةَ، ...... وَلَقَدْ عَلِمْتَ أَنَّ رَسُولَ اللَّهِ ﷺ خَطَبَ فَقَالَ " أَيُّمَا رَجُلٍ مِنْ أُمَّتِي سَبَبْتُهُ سَبَّةً أَوْ لَعَنْتُهُ لَعْنَةً فِي غَضَبِي - فَإِنَّمَا أَنَا مِنْ وَلَدِ آدَمَ أَغْضَبُ كَمَا يَغْضَبُونَ وَإِنَّمَا بَعَثَنِي رَحْمَةً لِلْعَالَمِينَ - فَاجْعَلْهَا عَلَيْهِمْ صَلَاةً يَوْمَ الْقِيَامَةِ ..... صحيح الألباني

'Amr b. Abl Qurrah said: ..... You know that the Messenger of Allah (May peace be upon him) addressed, saying: If I abused any person of my people, or cursed him in my anger. I am one of the children of Adam: I become angry as they become angry. He (Allah) has sent me as a mercy for all worlds. (O Allah!) make them (Abuse or curse) blessing for them on the day of judgment! .... : Sahih (Al-Albani). https://sunnah.com/abudawud/42/64.

He (SAS) has also been just with his wives as shown in the following narration:

عَنْ أَنَسٍ، قَالَ كَانَ النَّبِيُّ ﷺ عِنْدَ بَعْضِ نِسَائِهِ فَأَرْسَلَتْ إِحْدَى أُمَّهَاتِ الْمُؤْمِنِينَ بِصَحْفَةٍ فِيهَا طَعَامٌ، فَضَرَبَتِ الَّتِي النَّبِيُّ ﷺ فِي بَيْتِهَا يَدَ الْخَادِمِ فَسَقَطَتِ الصَّحْفَةُ فَانْفَلَقَتْ، فَجَمَعَ النَّبِيُّ ﷺ فِلَقَ الصَّحْفَةِ، ثُمَّ جَعَلَ يَجْمَعُ فِيهَا الطَّعَامَ الَّذِي كَانَ فِي الصَّحْفَةِ وَيَقُولُ " غَارَتْ أُمُّكُمْ "، ثُمَّ حَبَسَ الْخَادِمَ حَتَّى أُتِيَ بِصَحْفَةٍ مِنْ عِنْدِ الَّتِي هُوَ فِي بَيْتِهَا، فَدَفَعَ الصَّحْفَةَ الصَّحِيحَةَ إِلَى الَّتِي كُسِرَتْ صَحْفَتُهَا، وَأَمْسَكَ الْمَكْسُورَةَ فِي بَيْتِ الَّتِي كَسَرَتْ فِيهِ. رواه البخاري

Narrated Anas: While the Prophet (ﷺ) was in the house of one of his wives, one of the mothers of the believers sent a meal in a dish. The wife at whose house the Prophet (ﷺ) was, struck the hand of the servant, causing the dish to fall and break. The Prophet (ﷺ) gathered the broken pieces of the dish and then started collecting on them the food which had been in the dish and said, "Your mother (my wife) felt jealous." Then he detained the servant till a (sound) dish was brought from the wife at whose house he was. He gave the sound dish to the wife whose dish had been broken and kept the broken one at the house where it had been broken. Sahih al-Bukhari 5225. https://sunnah.com/bukhari/67/158.

The Prophet (SAS) has been just in lawful matters, without looking at the status of the sinner, as shown in the following narration:

عَنِ الزُّهْرِيِّ، قَالَ أَخْبَرَنِي عُرْوَةُ بْنُ الزُّبَيْرِ، أَنَّ امْرَأَةً، سَرَقَتْ فِي عَهْدِ رَسُولِ اللَّهِ ﷺ فِي غَزْوَةِ الْفَتْحِ - مُرْسَلٌ - فَفَزِعَ قَوْمُهَا إِلَى أُسَامَةَ بْنِ زَيْدٍ يَسْتَشْفِعُونَهُ - قَالَ عُرْوَةُ - فَلَمَّا كَلَّمَهُ أُسَامَةُ تَلَوَّنَ وَجْهُ رَسُولِ اللَّهِ ﷺ فَقَالَ " أَتُكَلِّمُنِي فِي حَدٍّ مِنْ حُدُودِ اللَّهِ " . قَالَ أُسَامَةُ اسْتَغْفِرْ لِي يَا رَسُولَ اللَّهِ . فَلَمَّا كَانَ الْعَشِيُّ قَامَ رَسُولُ اللَّهِ ﷺ خَطِيبًا فَأَثْنَى عَلَى اللَّهِ بِمَا هُوَ أَهْلُهُ ثُمَّ قَالَ " أَمَّا بَعْدُ فَإِنَّمَا هَلَكَ النَّاسُ قَبْلَكُمْ أَنَّهُمْ كَانُوا إِذَا سَرَقَ فِيهِمُ الشَّرِيفُ تَرَكُوهُ وَإِذَا سَرَقَ فِيهِمُ الضَّعِيفُ أَقَامُوا عَلَيْهِ الْحَدَّ وَالَّذِي نَفْسُ مُحَمَّدٍ بِيَدِهِ لَوْ أَنَّ فَاطِمَةَ بِنْتَ مُحَمَّدٍ سَرَقَتْ لَقَطَعْتُ يَدَهَا " . ثُمَّ أَمَرَ رَسُولُ اللَّهِ ﷺ بِيَدِ تِلْكَ الْمَرْأَةِ فَقُطِعَتْ فَحَسُنَتْ تَوْبَتُهَا بَعْدَ ذَلِكَ . قَالَتْ عَائِشَةُ رضى الله عنها وَكَانَتْ تَأْتِينِي بَعْدَ ذَلِكَ فَأَرْفَعُ حَاجَتَهَا إِلَى رَسُولِ اللَّهِ ﷺ . سنن النسائي

It was narrated that Az-Zuhri said: "Urwah bin Az-Zubair told me that a woman stole at the time of the Messenger of Allah, during the Conquest. Her people went to Uswamah bin Zaid, to ask him to intercede." 'Urwah said: "When Usamah spoke to him concerning her, the face of the Messenger of Allah changed color and he said: 'Are you speaking to me concerning one of the Hadd punishments of Allah?" Usamah said: 'Pray to Allah for forgiveness for me, O Messenger of Allah.' When evening came, the Messenger of Allah stood up to deliver a speech. He praised Allah as He deserves, then he said: 'The people who came before you were destroyed because, whenever a noble person among them stole, they would carry out the Hadd punishment on him. By the One in whose hand is my soul, if Fatimah bint Muhammad were to steal, I would cut off her hand.' Then the Messenger of Allah ordered that the hand of that woman be cut off. After that she repented sincerely, and 'Aishah said: 'She used to come to me after that, and I would convey her needs to the Messenger of Allah.'" Sunan an-Nasa'i 4903 (Sahih). https://sunnah.com/nasai/46/34.

It is quite clear that he (SAS) has been just in all matters because he has implemented the law of Allah (SWT) with no discrepancy due to friendship, blood relationship, status, belief, gender, race, color, etc. He has implemented justice in its comprehensive, perfect, and truthful way. The companions have learned the lessons from him (SAS) and spread justice worldwide wherever they go. This is another main character that characterize Islam and its teachings.

Character of Forbearance
Another great character that is hard to find these days, which is forbearance. It is the secret of attracting the good hearts to the Prophet (SAS) because his forbearance always defeat his anger. Look at the following narration and tell me what you would do if you are in the position of the Prophet (SAS):

وعن أنس رضي الله عنه قال: كنت أمشى مع رسول الله ﷺ، وعليه برد نجرانى غليظ الحاشية، فأدركه أعرابى، فجبذه بردائه جبذة شديدة، فنظرت إلى صفحة عاتق النبى ﷺ، وقد أثرت بها حاشية البرد من شدة فضحك، ثم قال: يا محمد مر لى من مال الله الذى عندك، فالتفت إليه فضحك ثم أمر له بعطاء. (متفق عليه)

Anas (May Allah be pleased with him) reported: I was walking with Messenger of Allah (ﷺ) who was wearing a Najrani cloak with a very thick border when a bedouin happened to meet him. He took hold of the side of his cloak and drew it violently. I noticed that the violence of jerk had bruised the neck of Messenger of Allah (ﷺ). The bedouin said: "O Muhammad! Give me out of Allah's wealth that you possess." Messenger of Allah (ﷺ) turned to him and smiled and directed that he should be given something. [Al-Bukhari and Muslim]. https://sunnah.com/riyadussalihin/introduction/644.

Usually in such situations, we get angry in which our minimum response is to reject this person's request. We might push back and generate a big fight with such ignorant harsh person. This is the common practice nowadays wherever you go. However, the case is different with the Prophet (SAS). He reacted differently with high standards of ethics and behavior. He gave the man what he wanted with a smile on his face (SAS). What a great character is this? Which school did he (SAS) learn this character in? Or who teaches him such great character? Allah teaches him (SAS) that He (SWT) is forbearer and loves forbearance. Therefore, he (SAS) has always practiced forbearance with others to be close to Allah and act upon His likings (SWT). This is clearer in the following narration:

وعنها أن النبى ﷺ قال: " إن الله رفيق يحب الرفق، ويعطى على الرفق ما لا يعطى على العنف ومالا يعطى على ما سواه" (رواه مسلم).

'Aishah (May Allah be pleased with him) reported: The Prophet (ﷺ) said, "Allah is Forbearer and He loves forbearance, and rewards for forbearance while He does not reward severity, and does not give for anything besides it (forbearance)." [Muslim] https://sunnah.com/riyadussalihin/introduction/633.

The Prophet (SAS) has taught his companions that whoever does not sustain forbearance and gentleness, he/she is the loser as shown in the following narration:

وعن جرير بن عبد الله رضي الله عنه قال: سمعت رسول الله ﷺ يقول: "من يحرم الرفق يحرم الخير كله" (رواه مسلم).

Jarir bin 'Abdullah (May Allah be pleased with him) reported: Messenger of Allah (ﷺ) said, "He who is deprived of forbearance and gentleness is, in fact, deprived of all good." [Muslim]. https://sunnah.com/riyadussalihin/introduction/637.

Do we want to be away from Hellfire? The answer is yes, then, we should practice forbearance and be approachable easy people. This is obvious in the following narration:

وعن ابن مسعود رضي الله عنه قال: قال رسول الله ﷺ: "ألا أخبركم بمن يحرم على النار -أو بمن تحرم عليه النار؟- تحرم على كل قريب هين لين سهل". (رواه الترمذي وقال: حديث حسن).

Ibn Mas'ud (May Allah be pleased with him) reported: Messenger of Allah (ﷺ) said, "Shall I not tell you whom the (Hell) Fire is forbidden to touch? It is forbidden to touch a man who is always accessible, having polite and tender nature." [At- Tirmidhi, Hadith Hasan]. https://sunnah.com/riyadussalihin/introduction/641.

Finally, here is another level or dimension of forbearance that is for people who tortured you. Usually, you will have hard feelings towards them. However, the case is different with those who have a message to promote in this life. They do not carry any hard feelings to others no matter what others are doing to them. This is the highest level of character that characterize the messengers and their followers who would like to accompany them in Paradise. Look at the following narration to explain such character:

وعن ابن مسعود رضي الله عنه قال: كأني أنظر إلى رسول الله ﷺ يحكي نبياً من الأنبياء، صلوات الله وسلامه عليهم، ضربه قومه فأدموه وهو يمسح الدم عن وجهه، ويقول: "اللهم اغفر لقومي فإنهم لا يعلمون" (متفق عليه).

Ibn Mas'ud (May Allah be pleased with him) reported: I can see the Messenger of Allah (ﷺ) look like one of the Prophets of Allah whose people beat and made him bleed while he was wiping the blood from his face and supplicating: "O Allah, forgive my people because they know not." [Al-Bukhari and Muslim]. https://sunnah.com/riyadussalihin/introduction/645.

Based upon the above discussion, acquiring forbearance character is a must for all messengers and their followers who carry their message to humanity. This forbearance should be practiced among the followers themselves before the others. This character represents a top secret in attracting the hearts and minds of others towards the message we carry.

Character of Courage

The Prophet (SAS), who has been merciful, forbearer, and kind, has also been a strong and a brave person. He has not been timid at any action. His actions have always been directly related to the situation he is in. If the situation needs a merciful character, he is the best to implement such mercy. If the situation needs a strong personality with high level of courage, he is the one who is ahead of others in practicing such courage. This is what Ali Ibn Abi Taleb has described in the following narration:

عَنْ عَلِيٍّ، رَضِيَ اللهُ عَنْهُ قَالَ كُنَّا إِذَا احْمَرَّ الْبَأْسُ وَلَقِيَ الْقَوْمُ الْقَوْمَ اتَّقَيْنَا بِرَسُولِ اللهِ ﷺ فَمَا يَكُونُ مِنَّا أَحَدٌ أَدْنَى مِنَ الْقَوْمِ مِنْهُ. مسند الإمام أحمد

It was narrated that 'Ali (رضي الله عنه) said: When the fighting intensified and the two sides met in battle, we sought shelter with the Messenger of Allah (ﷺ) and no one was closer to the enemy than him. Musnad Ahmad 1347 (Sahih). https://sunnah.com/ahmad/5/747.

In the situation of a battle, the Prophet (SAS) has been in the front lines to defend the truth with bravery actions. This has been very clear in all battles including the battle of Hunain when all the companions ran away from the field and left him (SAS) alone with very few others. He did not fear nor returned back. On the contrary, he called all the runners to come back to him and was able to win the battle with few around him (SAS). The following narration shows such incident:

عَنْ أَبِي إِسْحَاقَ، قِيلَ لِلْبَرَاءِ وَأَنَا أَسْمَعُ، أَوَلَّيْتُمْ مَعَ النَّبِيِّ ﷺ يَوْمَ حُنَيْنٍ فَقَالَ أَمَّا النَّبِيُّ ﷺ فَلاَ، كَانُوا رُمَاةً فَقَالَ "أَنَا النَّبِيُّ لاَ كَذِبْ أَنَا ابْنُ عَبْدِ الْمُطَّلِبْ". رواه البخاري

Narrated Abu 'Is-haq: Al-Bara' was asked while I was listening, "Did you flee (before the enemy) along with the Prophet (ﷺ) on the day of (the battle of) Hunain?" He replied, "As for the Prophet, he did not (flee). The enemy were good archers and the Prophet (ﷺ) was saying, "I am the Prophet (ﷺ) undoubtedly; I am the son of `Abdul Muttalib." Sahih al-Bukhari 4316. https://sunnah.com/bukhari/64/347.

He (SAS) has always recommended his followers to be strong and brave because sustenance and death are in the hands of Allah (SWT). No one can control them. So, why should we fear? Or what are we afraid of? The following narration shows the teachings of the Prophet (SAS) to his companions and followers:

عَنْ أَبِي هُرَيْرَةَ، قَالَ قَالَ رَسُولُ اللَّهِ ﷺ "الْمُؤْمِنُ الْقَوِيُّ خَيْرٌ وَأَحَبُّ إِلَى اللَّهِ مِنَ الْمُؤْمِنِ الضَّعِيفِ وَفِي كُلٍّ خَيْرٌ احْرِصْ عَلَى مَا يَنْفَعُكَ وَاسْتَعِنْ بِاللَّهِ وَلاَ تَعْجِزْ وَإِنْ أَصَابَكَ شَيْءٌ فَلاَ تَقُلْ لَوْ أَنِّي فَعَلْتُ كَانَ كَذَا وَكَذَا . وَلَكِنْ قُلْ قَدَرُ اللَّهِ وَمَا شَاءَ فَعَلَ فَإِنَّ لَوْ تَفْتَحُ عَمَلَ الشَّيْطَانِ". رواه مسلم

Abu Huraira reported Allah's Messenger (ﷺ) as saying: A strong believer is better and is more lovable to Allah than a weak believer, and there is good in everyone, (but) cherish that which gives you benefit (in the Hereafter) and seek help from Allah and do not lose heart, and if anything (in the form of trouble) comes to you, don't say: If I had not done that, it would not have happened so and so, but say: Allah did that what He had ordained to do and your" if" opens the (gate) for the Satan. Sahih Muslim 2664. https://sunnah.com/muslim/46/52.

If you live in our era, you will know the role of thumb, i.e., you are strong if you are able to defeat others in terms of power. The case is different to the Prophet (SAS) and his teachings to others where the strong person/country is the one who controls his/its anger. This character would have saved a lot of souls if it has been implemented along the history of mankind. Until today, implementing such character is hard and unusual. If you have been bothered by a person and has softly responded, you will be considered weak and such person will continue bothering you. Similarly, the case with countries which fight each other for weak or no reasons. The following narration represents a golden statement, which if implemented, we will never have the level of frustration that we have today worldwide:

وعن أبى هريرة رضي الله عنه أن رسول الله ﷺ قال: ليس الشديد بالصرعة، إنما الشديد الذى يملك نفسه عند الغضب" (متفق

عليه)

Abu Hurairah (May Allah be pleased with him) reported: Messenger of Allah (ﷺ) said, "The strong man is not the one who wrestles, but the strong man is in fact the one who controls himself in a fit of rage." [Al-Bukhari and Muslim]. https://sunnah.com/riyadussalihin/introduction/646.

This is the level of courage that the Prophet (SAS) attained and asked us to mimic him in such courage. Courage is a character that is missed in our society due to the high level of oppression and injustice.

Character of Humbleness

There is no words to describe the Prophet's humbleness (SAS). Although he is the best creation whom Allah (SWT) has created, he has been very humble in dealing with all people. He has been humble among his companions as shown in the following narration:

عَنْ أَبِي ذَرٍّ، وَأَبِي، هُرَيْرَةَ قَالاَ كَانَ رَسُولُ اللَّهِ ﷺ يَجْلِسُ بَيْنَ ظَهْرَىْ أَصْحَابِهِ فَيَجِيءُ الْغَرِيبُ فَلاَ يَدْرِي أَيُّهُمْ هُوَ حَتَّى يَسْأَلَ فَطَلَبْنَا إِلَى رَسُولِ اللَّهِ ﷺ أَنْ نَجْعَلَ لَهُ مَجْلِسًا يَعْرِفُهُ الْغَرِيبُ إِذَا أَتَاهُ ـ قَالَ ـ فَبَنَيْنَا لَهُ دُكَّانًا مِنْ طِينٍ فَجَلَسَ عَلَيْهِ وَكُنَّا نَجْلِسُ بِجَنْبَتَيْهِ وَذَكَرَ نَحْوَ هَذَا الْخَبَرِ فَأَقْبَلَ رَجُلٌ فَذَكَرَ هَيْئَتَهُ حَتَّى سَلَّمَ مِنْ طَرَفِ السِّمَاطِ فَقَالَ السَّلاَمُ عَلَيْكَ يَا مُحَمَّدُ . قَالَ فَرَدَّ عَلَيْهِ النَّبِيُّ ﷺ . صحيح الألباني

Narrated AbuDharr and AbuHurayrah: The Messenger of Allah (ﷺ) used to sit among his Companions. A stranger would come and not recognize him (the Prophet) until he asked (about him). So we asked the Messenger of Allah (ﷺ) to make a place where he might take his seat so that when a stranger came, he might recognise him. So we built a terrace of soil on which he would take his seat, and we would sit beside him. He then mentioned something similar to this Hadith saying: A man came, and he described his appearance. He saluted from the side of the assembly, saying: Peace be upon you, Muhammad. The Prophet (ﷺ) then responded to him. Sunan Abi Dawud 4698. Sahih (Al-Albani). https://sunnah.com/abudawud/42/103.

He (SAS) has been humble when he is invited to food or any other aspects as shown in the following narration:

عَنْ أَنَسِ بْنِ مَالِكٍ، قَالَ: كَانَ النَّبِيُّ ﷺ، يُدْعَى إِلَى خُبْزِ الشَّعِيرِ، وَالإِهَالَةِ السَّنِخَةِ، فَيُجِيبُ وَلَقَدْ كَانَ لَهُ دِرْعٌ عِنْدَ يَهُودِيٍّ، فَمَا وَجَدَ مَا يَفُكُّهَا حَتَّى مَاتَ. الشمائل المحمدية

Anas Radiyallahu 'Anhu reports: "Rasulullah Sallallahu 'Alayhi Wasallam accepted and attended invitations where bread made of barley, and stale fat a few days old was served (Without hesitation he accepted these invitations). Rasulullah Sallallahu 'Alayhi Wasallam had pawned his armour to a Jew. Till the end of his life Rasulullah Sallallahu 'Alayhi Wasallam did not possess a sufficient amount to release that armour'". Ash-Shama'il Al-Muhammadiyah 332 (Sahih). https://sunnah.com/shamail/47/4.

He (SAS) has always recommended his companions and followers to be humble and to be away from arrogance as both lead to different ways in the Hereafter. Being humble leads to Paradise and vice versa. So, humbleness is a pillar character for a believer. This is clear in the following narration:

وعن عبد الله بن مسعود رضي الله عنه عن النبى ﷺ قال: "لا يدخل الجنة من كان في قلبه مثقال ذرة من كبر" فقال رجل" إن الرجل يحب أن يكون ثوبه حسناً ونعله حسناً؟ قال: "إن الله جميل يحب الجمال الكبر بطر الحق وغمط الناس "(رواه مسلم).

'Abdullah bin Mas'ud (May Allah be pleased with him) reported: The Prophet (ﷺ) said,

"He who has, in his heart, an ant's weight of arrogance will not enter Jannah." Someone said: "A man likes to wear beautiful clothes and shoes?" Messenger of Allah (ﷺ) said, "Allah is Beautiful, He loves beauty. Arrogance means ridiculing and rejecting the Truth and despising people." [Muslim]. https://sunnah.com/riyadussalihin/introduction/611.

Let me ask myself and also ask you: have you seen any leader who is humble nowadays except very few? This character is also scarce in our world today. This shows the greatness of our beloved Prophet (SAS) who has the ability to practice such abundant character.

Character of Generosity

Generosity was a clear character in the Prophet (SAS) with high impact on his companions' life. He has been very generous, particularly in the month of Ramadan. This is obvious in the following narration:

عَنِ ابْنِ عَبَّاسٍ ـ رضى الله عنهما ـ قَالَ كَانَ النَّبِيُّ ﷺ أَجْوَدَ النَّاسِ بِالْخَيْرِ، وَأَجْوَدُ مَا يَكُونُ فِي شَهْرِ رَمَضَانَ لأَنَّ جِبْرِيلَ كَانَ يَلْقَاهُ فِي كُلِّ لَيْلَةٍ فِي شَهْرِ رَمَضَانَ حَتَّى يَنْسَلِخَ يَعْرِضُ عَلَيْهِ رَسُولُ اللَّهِ ﷺ الْقُرْآنَ، فَإِذَا لَقِيَهُ جِبْرِيلُ كَانَ أَجْوَدَ بِالْخَيْرِ مِنَ الرِّيحِ الْمُرْسَلَةِ. رواه البخاري

Narrated Ibn `Abbas: The Prophet (ﷺ) was the most generous person, and he used to become more so (generous) particularly in the month of Ramadan because Gabriel used to meet him every night of the month of Ramadan till it elapsed. Allah's Messenger (ﷺ) used to recite the Qur'an for him. When Gabriel met him, he used to become more generous than the fast wind in doing good. Sahih al-Bukhari 4997. https://sunnah.com/bukhari/66/19.

He (SAS) has practiced such generosity and has also taught his companions to practice generosity in their daily life activities. He has always recommended the continuous giving to others in terms of knowledge, money, efforts, etc. The following narration shows how the Prophet (SAS) contemplates about money. He does not need money to stay in his house more than three nights without benefiting everyone around him from such sustenance.

قَالَ أَبُو هُرَيْرَةَ ـ رضى الله عنه ـ قَالَ رَسُولُ اللَّهِ ﷺ " لَوْ كَانَ لِي مِثْلُ أُحُدٍ ذَهَبًا لَسَرَّنِي أَنْ لاَ تَمُرَّ عَلَىَّ ثَلاَثُ لَيَالٍ وَعِنْدِي مِنْهُ شَىْءٌ، إِلاَّ شَيْئًا أَرْصِدُهُ لِدَيْنٍ ". رواه البخاري

Narrated Abu Huraira: Allah Apostle said, "If I had gold equal to the mountain of Uhud, it would not please me that anything of it should remain with me after three nights (i.e., I would spend all of it in Allah's Cause) except what I would keep for repaying debts." Sahih al-Bukhari 6445. https://sunnah.com/bukhari/81/34.

Can we imagine what will happen if we practice such character today? Do you think our life would have been different? The answer is yes. Life is now hard because we do not practice generosity as it is supposed to be. We do not deal with money and sustenance the way he (SAS) has dealt with. This is one of the reasons behind being depressed in this life. There are lots of crises everywhere in our world due to many problems including being ungenerous and stop giving for His sake (SWT).

Character of Modesty

Modesty was the sugar coating character for the Prophet (SAS). He was more modest or shier than a virgin girl as shown in the following narration:

عَنْ أَبِي سَعِيدٍ الْخُدْرِيِّ ـ رضى الله عنه ـ قَالَ كَانَ النَّبِيُّ ﷺ أَشَدَّ حَيَاءً مِنَ الْعَذْرَاءِ فِي خِدْرِهَا. رواه البخارى

Narrated Abu Sa`id Al-Khudri: The Prophet (ﷺ) was shier than a veiled virgin girl. Sahih al-Bukhari 3562. https://sunnah.com/bukhari/61/71.

He (SAS) has also been a modest person with sinners or wrong doers. He has never confronted them by name; however, he was merciful and modest to them in the advice as shown in the following narration:

عَنْ عَائِشَةَ، رضى الله عنها قَالَتْ كَانَ النَّبِيُّ ﷺ إِذَا بَلَغَهُ عَنِ الرَّجُلِ الشَّىْءُ لَمْ يَقُلْ مَا بَالُ فُلاَنٍ يَقُولُ وَلَكِنْ يَقُولُ " مَا بَالُ أَقْوَامٍ يَقُولُونَ كَذَا وَكَذَا " . صحيح الألباني

Narrated Aisha, Ummul Mu'minin: When the Prophet (ﷺ) was informed of anything of a certain man, he would not say: What is the matter with so and so that he says? But he would say: What is the matter with the people that they say such and such? Sunan Abi Dawud 478. Sahih (Al-Albani). https://sunnah.com/abudawud/43/16

The character of modesty has been clear in the Prophet (SAS) where Allah (SWT) explains it to the believers as shown in the following verse:

يَا أَيُّهَا الَّذِينَ آمَنُوا لَا تَدْخُلُوا بُيُوتَ النَّبِيِّ إِلَّا أَن يُؤْذَنَ لَكُمْ إِلَىٰ طَعَامٍ غَيْرَ نَاظِرِينَ إِنَاهُ وَلَٰكِنْ إِذَا دُعِيتُمْ فَادْخُلُوا فَإِذَا طَعِمْتُمْ فَانتَشِرُوا وَلَا مُسْتَأْنِسِينَ لِحَدِيثٍ ۚ إِنَّ ذَٰلِكُمْ كَانَ يُؤْذِي النَّبِيَّ فَيَسْتَحْيِي مِنكُمْ ۖ وَاللَّهُ لَا يَسْتَحْيِي مِنَ الْحَقِّ ۚ .... (53) سورة الأحزاب

Chapter Al-Ahzab **(53) O you who have believed, do not enter the houses of the Prophet except when you are permitted for a meal, without awaiting its readiness. But when you are invited, then enter; and when you have eaten, disperse without seeking to remain for conversation. Indeed, that [behavior] was troubling the Prophet, and he is shy of [dismissing] you. But Allah is not shy of the truth. ......**

We should try to practice such decent character.

Character of Asceticism

The Prophet (SAS) has lived as ascetic providing that he would have been given a better life if he asked for. However, he has preferred such life over anything else in this world because he has understood the reality of life. He has known that life is short, it is a period of preparation for a better life afterwards in the Hereafter, and it is deceiving. Therefore, he (SAS) has tried to be ascetic in this life. This is clear in the following narration:

حَدَّثَنَا أَنَسُ بْنُ مَالِكٍ قَالَ: دَخَلْتُ عَلَى النَّبِيِّ ﷺ وَهُوَ عَلَى سَرِيرٍ مَرْمُولٍ بِشَرِيطٍ، تَحْتَ رَأْسِهِ وِسَادَةٌ مِنْ أَدَمٍ حَشْوُهَا لِيفٌ، مَا بَيْنَ جِلْدِهِ وَبَيْنَ السَّرِيرِ ثَوْبٌ، فَدَخَلَ عَلَيْهِ عُمَرُ فَبَكَى، فَقَالَ لَهُ النَّبِيُّ ﷺ: مَا يُبْكِيكَ يَا عُمَرُ؟ قَالَ: أَمَا وَاللَّهِ مَا أَبْكِي يَا رَسُولَ اللَّهِ، أَلَّا أَكُونَ أَعْلَمُ أَنَّكَ أَكْرَمُ عَلَى اللَّهِ مِنْ كِسْرَى وَقَيْصَرَ، فَهُمَا يَعِيشَانِ فِيمَا يَعِيشَانِ فِيهِ مِنَ الدُّنْيَا، وَأَنْتَ يَا رَسُولَ اللَّهِ بِالْمَكَانِ الَّذِي أَرَى، فَقَالَ النَّبِيُّ ﷺ: أَمَا تَرْضَى يَا عُمَرُ أَنْ تَكُونَ لَهُمُ الدُّنْيَا وَلَنَا الْآخِرَةُ؟ قُلْتُ: بَلَى يَا رَسُولَ اللَّهِ، قَالَ: فَإِنَّهُ كَذَلِكَ. حسن صحيح الألباني

Anas ibn Malik said, "I came to the Prophet, May Allah bless him and grant him peace, while he was on a seat with a bad woven on it. He had a pillow under his head made of skin stuffed with fibre. There was a cloth between his skin and the seat. 'Umar visited him and wept. The Prophet, May Allah bless him and grant him peace, said, 'What made you weep, 'Umar?' He said, 'By Allah, Messenger of Allah, I am only weeping since I know that you are nobler with Allah than Chosroes and Caesar. They both live in what they live of this world while you, Messenger of Allah, are in the place I see.' The Prophet, May Allah bless him and grant him peace, said, 'Are you not content, 'Umar, that they have this world while we have the Next?' I replied, 'Yes, Messenger of Allah.' He said, 'That is the way of it.'" Hasan Sahih (Al-Albani). https://sunnah.com/adab/47/10

It is astonishing when we see that a Prophet of Allah (SWT), the best creation on earth, is living such harsh life. For us, such life is considered very harsh. Anyone of us might have in his/her house luxury staff that are thousands of times as much as what the Prophet (SAS) has in his house. Even though we consider ourselves as humble who are living a tough life. The difference between us and him (SAS) is that we love this life much more than him. We do not understand the secret of life as much as he (SAS) has understood. We value life more than what he (SAS) has valued. Unfortunately, we are far away from his teachings (SAS) related to life and its position in our hearts. This is one of the major rationale for being unhappy in our lives. Look at the following narrations and tell me how would feel about your life:

وعن عروة عن عائشة، رضي الله عنها، أنها كانت تقول: والله يا ابن اختي إن كنا لننظر إلى الهلال، ثم الهلال: ثلاثة أهلة في شهرين، وما أوقد في أبيات رسول ﷺ ، نار. قلت: يا خالة فما كان يعيشكم؟ قالت: الأسودان: التمر والماء، إلا أنه قد كان لرسول الله ﷺ جيران من الأنصار، وكانت لهم منائح وكانوا يرسلون إلى رسول الله من ألبانها فيسقينا. (متفق عليه).

'Urwah from 'Aishah (May Allah be pleased with her) reported that she used to say to Urwah (May Allah be pleased with him): "O son of my sister, by Allah, I used to see the new moon, then the new moon, then the new moon, i.e., three moons in two months, and a fire was not kindled in the house of Messenger of Allah (ﷺ). "I ('Urwah) said, "O my aunt, what were your means of sustenance?" She said; "Dates and water. But it (so happened) that Messenger of Allah (ﷺ) had some Ansar neighbours who had milch animals. They used to send Messenger of Allah (ﷺ) some milk of their (animals) and he gave that to us to drink." [Al-Bukhari and Muslim]. https://sunnah.com/riyadussalihin/introduction/491

عَنِ ابْنِ عَبَّاسٍ، قَالَ كَانَ رَسُولُ اللَّهِ ﷺ يَبِيتُ اللَّيَالِيَ الْمُتَتَابِعَةَ طَاوِيًا وَأَهْلُهُ لاَ يَجِدُونَ عَشَاءً وَكَانَ أَكْثَرُ خُبْزِهِمْ خُبْزَ الشَّعِيرِ . قَالَ أَبُو عِيسَى هَذَا حَدِيثٌ حَسَنٌ صَحِيحٌ . الترمذى

Ibn 'Abbas said: "The Messenger of Allah (s.a.w) would spend many consecutive nights and his family did not have supper, and most of the time their bread was barley bread." Jami` at-Tirmidhi 2360 (Sahih). https://sunnah.com/tirmidhi/36/57

Can we visualize our houses with no food for more than three months? If your children has meals without meat for one day, they will consider themselves living a miserable life. How about three months or more? I think we are now living an extremely luxury life compared to that of the Prophet (SAS) and his companions. However, the big difference is that life has not been in their hearts but in their hands. They have been able to control life without being deceived by its decoration. On the contrary, life is getting closer to our hearts in which, in general, it controls us. This is why we are weak and getting weaker every day. Asceticism character is a key performance indicator of our belief and the practices of our true understanding for the Prophet's (SAS) teachings.

Character of Patience
Patience is the pillar of success in the life of a human being. Without such character, one cannot achieve much in this life. The Prophet (SAS) has practiced patience in all matters, particularly with the actions of disbelievers. They have been torturing him (SAS) and his

companions for long times and sometimes until death. He never lost patience as shown in the following verse:

فَاصْبِرْ عَلَىٰ مَا يَقُولُونَ وَسَبِّحْ بِحَمْدِ رَبِّكَ قَبْلَ طُلُوعِ الشَّمْسِ وَقَبْلَ الْغُرُوبِ(39) سورة ق

Chapter Qaf (39) So be patient, [O Muhammad], over what they say and exalt [Allah] with praise of your Lord before the rising of the sun and before its setting,

Due to the fact that torture and bad actions from disbelievers have been incredible and unbearable, he (SAS) should have been very patient. This has been the only way to pass through such difficulties in life. No other messenger was sent to people unless he should be patient because he would face difficulties with the disbelievers. This is what Allah (SWT) recommends the Prophet (SAS) in the following verse:

فَاصْبِرْ كَمَا صَبَرَ أُولُو الْعَزْمِ مِنَ الرُّسُلِ وَلَا تَسْتَعْجِل لَّهُمْ ۚ كَأَنَّهُمْ يَوْمَ يَرَوْنَ مَا يُوعَدُونَ لَمْ يَلْبَثُوا إِلَّا سَاعَةً مِّن نَّهَارٍ ۚ بَلَاغٌ ۚ فَهَلْ يُهْلَكُ إِلَّا الْقَوْمُ الْفَاسِقُونَ(35) سورة الأحقاف

Chapter Al-Ahqaf (35) So be patient, [O Muhammad], as were those of determination among the messengers and do not be impatient for them. It will be - on the Day they see that which they are promised - as though they had not remained [in the world] except an hour of a day. [This is] notification. And will [any] be destroyed except the defiantly disobedient people?

The character, which helps the Prophet (SAS) to attain and practice all the above morals, is patience. It is the main pillar of all characters of success. Therefore, no success without patience in any life matters and even for matters related to the Hereafter. We cannot achieve success in our work, study, family life, raising children, dealing with people, etc, without lots of patience. We cannot accomplish success in the Hereafter without lots of patience on worshiping Allah (SWT) in terms of prayer, fasting, charity, and implementing all Islamic principles. Therefore, we should exert much effort to attain such backbone character in our life, i.e., patience.

In conclusion, what would you do when you find a person who has all the above characters? If we find a person who has only one of these characters, we position him high in our minds and hearts. What about if he has all the above and more? We should value him much and position him high in our minds, hearts and life. This is my response to those people who are trying to insult our beloved Prophet (SAS). If you are insulting or undermining the person who has all the above characters, you are the devil himself. I supplicate to Allah (SWT) to guide you to the best and to know the Prophet (SAS) more. This might change your life and your place in the Hereafter.

Recommendations:
I tried my best to be brief in explaining the different personal characters of our beloved Prophet (SAS). I also tried to make every character presented in very few pages in order to make it easy for the readers to share with others and discuss with their children. Therefore, it is recommended that you do the following activities in order to positively defend our beloved Prophet (SAS):
- 1- Share the individual characters with your groups of friends and followers to benefit from such information and spread the good things about our beloved Prophet who is under attack from a few ignorant individuals.

2- Print each character and discuss with your children in order to immune them against all actions of disbelievers who are trying to dilute his reputation (SAS). This action will give them the appropriate minimum knowledge about him (SAS), which will serve two purposes: (a) increase their knowledge about the Prophet (SAS) and (b) encourage them to practice such great characters in their daily life activities.
3- Make a short and long term plans to practice these characters in the individual and family levels. This is crucial to be role models of good characters in an era that is full of bad characters and behaviors.

Chapter II

Remarkable Social Intelligence of our Beloved Prophet

In the previous chapters, we discussed the personal characters of our beloved Prophet (SAS). We have seen the exceptional characters that he (SAS) attained as described by Allah (SWT) and his companions. The discussion reveals high level of standards in ethics, morals and behavior of the Prophet (SAS). In this chapter, I will walk you through the Prophet's outstanding social intelligence that distinguishes him from other human beings and makes him the most beloved prophet to Allah (SWT). It introduces how he (SAS) has dealt with his opponents, ignorant people and wrong doers, animals, followers, servants, and employees.

(i) **The Prophet's Characters with Opponents**:
To show his character in dealing with his opponents, the Prophet (SAS) has been very patient, merciful, and forbearer with them. The following incidents have been evident of such character:

1- *A situation with a Jewish group*:

Aishah, may Allah pleased with her, reported a situation with a Jewish group who came to the Prophet (SAS) and greeted him saying "death be upon you" instead of "peace be upon you". Both words are close in Arabic pronunciation. The Prophet responded "and on you". He kept calm and quite with lots of patience on this abnormal action of this group of people. He was able to respond in a harsh way but he did not. When Aishah tried to respond firmly, he (SAS) asked her to be calm and patient as explained in the following narration:

عَنِ الزُّهْرِيِّ، قَالَ أَخْبَرَنِي عُرْوَةُ، أَنَّ عَائِشَةَ ـ رضى الله عنها ـ قَالَتْ دَخَلَ رَهْطٌ مِنَ الْيَهُودِ عَلَى رَسُولِ اللَّهِ صلى الله عليه وسلم فَقَالُوا السَّامُ عَلَيْكَ. فَفَهِمْتُهَا فَقُلْتُ عَلَيْكُمُ السَّامُ وَاللَّعْنَةُ. فَقَالَ رَسُولُ اللَّهِ صلى الله عليه وسلم " مَهْلاً يَا عَائِشَةُ، فَإِنَّ اللَّهَ يُحِبُّ الرِّفْقَ فِي الأَمْرِ كُلِّهِ ". فَقُلْتُ يَا رَسُولَ اللَّهِ أَوَلَمْ تَسْمَعْ مَا قَالُوا قَالَ رَسُولُ اللَّهِ صلى الله عليه وسلم " فَقَدْ قُلْتُ وَعَلَيْكُمْ ". (رواه البخارى).

Narrated `Aisha: A group of Jews came to Allah's Messenger (ﷺ) and said, "Death be on you, and I understood it and said to them, "Death and curse be on you." Allah's Apostle said, "Be calm! O `Aisha, for Allah loves that one should be kind and lenient in all matters." I said. "O Allah's Messenger (ﷺ)! Haven't you heard what they have said?" Allah's Messenger (ﷺ) said, "I have (already) said (to them), 'upon you.' " Sahih al-Bukhari 6256. https://sunnah.com/bukhari/79/30

2- Another situation with a Bedouin:

When a Bedouin was very harsh to the Prophet (SAS), he (SAS) was very patient and calm dealing with him as shown in the following narration:

عَنْ أَنَسِ بْنِ مَالِكٍ ـ رضى الله عنه قَالَ كُنْتُ أَمْشِي مَعَ النَّبِيِّ ﷺ وَعَلَيْهِ بُرْدٌ نَجْرَانِيٌّ غَلِيظُ الْحَاشِيَةِ، فَأَدْرَكَهُ أَعْرَابِيٌّ فَجَذَبَهُ جَذْبَةً شَدِيدَةً، حَتَّى نَظَرْتُ إِلَى صَفْحَةِ عَاتِقِ النَّبِيِّ ﷺ قَدْ أَثَّرَتْ بِهِ حَاشِيَةُ الرِّدَاءِ مِنْ شِدَّةِ جَذْبَتِهِ، ثُمَّ قَالَ مُرْ لِي مِنْ مَالِ اللَّهِ الَّذِي عِنْدَكَ. فَالْتَفَتَ إِلَيْهِ، فَضَحِكَ ثُمَّ أَمَرَ لَهُ بِعَطَاءٍ. (رواه البخارى).

Narrated Anas bin Malik: While I was walking with the Prophet (ﷺ) who was wearing a Najrani outer garment with a thick hem, a bedouin came upon the Prophet (ﷺ) and pulled his garment so violently that I could recognize the impress of the hem of the garment on his shoulder, caused by the violence of his pull. Then the bedouin said, "Order for me something from Allah's Fortune which you have." The Prophet (ﷺ) turned to him and smiled, and ordered that a gift be given to him. Sahih al-Bukhari 3149. https://sunnah.com/bukhari/57/57

The main goal of the Prophet's existence is to guide people with utmost mercy and kindness. Therefore, he has kept considerable amount of energy to be patient to and kind with those harsh people, i.e., opponents, hoping to attract the attention of their minds and hearts to the right path. He has never forgotten his core message (SAS) of being a mercy to mankind in order to pull them out of the darkness of disbelief to the light of belief. He has tried continuously and untiredly with opponents until his death (SAS). Then, his companions and followers have carried the message and the guidance to humanity until today. It will continue until the day Judgment following the practices and traditions of our beloved Prophet (SAS).

(ii) **The Prophet's Characters with Ignorant People**
The Prophet (SAS) has a great philosophy and conceptual vision in dealing with ignorant people. He (SAS) has implemented such a vision in all life matters. For example, in the following narration, a man once urinated in the mosque, i.e., the place of prayer that should always be kept clean. It is an unusual act that might be due to ignorance, negligence, or hatred. In a situation like that, a human being will be very angry, irritated and bothered. However, the response of the Prophet (SAS) has been totally different, which shows his conceptual behavior with this man. He (SAS) has stopped his companions from hurting this ignorant man and has explained to them the conceptual character of being sent to humanity to make things easy (for the people) as shown in the following narration:

أَنَّ أَبَا هُرَيْرَةَ، أَخْبَرَهُ أَنَّ أَعْرَابِيًّا بَالَ فِي الْمَسْجِدِ، فَثَارَ إِلَيْهِ النَّاسُ لِيَقَعُوا بِهِ فَقَالَ لَهُمْ رَسُولُ اللَّهِ ﷺ " دَعُوهُ، وَأَهْرِيقُوا عَلَى بَوْلِهِ ذَنُوبًا مِنْ مَاءٍ ـ أَوْ سَجْلاً مِنْ مَاءٍ ـ فَإِنَّمَا بُعِثْتُمْ مُيَسِّرِينَ، وَلَمْ تُبْعَثُوا مُعَسِّرِينَ ". (رواه البخاري).

Narrated Abu Huraira: A bedouin urinated in the mosque, and the people rushed to beat him. Allah's Messenger (ﷺ) ordered them to leave him and pour a bucket or a tumbler (full) of water over the place where he has passed urine. The Prophet then said, "You have been sent to make things easy (for the people) and you have not been sent to make things difficult for them." Sahih al-Bukhari 6128. https://sunnah.com/bukhari/78/155

The Prophet (SAS) has been implementing the Quranic concept of soft dealings with ignorant people as shown in the following verse:

وَإِذَا سَمِعُوا اللَّغْوَ أَعْرَضُوا عَنْهُ وَقَالُوا لَنَا أَعْمَالُنَا وَلَكُمْ أَعْمَالُكُمْ سَلَامٌ عَلَيْكُمْ لَا نَبْتَغِي الْجَاهِلِينَ(55) سورة القصص

Chapter Al-Qasas **(55) And when they hear ill speech, they turn away from it and say, "For us are our deeds, and for you are your deeds. Peace will be upon you; we seek not the ignorant."**

He (SAS) has practiced the character of servants of Allah (SWT) who are humble and peaceful to those who are ignorant as shown in the following verse:

وَعِبَادُ الرَّحْمَنِ الَّذِينَ يَمْشُونَ عَلَى الْأَرْضِ هَوْنًا وَإِذَا خَاطَبَهُمُ الْجَاهِلُونَ قَالُوا سَلَامًا(63) سورة الفرقان

Chapter Al-Furqan **(63) And the servants of the Most Merciful are those who walk upon the earth easily, and when the ignorant address them [harshly], they say** [words of] peace.

(iii) The Prophet's Characters with Wrong Doers

Wrong doers are always treated harshly by the society they live in. They are usually under attack due to their bad actions that harm others. However, if the society considers their bad actions as psychological problems that need attention and good treatment, they will be treated differently. This is what the Prophet (SAS) has already done with his wisdom and the help of Allah's revelation. He (SAS) has been very kind, merciful, and forbearer with the wrong doers. In the following narration, he (SAS) is supposed to get angry because the companions have traded with interest, i.e., one of the obvious largest mistakes in the religion. However, he (SAS) has used the calm and soft response to teach his companions how to deal with such situations as follows:

عَنْ أَبِي سَعِيدٍ، قَالَ أُتِيَ رَسُولُ اللَّهِ ﷺ بِتَمْرٍ فَقَالَ " مَا هَذَا التَّمْرُ مِنْ تَمْرِنَا " . فَقَالَ الرَّجُلُ يَا رَسُولَ اللَّهِ بِعْنَا تَمْرَنَا صَاعَيْنِ بِصَاعٍ مِنْ هَذَا . فَقَالَ رَسُولُ اللَّهِ ﷺ " هَذَا الرِّبَا فَرُدُّوهُ ثُمَّ بِيعُوا تَمْرَنَا وَاشْتَرُوا لَنَا مِنْ هَذَا " . (رواه مسلم).

Abu Sa'id (Allah be pleased with him) reported: Dates were brought to Allah's Messenger (ﷺ), and he said: These dates are not like our dates, whereupon a man said: We sold two sa's of our dates (in order to get) one sa', of these (fine dates), whereupon Allah's Messenger (ﷺ) said: That is interest; so return (these dates of fine quality), and get your (inferior dates) ; then sell our dates (for money) and buy for us (with the help of money) such (fine dates). Sahih Muslim 1594 b, https://sunnah.com/muslim/22/123

In another incident, when Usama Ibn Zaid has tried to intercede for a woman that has stolen something and her tribe did not want her to be punished for such an action. It was not a wise action from Usama Ibn Zaid to commit such a sin. However, the Prophet (SAS) politely rejected his request. Then, he (SAS) has spoken to people not to do such actions because they cause destruction to the society as shown in the following narration:

قَالَ أَخْبَرَنِي عُرْوَةُ بْنُ الزُّبَيْرِ، أَنَّ امْرَأَةً، سَرَقَتْ فِي عَهْدِ رَسُولِ اللَّهِ ﷺ فِي غَزْوَةِ الْفَتْحِ، فَفَزِعَ قَوْمُهَا إِلَى أُسَامَةَ بْنِ زَيْدٍ يَسْتَشْفِعُونَهُ، قَالَ عُرْوَةُ فَلَمَّا كَلَّمَهُ أُسَامَةُ فِيهَا تَلَوَّنَ وَجْهُ رَسُولِ اللَّهِ ﷺ فَقَالَ " أَتُكَلِّمُنِي فِي حَدٍّ مِنْ حُدُودِ اللَّهِ ". قَالَ أُسَامَةُ اسْتَغْفِرْ لِي يَا رَسُولَ اللَّهِ. فَلَمَّا كَانَ الْعَشِيُّ قَامَ رَسُولُ اللَّهِ ﷺ خَطِيبًا، فَأَثْنَى عَلَى اللَّهِ بِمَا هُوَ أَهْلُهُ ثُمَّ قَالَ " أَمَّا بَعْدُ، فَإِنَّمَا أَهْلَكَ النَّاسَ قَبْلَكُمْ أَنَّهُمْ كَانُوا إِذَا سَرَقَ فِيهِمُ الشَّرِيفُ تَرَكُوهُ، وَإِذَا سَرَقَ فِيهِمُ الضَّعِيفُ أَقَامُوا عَلَيْهِ الْحَدَّ، وَالَّذِي نَفْسُ مُحَمَّدٍ بِيَدِهِ، لَوْ أَنَّ فَاطِمَةَ بِنْتَ مُحَمَّدٍ سَرَقَتْ لَقَطَعْتُ يَدَهَا ". ثُمَّ أَمَرَ رَسُولُ اللَّهِ ﷺ بِتِلْكَ الْمَرْأَةِ، فَقُطِعَتْ يَدُهَا، فَحَسُنَتْ تَوْبَتُهَا بَعْدَ ذَلِكَ وَتَزَوَّجَتْ. قَالَتْ عَائِشَةُ فَكَانَتْ تَأْتِي بَعْدَ ذَلِكَ فَأَرْفَعُ حَاجَتَهَا إِلَى رَسُولِ اللَّهِ ﷺ. (رواه البخارى).

Narrated `Urwa bin Az-Zubair: A lady committed theft during the lifetime of Allah's Messenger (ﷺ) in the Ghazwa of Al-Fath, ((i.e. Conquest of Mecca). Her folk went to Usama bin Zaid to intercede for her (with the Prophet). When Usama interceded for her with Allah's Messenger (ﷺ), the color of the face of Allah's Messenger (ﷺ) changed and he said, "Do you intercede with me in a matter involving one of the legal punishments prescribed by Allah?" Usama said, "O Allah's Messenger (ﷺ)! Ask Allah's Forgiveness for me." So in the afternoon, Allah's Apostle got up and addressed the people. He praised Allah as He deserved and then said, "Amma ba'du ! The nations prior to you were destroyed because if a noble amongst them stole, they used to excuse him, and if a poor person amongst them stole, they would apply (Allah's) Legal Punishment to him. By Him in Whose Hand Muhammad's soul is, if Fatima, the daughter of Muhammad stole, I would cut her hand." Then Allah's Messenger (ﷺ) gave his order in the case of that woman and her hand was cut off. Afterwards her repentance proved sincere and she got married. `Aisha said, "That lady used to visit me and I used to convey her demands to Allah's

Messenger (ﷺ)." Sahih al-Bukhari 4304, https://sunnah.com/bukhari/64/337

The following incident has been the worst when a believer has asked the Prophet (SAS) to give him a permission to commit adultery. This is a big sin in Islam that is strictly prohibited. The Prophet's companions have been irritated with such a request. However, the Prophet (SAS) has been totally different and dealt with such incident with full wisdom and kindness. Such action has made the person who asked the question fully satisfied and disliked what he has asked for:

وَعَنْ أَبِي أُمَامَةَ، قَالَ: إِنَّ فَتًى شَابًّا أَتَى النَّبِيَّ ﷺ فَقَالَ: يَا رَسُولَ اللَّهِ، ائْذَنْ لِي بِالزِّنَا، فَأَقْبَلَ الْقَوْمُ عَلَيْهِ، فَزَجَرُوهُ، قَالُوا: مَهْ مَهْ، فَقَالَ: " ادْنُهْ "، فَدَنَا مِنْهُ قَرِيبًا، قَالَ: فَجَلَسَ، قَالَ: " أَتُحِبُّهُ لِأُمِّكَ؟ "، قَالَ: لَا وَاللَّهِ، جَعَلَنِي اللَّهُ فِدَاءَكَ، قَالَ " :وَلَا النَّاسُ يُحِبُّونَهُ لِأُمَّهَاتِهِمْ "، قَالَ: " أَفَتُحِبُّهُ لِابْنَتِكَ؟ "، قَالَ: لَا وَاللَّهِ يَا رَسُولَ اللَّهِ، جَعَلَنِي اللَّهُ فِدَاءَكَ، قَالَ: " وَلَا النَّاسُ يُحِبُّونَهُ لِبَنَاتِهِمْ، قَالَ: أَفَتُحِبُّهُ لِأُخْتِكَ؟ "، قَالَ: لَا وَاللَّهِ، جَعَلَنِي اللَّهُ فِدَاءَكَ، قَالَ: " وَلَا النَّاسُ يُحِبُّونَهُ لِأَخَوَاتِهِمْ، قَالَ: أَفَتُحِبُّهُ لِعَمَّتِكَ؟ "، قَالَ: لَا وَاللَّهِ، جَعَلَنِي اللَّهُ فِدَاءَكَ، قَالَ: " وَلَا النَّاسُ يُحِبُّونَهُ لِعَمَّاتِهِمْ، قَالَ: أَفَتُحِبُّهُ لِخَالَتِكَ؟ "، قَالَ: لَا وَاللَّهِ، جَعَلَنِي اللَّهُ فِدَاءَكَ، قَالَ: " وَلَا النَّاسُ يُحِبُّونَهُ لِخَالَاتِهِمْ، قَالَ: فَوَضَعَ يَدَهُ عَلَيْهِ، وَقَالَ: " اللَّهُمَّ اغْفِرْ ذَنْبَهُ، وَطَهِّرْ قَلْبَهُ، وَحَصِّنْ فَرْجَهُ "، فَلَمْ يَكُنْ بَعْدَ ذَلِكَ الْفَتَى يَلْتَفِتُ إِلَى شَيْءٍ. (رواه الإمام أحمد [21708] ورواته ثقات).

Abi Umamah narrated that a young man came to the Prophet, may Allah's prayers and peace be upon him, and said: O Prophet of Allah, do you permit me to commit adultery? The people shouted at him, then the Prophet, may Allah bless him and grant him peace, said, "Get him closer to me until the man sat before the Prophet." So the Prophet, may peace and blessings be upon him, said: Do you like your mother to commit adultery? The man said: No, may Allah made me redeem you, he said: Likewise people do not like it for their mothers. He said: do you like it for your daughter? The man said No, may Allah made me redeem you, he said: Likewise people do not like it for their daughters. Do you like it for your sister? The man said No, may Allah made me redeem you, he said: Likewise people do not like it for their sisters. Do you like it for your aunt? The man said No, may Allah made me redeem you, he said: Likewise people do not like it for their aunts. Then, the Prophet (SAS) put his hands on the man's chest and said: O Allah, forgive his sin, purify his heart, and protect his private organs, so nothing was more hateful to this young man than adultery. Narrated by Ahmed. https://dorar.net/hadith/sharh/112427

The Previous incidents, like many other ones, have continually occurred to the Prophet (SAS) during his entire life. His response (SAS) has been always the same where the wrong doers have converted their positions before and after the sin. It is always the wisdom, mercy, and kindness that cause such dramatical change in the position of people. What power that makes the Prophet (SAS) do such a change in the minds and hearts of people. It is the power of always being with Allah (SWT), of following His orders, and of always remembering Him.

(iv) The Prophet's Characters with People Who Hurt Him and His Companions
Look at the surprising response of the Prophet (SAS) and his dealings with the disbelievers who have tortured him and his companions for 13 years in Makkah and have fought them for 8 years afterwards. The disbelievers have killed the Prophet's uncle and many of his companions in very tough battles with no mercy. Despite all of the above, he has forgiven them all and has dealt with them with exceptional high level of mercy that never occurs in the past nor the modern history. The Prophet's response is shown in the following narration:

عَنْ ابْنِ عَبَّاسٍ، قَالَ لَمَّا نَزَلَ رَسُولُ اللَّهِ ﷺ مَرَّ الظَّهْرَانَ قَالَ الْعَبَّاسُ قُلْتُ وَاللَّهِ لَئِنْ دَخَلَ رَسُولُ اللَّهِ ﷺ مَكَّةَ عَنْوَةً قَبْلَ أَنْ يَأْتُوهُ فَيَسْتَأْمِنُوهُ إِنَّهُ لَهَلَاكُ قُرَيْشٍ فَجَلَسْتُ عَلَى بَغْلَةِ رَسُولِ اللَّهِ ﷺ فَقُلْتُ لَعَلِّي أَجِدُ ذَا حَاجَةٍ يَأْتِي مَكَّةَ فَيُخْبِرُهُمْ بِمَكَانِ رَسُولِ اللَّهِ ﷺ لِيَخْرُجُوا إِلَيْهِ فَيَسْتَأْمِنُوهُ فَإِنِّي لَأَسِيرُ إِذْ سَمِعْتُ كَلَامَ أَبِي سُفْيَانَ وَبُدَيْلِ بْنِ وَرْقَاءَ فَقُلْتُ يَا أَبَا حَنْظَلَةَ فَعَرَفَ صَوْتِي فَقَالَ أَبُو الْفَضْلِ قُلْتُ نَعَمْ . قَالَ مَا لَكَ فِدَاكَ أَبِي وَأُمِّي قُلْتُ هَذَا رَسُولُ اللَّهِ ﷺ وَالنَّاسُ . قَالَ فَمَا الْحِيلَةُ قَالَ فَرَكِبَ خَلْفِي وَرَجَعَ صَاحِبُهُ فَلَمَّا أَصْبَحَ غَدَوْتُ بِهِ عَلَى رَسُولِ اللَّهِ ﷺ فَأَسْلَمَ قُلْتُ يَا رَسُولَ اللَّهِ إِنَّ أَبَا سُفْيَانَ رَجُلٌ يُحِبُّ هَذَا الْفَخْرَ فَاجْعَلْ لَهُ شَيْئًا . قَالَ " نَعَمْ مَنْ دَخَلَ دَارَ أَبِي سُفْيَانَ فَهُوَ آمِنٌ وَمَنْ أَغْلَقَ عَلَيْهِ دَارَهُ فَهُوَ آمِنٌ وَمَنْ دَخَلَ الْمَسْجِدَ فَهُوَ آمِنٌ " . قَالَ فَتَفَرَّقَ النَّاسُ إِلَى دُورِهِمْ وَإِلَى الْمَسْجِدِ . حسن - الألباني

Narrated Abdullah Ibn Abbas: When the Prophet (ﷺ) alighted at Marr az-Zahran, al-Abbas said: I thought, I swear by Allah, if the Messenger of Allah (ﷺ) enters Mecca with the army by force before the Quraysh come to him and seek protection from him, it will be their total ruin. So I rode on the mule of the Messenger of Allah (ﷺ) and thought, Perhaps I may find a man coming for his needs who will to the people of Mecca and inform them of the position of the Messenger of Allah (ﷺ), so that they may come to him and seek protection from him. While I was on my way, I heard AbuSufyan and Budayl ibn Warqa' speaking.

I said: O AbuHanzalah! He recognized my voice and said: AbulFadl? I replied: Yes. He said: who is with you, may my parents be a sacrifice for you? I said: Here are the Messenger of Allah (ﷺ) and his people (with him).
He asked: Which is the way out? He said: He rode behind me, and his companion returned. When the morning came, I brought him to the Messenger of Allah (ﷺ) and he embraced Islam.
I said: Messenger of Allah, AbuSufyan is a man who likes this pride, do something for him. He said: Yes, **he who enters the house of AbuSufyan is safe; he who closes the door upon him is safe; and he who enters the mosque is safe. The people scattered to their houses and in the mosque**. Hasan (Al-Albani).
https://sunnah.com/abudawud/20/95

Can you imagine such action of forgiveness to those who have killed, tortured, and fought you for 21 years? This is an unbelievable character. What kind of heart the Prophet has. It is beyond expectations to forgive at the time you are able to revenge and deal with the disbelievers in a similar manner to what they have done to your relatives and friends. This has not been only the Prophet's character, it was also the companions' character. They did not even think of taking revenge from those who killed their family members, friends, and/or relatives. All of them have been obedient to their leader (SAS). I think such actions and great behavior are valued by great principled people. However, those who do not value such great actions are representing the devil on earth.

(v) The Prophet's Characters with Disbelievers
Whenever I walk through the Prophet's characters with different social sectors of his society, I realize his social intelligence (SAS) in dealing with all sectors. In the case of disbelievers, he (SAS) has dealt with them in a high level of mercy and kindness. Look at the following narration when he (SAS) has given them generously:

عَنْ مُوسَى بْنِ أَنَسٍ، عَنْ أَبِيهِ، قَالَ مَا سُئِلَ رَسُولُ اللَّهِ ﷺ عَلَى الإِسْلاَمِ شَيْئًا إِلاَّ أَعْطَاهُ - قَالَ - فَجَاءَهُ رَجُلٌ فَأَعْطَاهُ غَنَمًا بَيْنَ جَبَلَيْنِ فَرَجَعَ إِلَى قَوْمِهِ فَقَالَ يَا قَوْمِ أَسْلِمُوا فَإِنَّ مُحَمَّدًا يُعْطِي عَطَاءً لاَ يَخْشَى الْفَاقَةَ . (رواه مسلم).

Musa b. Anas reported on the authority of his father: It never happened that Allah's

Messenger (ﷺ) was asked anything for the sake of Islam and he did not give that. There came to him a person and he gave him a large flock (of sheep and goats) and he went back to his people and said: My people, embrace Islam, for Muhammad gives so much charity as if he has no fear of want. Sahih Muslim 2312 a. https://sunnah.com/muslim/43/78

He (SAS) also has recommended all the companions to respect the treaty with the disbelievers as shown in the following narration:

عَنْ عَبْدِ اللَّهِ بْنِ عَمْرٍو ـ رضى الله عنهما ـ عَنِ النَّبِيِّ ﷺ قَالَ " مَنْ قَتَلَ مُعَاهَدًا لَمْ يَرَحْ رَائِحَةَ الْجَنَّةِ، وَإِنَّ رِيحَهَا تُوجَدُ مِنْ مَسِيرَةِ أَرْبَعِينَ عَامًا ". (رواه البخارى).

Narrated `Abdullah bin `Amr: The Prophet (ﷺ) said, "Whoever killed a person having a treaty with the Muslims, shall not smell the smell of Paradise though its smell is perceived from a distance of forty years." Sahih al-Bukhari 3166. https://sunnah.com/bukhari/58/8

The following narration shows how his mercy (SAS) was the reason for disbelievers to change their minds and hearts and convert to Islam:

أَنَّهُ سَمِعَ أَبَا هُرَيْرَةَ ـ رضى الله عنه ـ قَالَ بَعَثَ النَّبِيُّ ﷺ خَيْلاً قِبَلَ نَجْدٍ، فَجَاءَتْ بِرَجُلٍ مِنْ بَنِي حَنِيفَةَ يُقَالُ لَهُ ثُمَامَةُ بْنُ أُثَالٍ، فَرَبَطُوهُ بِسَارِيَةٍ مِنْ سَوَارِي الْمَسْجِدِ، فَخَرَجَ إِلَيْهِ النَّبِيُّ ﷺ فَقَالَ " مَا عِنْدَكَ يَا ثُمَامَةُ ". فَقَالَ عِنْدِي خَيْرٌ يَا مُحَمَّدُ، إِنْ تَقْتُلْنِي تَقْتُلْ ذَا دَمٍ، وَإِنْ تُنْعِمْ تُنْعِمْ عَلَى شَاكِرٍ، وَإِنْ كُنْتَ تُرِيدُ الْمَالَ فَسَلْ مِنْهُ مَا شِئْتَ. حَتَّى كَانَ الْغَدُ ثُمَّ قَالَ لَهُ " مَا عِنْدَكَ يَا ثُمَامَةُ ". قَالَ مَا قُلْتُ لَكَ إِنْ تُنْعِمْ تُنْعِمْ عَلَى شَاكِرٍ. فَتَرَكَهُ حَتَّى كَانَ بَعْدَ الْغَدِ، فَقَالَ " مَا عِنْدَكَ يَا ثُمَامَةُ ". فَقَالَ عِنْدِي مَا قُلْتُ لَكَ. فَقَالَ " أَطْلِقُوا ثُمَامَةَ "، فَانْطَلَقَ إِلَى نَخْلٍ قَرِيبٍ مِنَ الْمَسْجِدِ ثُمَّ دَخَلَ الْمَسْجِدَ فَقَالَ أَشْهَدُ أَنْ لاَ إِلَهَ إِلاَّ اللَّهُ، وَأَشْهَدُ أَنَّ مُحَمَّدًا رَسُولُ اللَّهِ، يَا مُحَمَّدُ وَاللَّهِ مَا كَانَ عَلَى الأَرْضِ وَجْهٌ أَبْغَضَ إِلَىَّ مِنْ وَجْهِكَ، فَقَدْ أَصْبَحَ وَجْهُكَ أَحَبَّ الْوُجُوهِ إِلَىَّ، وَاللَّهِ مَا كَانَ مِنْ دِينٍ أَبْغَضَ إِلَىَّ مِنْ دِينِكَ، فَأَصْبَحَ دِينُكَ أَحَبَّ الدِّينِ إِلَىَّ، وَاللَّهِ مَا كَانَ مِنْ بَلَدٍ أَبْغَضَ إِلَىَّ مِنْ بَلَدِكَ، فَأَصْبَحَ بَلَدُكَ أَحَبَّ الْبِلاَدِ إِلَىَّ، وَإِنَّ خَيْلَكَ أَخَذَتْنِي وَأَنَا أُرِيدُ الْعُمْرَةَ، فَمَاذَا تَرَى فَبَشَّرَهُ رَسُولُ اللَّهِ ﷺ وَأَمَرَهُ أَنْ يَعْتَمِرَ، فَلَمَّا قَدِمَ مَكَّةَ قَالَ لَهُ قَائِلٌ صَبَوْتَ. قَالَ لاَ، وَلَكِنْ أَسْلَمْتُ مَعَ مُحَمَّدٍ رَسُولِ اللَّهِ ﷺ ، وَلاَ، وَاللَّهِ لاَ يَأْتِيكُمْ مِنَ الْيَمَامَةِ حَبَّةُ حِنْطَةٍ حَتَّى يَأْذَنَ فِيهَا النَّبِيُّ ﷺ . (رواه البخارى).

Narrated Abu Huraira: The Prophet (ﷺ) sent some cavalry towards Najd and they brought a man from the tribe of Banu Hanifa who was called Thumama bin Uthal. They fastened him to one of the pillars of the Mosque. The Prophet went to him and said, "What have you got, O Thumama?" He replied," I have got a good thought, O Muhammad! If you should kill me, you would kill a person who has already killed somebody, and if you should set me free, you would do a favor to one who is grateful, and if you want property, then ask me whatever wealth you want." He was left till the next day when the Prophet (ﷺ) said to him, "What have you got, Thumama? He said, "What I told you, i.e. if you set me free, you would do a favor to one who is grateful." The Prophet (ﷺ) left him till the day after, when he said, "What have you got, O Thumama?" He said, "I have got what I told you. "On that the Prophet (ﷺ) said, "Release Thumama." So he (i.e. Thumama) went to a garden of date-palm trees near to the Mosque, took a bath and then entered the Mosque and said, "I testify that None has the right to be worshipped except Allah, and also testify that Muhammad is His Apostle! By Allah, O Muhammad! There was no face on the surface of the earth most disliked by me than yours, but now your face has become the most beloved face to me. By Allah, there was no religion most disliked by me than yours, but now it is the most beloved religion to me. By Allah, there was no town most disliked by me than your town, but now it is the most beloved town to me. Your cavalry arrested me (at the time) when I was intending to perform the `Umra. And now what do you think?" The Prophet (ﷺ) gave him good tidings (congratulated him) and ordered him to perform the `Umra. So when he came to Mecca, someone said to him, "You have become a

Sabian?" Thumama replied, "No! By Allah, I have embraced Islam with Muhammad, Apostle of Allah. No, by Allah! Not a single grain of wheat will come to you from Yamamah unless the Prophet gives his permission." Sahih al-Bukhari 4372. https://sunnah.com/bukhari/64/398

The Prophet (SAS) has been simply applying the following verse in all his dealings with the disbelievers:

لَا يَنْهَاكُمُ اللَّهُ عَنِ الَّذِينَ لَمْ يُقَاتِلُوكُمْ فِي الدِّينِ وَلَمْ يُخْرِجُوكُم مِّن دِيَارِكُمْ أَن تَبَرُّوهُمْ وَتُقْسِطُوا إِلَيْهِمْ ۚ إِنَّ اللَّهَ يُحِبُّ الْمُقْسِطِينَ (8) سورة الممتحنة

Chapter Al-Mumtahanah **(8) Allah does not forbid you from those who do not fight you because of religion and do not expel you from your homes - from being righteous toward them and acting justly toward them. Indeed, Allah loves those who act justly.**

You can realize from this verse and its implementation by the Prophet (SAS) and his companions all principles of love, forbearance, and pure hearts. It also complies high level of ethics and social intelligence. The hearts of the Prophet (SAS), his companions, and the followers until the Day of Judgement have no hard feeling against their enemies or opponents. On the contrary, they like to their enemies all the best and hope for them the guidance in life and the great reward in the Hereafter. It becomes a role, until the day of judgement, that believers do not carry any hard feeling against disbelievers who do not harm or expel them from their homes/lands. Allah (SWT) asked the believers to be righteous and just to the disbelievers because they are brothers and sisters in humanity. It is one of the core principles that made Muslims and all other religions live together in the same places for hundreds of years in peace with no conflict. The conflict has always occurred only with the disbelievers who represent the devil and hate to co-live with others in the same place.

(vi) The Prophet's Characters with Animals

The great hearts do not always distinguish between different creatures, i.e., humans, animals, plants, etc, in their dealings. This case is obvious with the Prophet (SAS) who has dealt with complete mercy and kindness with animals in many occasions. The following narration explains his approach towards animals when he advised Aisha (may Allah be pleased with her) to be kind and sympathized with the animal:

سَمِعْتُ عَائِشَةَ تَقُولُ: كُنْتُ عَلَى بَعِيرٍ فِيهِ صُعُوبَةٌ، فَجَعَلْتُ أَضْرِبُهُ، فَقَالَ النَّبِيُّ ﷺ : عَلَيْكِ بِالرِّفْقِ، فَإِنَّ الرِّفْقَ لاَ يَكُونُ فِي شَيْءٍ إِلاَّ زَانَهُ، وَلاَ يُنْزَعُ مِنْ شَيْءٍ إِلاَّ شَانَهُ. صحيح الألباني

'A'isha said, "I was on a camel that was somewhat intractable and I began to beat it. The Prophet, may Allah bless him and grant him peace, said, 'You must be compassionate. Whenever there is compassion in something, it adorns it, and whenever it is removed from something it disgraces it." Sahih (Al-Albani). https://sunnah.com/adab/27/14

In several other situations, he (SAS) has shown his companions the necessity of being kind to animals and how this might grant them Paradise with great rewards in the Hereafter as indicated in the following narration:

عَنْ أَبِي هُرَيْرَةَ ـ رضي الله عنه ـ أَنَّ رَسُولَ اللَّهِ ﷺ قَالَ " بَيْنَا رَجُلٌ يَمْشِي فَاشْتَدَّ عَلَيْهِ الْعَطَشُ، فَنَزَلَ بِئْرًا فَشَرِبَ مِنْهَا، ثُمَّ خَرَجَ فَإِذَا هُوَ بِكَلْبٍ يَلْهَثُ، يَأْكُلُ الثَّرَى مِنَ الْعَطَشِ، فَقَالَ لَقَدْ بَلَغَ هَذَا مِثْلُ الَّذِي بَلَغَ بِي فَمَلأَ خُفَّهُ ثُمَّ أَمْسَكَهُ بِفِيهِ، ثُمَّ رَقِيَ، فَسَقَى الْكَلْبَ

فَشَكَرَ اللَّهُ لَهُ، فَغَفَرَ لَهُ ". قَالُوا يَا رَسُولَ اللَّهِ، وَإِنَّ لَنَا فِي الْبَهَائِمِ أَجْرًا قَالَ " فِي كُلِّ كَبِدٍ رَطْبَةٍ أَجْرٌ ". تَابَعَهُ حَمَّادُ بْنُ سَلَمَةَ وَالرَّبِيعُ بْنُ مُسْلِمٍ عَنْ مُحَمَّدِ بْنِ زِيَادٍ. (رواه البخاري).

Narrated Abu Huraira: Allah's Messenger (ﷺ) said, "While a man was walking he felt thirsty and went down a well and drank water from it. On coming out of it, he saw a dog panting and eating mud because of excessive thirst. The man said, 'This (dog) is suffering from the same problem as that of mine. So he (went down the well), filled his shoe with water, caught hold of it with his teeth and climbed up and watered the dog. Allah thanked him for his (good) deed and forgave him." The people asked, "O Allah's Messenger (ﷺ)! Is there a reward for us in serving (the) animals?" He replied, "Yes, there is a reward for serving any animate." Sahih al-Bukhari 2363. https://sunnah.com/bukhari/42/11

The great reward from Allah (SWT) always comes with kindness and mercy to any creation. The Prophet (SAS) has indicated the forgiveness of Allah (SWT) to wrong doers who are merciful and sympathized with animals. Look at the excessive reward for a lady, who is a sinner, in this narration:

عَنْ أَبِي هُرَيْرَةَ ـ رضى الله عنه ـ عَنْ رَسُولِ اللَّهِ ﷺ قَالَ " غُفِرَ لاِمْرَأَةٍ مُومِسَةٍ مَرَّتْ بِكَلْبٍ عَلَى رَأْسِ رَكِيٍّ يَلْهَثُ، قَالَ كَادَ يَقْتُلُهُ الْعَطَشُ، فَنَزَعَتْ خُفَّهَا، فَأَوْثَقَتْهُ بِخِمَارِهَا، فَنَزَعَتْ لَهُ مِنَ الْمَاءِ، فَغُفِرَ لَهَا بِذَلِكَ ". (رواه البخاري).

Narrated Abu Huraira: Allah's Messenger (ﷺ) said, "A prostitute was forgiven by Allah, because, passing by a panting dog near a well and seeing that the dog was about to die of thirst, she took off her shoe, and tying it with her head-cover she drew out some water for it. So, Allah forgave her because of that." Sahih al-Bukhari 3321. https://sunnah.com/bukhari/59/127

Unlike of the above, he (SAS) has described the punishment of human beings who are harsh to animals. In the following narration, Allah (SWT) has punished a lady because she trapped a cat with no food and water until death. This action shows the lady's tough heart against the cat. The heart of a believer should be soft towards all creations of Allah (SWT) because He has made such a creation for a purpose. We should not behave like this lady towards others.

وَعَنْ اِبْنِ عُمَرَ رَضِيَ اَللَّهُ عَنْهُمَا; عَنْ اَلنَّبِيِّ ـ ﷺ ـ قَالَ : {عُذِّبَتْ اِمْرَأَةٌ فِي هِرَّةٍ سَجَنَتْهَا حَتَّى مَاتَتْ, فَدَخَلَتْ اَلنَّارَ فِيهَا, لَا هِيَ أَطْعَمَتْهَا وَسَقَتْهَا إِذْ هِيَ حَبَسَتْهَا, وَلَا هِيَ تَرَكَتْهَا, تَأْكُلُ مِنْ خَشَاشِ اَلْأَرْضِ} مُتَّفَقٌ عَلَيْهِ (صحيح رواه البخاري (3482)، ومسلم (2242)).

Narrated Ibn 'Umar (RA): The Prophet (ﷺ) said: "A woman was punished on account of a cat which she held captive till it died. Hence, she entered the Hell-Fire due to (her mistreatment of) the cat. She did not feed it or give it water while she held it captive, nor did she let it out so that it may eat the things that creep on the earth." [Agreed upon].

Even animals have benefitted from the mercy and kindness of the Prophet (SAS), his companions, and the followers until the Day of Judgement. A man like the Prophet (SAS) with such characters is a treasure in this world. We should highly regard him instead of mocking or spreading rumors about him.

(vii) The Prophet's Characters with his Companions

If he (SAS) has been kind and merciful to his opponents, disbelievers, and even animals, he has been the kindest person ever with his companions. He (SAS) has dealt with them with love, sympathy, forbearance, patience, and a list of all good characters. The companions for him (SAS) has represented the hope, the future, and the complete life. They have been the supporters, the message's future carriers, and the hope for humanity. He has carried out the complete adoration and brotherhood for his companions. Look at what he (SAS) told Mu'adh Ibn Jabal in the following narration:

عَنْ مُعَاذِ بْنِ جَبَلٍ قَالَ: أَخَذَ بِيَدِي النَّبِيُّ ﷺ فَقَالَ: يَا مُعَاذُ، قُلْتُ: لَبَّيْكَ، قَالَ: إِنِّي أُحِبُّكَ، قُلْتُ: وَأَنَا وَاللَّهِ أُحِبُّكَ، قَالَ: أَلَا أُعَلِّمُكَ كَلِمَاتٍ تَقُولُهَا فِي دُبُرِ كُلِّ صَلَاتِكَ؟ قُلْتُ: نَعَمْ، قَالَ: قُلِ: اللَّهُمَّ أَعِنِّي عَلَى ذِكْرِكَ، وَشُكْرِكَ، وَحُسْنِ عِبَادَتِكَ. صحيح الألباني

Mu'adh ibn Jabal said, "The Prophet, may Allah bless him and grant him peace, took my hand and then said, "Mu'adh!' 'At your service!' I said. He said, 'I love you.' I replied, 'And, by Allah, I love you.' He asked, 'Shall I teach you some words to say at the end of your prayer?' 'Yes,' I replied. He said, 'Say: "O Allah, help me to remember You and thank You and help me to the best manner of worshipping You."'" Sahih (Al-Albani) https://sunnah.com/urn/2306880

He (SAS) has not stopped at loving his companions but has spread the adoration and brotherhood among them all. He (SAS) has asked a companion to tell his brother in belief that he loves him as indicated in the following narration:

وعن أنس، رضي الله عنه ، أن رجلاً كان عند النبي، ﷺ ، فمر رجل به، فقال: يا رسول الله إني لأحب هذا، فقال له النبي ﷺ: "أأعلمته؟" قال: لا : قال: "أعلمه" فلحقه، فقال : إني أحبك في الله، فقال: أحبك الله الذي أحببتني له. ((رواه أبو داود بإسناد صحيح)).

Anas bin Malik (May Allah be pleased with him) reported: A man was with the Prophet (ﷺ) when another man passed by and the former said: "O Messenger of Allah! I love this man (for Allah's sake)". Messenger of Allah (ﷺ) asked, "Have you informed him?" He said, "No". Messenger of Allah (ﷺ) then said, "Tell him (that you love him)". So he went up to the man and said to him, "I love you for the sake of Allah;" and the other replied, "May Allah, for Whose sake you love me, love you." [Abu Dawud]. https://sunnah.com/riyadussalihin/introduction/385

He (SAS) has always been smiling in the faces of people without looking at their religion, race, color, etc. He has spread all meanings of love among people who are brothers in humanity. This is evident from the following narrations:

قَالَ جَرِيرُ بْنُ عَبْدِ اللَّهِ مَا حَجَبَنِي رَسُولُ اللَّهِ ﷺ مُنْذُ أَسْلَمْتُ وَلاَ رَآنِي إِلاَّ ضَحِكَ . (رواه مسلم).

Jarir b. 'Abdullah said: Allah's Messenger (ﷺ) never refused me permission to see him since I embraced Islam and never looked at me but with a smile. Sahih Muslim 2475 a. https://sunnah.com/muslim/44/193

عَنْ عَبْدِ اللَّهِ بْنِ الْحَارِثِ بْنِ جَزْءٍ، قَالَ مَا رَأَيْتُ أَحَدًا أَكْثَرَ تَبَسُّمًا مِنْ رَسُولِ اللَّهِ ﷺ . قَالَ أَبُو عِيسَى هَذَا حَدِيثٌ حَسَنٌ غَرِيبٌ . الترمذى

Narrated Ibn Jaz: "I have not seen anyone who smiled more than the Messenger of Allah (ﷺ)." Hasan, Al Termizi, https://sunnah.com/urn/735120

He (SAS) has always been easy to people and has recommended his companions to be easy in all matters. He has also recommended his companions to approach people with glad tidings or welcome and not to be repulsive. He always select the easy matter if he has been given the freedom to select as shown in the following narrations:

وعن أنس رضي الله عنه عن النبى ﷺ قال: "يسروا ولا تعسروا وبشروا ولا تنفروا ((متفق عليه)).

Anas (May Allah be pleased with him) reported: The Prophet (ﷺ) said, "Make things easy and do not make them difficult, cheer the people up by conveying glad tidings to them and do not repulse (them)." [Al-Bukhari and Muslim]. https://sunnah.com/riyadussalihin/introduction/636

عن عائشة رضي الله عنها قالت: ما خير رسول الله ﷺ بين أمرين قط إلا أخذ أيسرهما، ما لم يكن إثماً، فإن كان إثماً، كان أبعد الناس منه، وما انتقم رسول الله ﷺ لنفسه في شئ قط، إلا أن تنتهك حرمة الله، فينتقم لله تعالى. ((متفق عليه))

'Aishah (May Allah be pleased with her) reported: Whenever the Prophet (ﷺ) was given a choice between two matters, he would (always) choose the easier as long as it was not sinful to do so; but if it was sinful he was most strict in avoiding it. He never took revenge upon anybody for his own sake; but when Allah's Legal Bindings were outraged, he would take revenge for Allah's sake. [Al-Bukhari and Muslim]. https://sunnah.com/riyadussalihin/introduction/640

The Prophet (SAS) has also been a serious person despite his kindness and mercifulness. When he (SAS) talks, every one listens and memorizes his words because they are clear and full of wisdom as indicated in the following narration:

عَنْ عَائِشَةَ، قَالَتْ مَا كَانَ رَسُولُ اللَّهِ ﷺ يَسْرُدُ سَرْدَكُمْ هَذَا وَلَكِنَّهُ كَانَ يَتَكَلَّمُ بِكَلاَمٍ فَصْلٍ يَحْفَظُهُ مَنْ جَلَسَ إِلَيْهِ . قَالَ أَبُو عِيسَى هَذَا حَدِيثٌ حَسَنٌ صَحِيحٌ لاَ نَعْرِفُهُ إِلاَّ مِنْ حَدِيثِ الزُّهْرِيِّ وَقَدْ رَوَاهُ يُونُسُ بْنُ يَزِيدَ عَنِ الزُّهْرِيِّ . (رواه الترمذى).

Narrated 'Urwah: that 'Aishah said: "The Messenger of Allah (ﷺ) did not speak quickly like you do now, rather he would speak so clearly, unmistakably, that those who sat with him would memorize it." Sahih Al Termizi, https://sunnah.com/urn/735100

The Prophet (SAS) has never rejected any request for help from anyone. He has been close to people, approachable, and socially intelligent. No one has dealt with him (SAS) without loving and highly regarding him. He has never distinguished people based on their faith, status, wealth, or any life matters as supported by the following narration:

عَنْ أَنَسِ بْنِ مَالِكٍ، قَالَ إِنْ كَانَتِ الأَمَةُ مِنْ أَهْلِ الْمَدِينَةِ لَتَأْخُذُ بِيَدِ رَسُولِ اللَّهِ ـ ﷺ ـ فَمَا يَنْزِعُ يَدَهُ مِنْ يَدِهَا حَتَّى تَذْهَبَ بِهِ حَيْثُ شَاءَتْ مِنَ الْمَدِينَةِ فِي حَاجَتِهَا . (رواه ابن ماجه).

It was narrated that Anas bin Malik said: "If a female slave among the people of Al-Madinah were to take the hand of the Messenger of Allah (ﷺ), he would not take his hand away from hers until she had taken him wherever she wanted in Al-Madinah so that her needs may be met." Sahih Ibn Majeh, https://sunnah.com/ibnmajah/37/78

Although he (SAS) has practiced all the good characters with people, particularly, his companions, he has also recommended them to follow the same practices with others as shown in the following narration:

عَنْ جَابِرٍ، قَالَ كَانَ لِي خَالٌ يَرْقِي مِنَ الْعَقْرَبِ فَنَهَى رَسُولُ اللَّهِ ﷺ عَنِ الرُّقَى ـ قَالَ ـ فَأَتَاهُ فَقَالَ يَا رَسُولَ اللَّهِ إِنَّكَ نَهَيْتَ عَنِ الرُّقَى وَأَنَا أَرْقِي مِنَ الْعَقْرَبِ . فَقَالَ " مَنِ اسْتَطَاعَ مِنْكُمْ أَنْ يَنْفَعَ أَخَاهُ فَلْيَفْعَلْ " . (رواه مسلم).

Jabir b. 'Abdullah reported I had a maternal uncle who treated the sting of the scorpion with the help of incantation. Allah's Messenger (ﷺ) forbade incantation. He came to him and said: Allah's Messenger, you forbade to practice incantation, whereas I employ it for curing the sting of the scorpion, whereupon he said: He who amongst you is capable of employing it as a means to do good should do that. Sahih Muslim 2199 c. https://sunnah.com/muslim/39/83

The above is too little compared to the inherited large number of narrations that show how much love the Prophet (SAS) has carried for his companions. Such inherited authentic stories about his daily life dealings with his companions are immense to be listed in books. However, I tried to present a few of them to show, without exaggeration, how a great person he (SAS) is in all aspects.

(viii) The Prophet's Characters with his Servants and Employees

People, who have been working under the supervision of or serving the Prophet (SAS), have highly regarded him and have preferred him to their families. The popular story of Zaid Ibn Harithah before the Prophecy is an evidence of the above argument. The story is not traditionally authenticated as it has occurred before the Prophecy, however, it carries lots of meaningful concepts and reflections. Zaid was a victim of robbery to his mother's caravan during her travel. He was sold as a servant to Khadijah, may Allah be pleased with her, the wife of the Prophet and the mother of believers. She has assigned Zaid to serve the Prophet (SAS). Zaid's family knew about his location in Makkah and came to the Prophet (SAS) to buy and free him from being a servant. Zaid was given the freedom to select between continuing with the Prophet (SAS) and returning back to his tribe as a free man. He has preferred to be a servant to the Prophet and continue being with him (SAS). This was shocking to his father and uncle who asked Zaid "do you prefer being a servant to being a freeman?" He answered yes and continued expressing his rationale "I have seen from this man, i.e., the Prophet (SAS), lots of characters that forbade me from leaving him for anything else." At this moment, the Prophet (SAS) has gone to the largest square in Makkah and has announced that Zaid is a free man and has become my son by adoption.

Can we imagine a story like this to happen anywhere worldwide? I am completely doubtful of something like this to occur in our era. Even before the Prophecy, his characters (SAS) made Zaid prefer him over his family and tribe. To make matters more astonishing, he has preferred being a servant for a good man than being a freeman in his tribe. This is how people have highly regarded the Prophet (SAS) even before Islam.

During his time in Madeenah, the Prophet (SAS) has been given Anas Ibn Malik, may Allah be pleased with him, as a helper for nine years. Anas has described how the Prophet (SAS) has dealt with him during such long period of time as shown in the following narration:

قَالَ إِسْحَاقُ قَالَ أَنَسٌ كَانَ رَسُولُ اللَّهِ ﷺ مِنْ أَحْسَنِ النَّاسِ خُلُقًا فَأَرْسَلَنِي يَوْمًا لِحَاجَةٍ فَقُلْتُ وَاللَّهِ لاَ أَذْهَبُ . وَفِي نَفْسِي أَنْ أَذْهَبَ لِمَا أَمَرَنِي بِهِ نَبِيُّ اللَّهِ ﷺ فَخَرَجْتُ حَتَّى أَمُرَّ عَلَى صِبْيَانٍ وَهُمْ يَلْعَبُونَ فِي السُّوقِ فَإِذَا رَسُولُ اللَّهِ ﷺ قَدْ قَبَضَ بِقَفَاىَ مِنْ وَرَائِي - قَالَ - فَنَظَرْتُ إِلَيْهِ وَهُوَ يَضْحَكُ فَقَالَ " يَا أُنَيْسُ أَذَهَبْتَ حَيْثُ أَمَرْتُكَ " . قَالَ قُلْتُ نَعَمْ أَنَا أَذْهَبُ يَا رَسُولَ اللَّهِ . قَالَ أَنَسٌ وَاللَّهِ لَقَدْ خَدَمْتُهُ تِسْعَ سِنِينَ مَا عَلِمْتُهُ قَالَ لِشَيْءٍ صَنَعْتُهُ لِمَ فَعَلْتَ كَذَا وَكَذَا أَوْ لِشَيْءٍ تَرَكْتُهُ هَلاَّ فَعَلْتَ كَذَا وَكَذَا . (رواه مسلم).

Anas reported that Allah's Messenger (ﷺ) had the best disposition amongst people. He sent me on an errand one day, and I said: By Allah, I would not go. I had, however, this idea in my mind that I would do as Allah's Apostle (ﷺ) had commanded me to do. I went out until I happened to come across children who had been playing in the street. In the meanwhile, Allah's Messenger (ﷺ) came there and he caught me by the back of my neck from behind me. As I looked towards him I found him smiling and he said: Unais, did you go where I commanded you to go? I said: Allah's Messenger, yes, I am going. Anas further said: I served him for nine years but I know not that he ever said to me about a thing which I had done why I did that, or about a thing I had left as to why I had not done that. Sahih Muslim 2310 a, 2309 e. https://sunnah.com/muslim/43/74

He (SAS) has practiced the good character with his employees and servants and has recommended the companions to similarly deal with their servants and employees. This is clear in the following narration:

عَنْ عَلِيٍّ، رَضِيَ اللَّهُ عَنْهُ قَالَ كَانَ آخِرُ كَلَامِ رَسُولِ اللَّهِ صَلَّى اللَّهُ عَلَيْهِ وَسَلَّمَ الصَّلَاةَ الصَّلَاةَ اتَّقُوا اللَّهَ فِيمَا مَلَكَتْ أَيْمَانُكُمْ. مسند الأمام أحمد

It was narrated from Ali (May Allah pleased with him) that he said: "The last words of the Messenger of Allah (ﷺ) were: "Prayer, prayer! And fear Allah with regard to what your right hands possess, [i.e., female slaves]." Musnad Ahmad 585. https://sunnah.com/ahmad/5/23

He (SAS) has never punished any of his servants and workers as shown in the following narration:

وعنها قالت: ما ضرب رسول الله ﷺ شيئاً قط بيده، ولا امرأة ولا خادماً، إلا أن يجاهد في سبيل الله، وما نيل منه شئ قط فينتقم من صاحبه، إلا أن ينتهك شئ من محارم الله تعالى، فينتقم لله تعالى. (رواه مسلم).

With his servants: 'Aishah (May Allah be pleased with her) reported: Messenger of Allah (ﷺ) never hit anything with his hand neither a servant nor a woman but of course, he did fight in the Cause of Allah. He never took revenge upon anyone for the wrong done to him, but of course, he exacted retribution for the sake of Allah in case the Injunctions of Allah about unlawful acts were violated. [Muslim]. https://sunnah.com/riyadussalihin/introduction/643

I am really proud of being a follower of such a great man who has been sent as a mercy to mankind. He (SAS) has taught me how to behave and deal with people from all kinds. Whenever I am in a situation with any type of people, I always find guidance from him (SAS) in similar situations. I now deeply sense his feelings (SAS) when dealing with opponents, ignorant, or disbelievers and how much patience this might entail. I sincerely feel his state of mind (SAS) when dealing with employees and co-workers from different cultures with wide spectrum of values and practices. Now, I find the guidance in his teachings and practices with his great companions and followers. The Prophet (SAS) is the great role model to mankind in all aspects of life. One day, those who are trying to insult him (SAS), will know how great he is. I hope it will not be a miserable day for them. This type of people think that such day is far away, however, it is apparently closer than what they have expected.

Recommendations:
To defend the Prophet (SAS), first, it is necessary to follow his guidance in all matters. Because we are a little far away from all his teachings in many matters, we should work gradually to learn and apply them. I will start with the essentials, i.e., authentic Sunnah prayers per day, to establish a good base for future practical activities. So, I suggest that we follow his teachings (SAS) in these prayers first, then we can move to other traditions. Try to make a gradual plan to apply the authentic Sunnah for prayers as listed in the following narrations, i.e., 10 per day (two before Fajr & Zuhr prayers and two after Zuhr, Maghrib, and Isha prayers) or 12 per day (four before Zuhr prayer instead of two):

عَنْ عَائِشَةَ، قَالَتْ قَالَ رَسُولُ اللَّهِ ـ ﷺ ـ " مَنْ ثَابَرَ عَلَى ثِنْتَىْ عَشْرَةَ رَكْعَةً مِنَ السُّنَّةِ بُنِيَ لَهُ بَيْتٌ فِي الْجَنَّةِ أَرْبَعٌ قَبْلَ الظُّهْرِ

وَرَكْعَتَيْنِ بَعْدَ الظُّهْرِ وَرَكْعَتَيْنِ بَعْدَ الْمَغْرِبِ وَرَكْعَتَيْنِ بَعْدَ الْعِشَاءِ وَرَكْعَتَيْنِ قَبْلَ الْفَجْرِ " . (رواه ابن ماجه).

It was narrated that 'Aishah said: "The Messenger of Allah (ﷺ) said: 'Whoever persists in performing twelve Rak'ah from the Sunnah, a house will be built for him in Paradise: four before the Zuhr, two Rak'ah after Zuhr, two Rak'ah after Maghrib, two Rak'ah after the 'Isha' and two Rak'ah before Fajr.'" Ibn Majeh, https://sunnah.com/ibnmajah/5/338

وَعَنْ اِبْنِ عُمَرَ -رَضِيَ اَللَّهُ عَنْهُمَا- قَالَ : {حَفِظْتُ مِنْ اَلنَّبِيِّ - ﷺ -عَشْرَ رَكَعَاتٍ: رَكْعَتَيْنِ قَبْلَ اَلظُّهْرِ , وَرَكْعَتَيْنِ بَعْدَهَا , وَرَكْعَتَيْنِ بَعْدَ اَلْمَغْرِبِ فِي بَيْتِهِ , وَرَكْعَتَيْنِ بَعْدَ اَلْعِشَاءِ فِي بَيْتِهِ , وَرَكْعَتَيْنِ قَبْلَ اَلصُّبْحِ} مُتَّفَقٌ عَلَيْهِ. رواه البخاري (1180) ، ومسلم (729) ، واللفظ للبخاري .

Narrated Ibn 'Umar (RA): I memorized from the Prophet (ﷺ) ten (voluntary) Rak'at - two Rak'at before the Zuhr prayer and two after it; two Rak'at after Magbrib prayer in his house, and two Rak'at after 'Isha' prayer in his house, and two Rak'at before the Fajr prayer. [Agreed upon]. https://sunnah.com/bulugh/2/254

This plan should be realistic in adopting your current situation. If you do not apply any of these Sunnah prayers, then, you can start by a Sunnah of one prayer like after Zuhr prayer, for example. You continue doing it for a week or two, then, add another prayer, for example Maghrib, then, Isha, then, Fajr, then, four before Zuhr prayer. You continue week after week until you train yourself very well on these Sunnah prayers. Once you master all of them, you move to another target, which includes Dhoha and Qiyam prayers. You start with two Rak'ahs and increase gradually to the best of your ability.

In Fasting, you develop a gradual plan of voluntary fasting of one day a month, then, increase it gradually until you reach Mondays and Thursdays of every week. Similarly, you plan for charity and Zakat. You start small and gradually increase to the best of your ability. You start from your position in following the Sunnah of the Prophet (SAS) today and gradually increase until you reach the set targets for yourself. I pray to Allah (SWT) to help us achieve such good targets in a short period of time in order to be called: **Servants of Allah** (SWT).

Chapter III

The Prophet as a Role Model for Husbands

Overview

In the previous chapters, we have discussed the individual characters and the social intelligence of our beloved Prophet Muhammed (SAS). In the coming chapters including this one, we will analyze his personality (SAS) as a role model in all aspects of life. This is clearly stated by Allah (SWT) in the following verse:

لَقَدْ كَانَ لَكُمْ فِي رَسُولِ اللَّهِ أُسْوَةٌ حَسَنَةٌ لِّمَن كَانَ يَرْجُو اللَّهَ وَالْيَوْمَ الْآخِرَ وَذَكَرَ اللَّهَ كَثِيرًا (21) الأحزاب

Chapter Al-Ahzab **(21) There has certainly been for you in the Messenger of Allah an excellent role model for anyone whose hope is in Allah and the Last Day and [who] remembers Allah often.** https://quran.com/33/21/

Imam Al-Qurobi and most scholars of Quran interpretation have explained the necessity of following the Prophet (SAS) in his actions, particularly in acts of worship. There are differences among scholars about the obligation of following him (SAS) in the acts of life matters. Some have supported the opinion of being obligatory to follow him (SAS) and others have considered it as a preference not obligation. Whether it is a preference or obligation, it is mandatory to show the behavior of the Prophet (SAS) in different life matters. If you look therefore at the Prophet (SAS), you will find him an excellent role model as a husband, a father, a teacher, a leader, etc. In this chapter, we will briefly discuss the great personality of our beloved Prophet (SAS) as a role model for husbands.

Although the Prophet (SAS) has been an extremely busy man and leader, he did not forget his obligation towards his family, i.e., wives, children, and relatives. As a husband, he (SAS) has shown great characteristics of being so kind and fair to his wives, of working at home like everyone else, and of doing his personal staff. Let us walk through few evidences about these characters in the following sections.

Kind to his Wives

The Prophet (SAS) has been very kind to his wives. He has also recommended his companions to be kind and gentle to their wives as shown in the following narration:

عَنِ ابْنِ عَبَّاسٍ، عَنِ النَّبِيِّ ـ ﷺ ـ قَالَ " خَيْرُكُمْ خَيْرُكُمْ لأَهْلِهِ وَأَنَا خَيْرُكُمْ لأَهْلِي " . ابن ماجه

It was narrated from Ibn 'Abbas that: the Prophet said: "The best of you is the one who is best to his wife, and I am the best of you to my wives." Ibn Majeh, Hasan. https://sunnah.com/urn/1320540

Despite his business, he (SAS) has been giving his wives all their rights and utmost attention. He has always shown his interest and care as in the following narration:

عَنْ عَائِشَةَ ـ رضى الله عنها ـ كَانَ رَسُولُ اللَّهِ ﷺ إِذَا انْصَرَفَ مِنَ الْعَصْرِ دَخَلَ عَلَى نِسَائِهِ، فَيَدْنُو مِنْ إِحْدَاهُنَّ، فَدَخَلَ عَلَى حَفْصَةَ، فَاحْتَبَسَ أَكْثَرَ مَا كَانَ يَحْتَبِسُ. البخاري

Narrated `Aisha: Whenever Allah's Messenger (ﷺ) finished his `Asr prayer, he would enter upon his wives and stay with one of them. One day he went to Hafsa and stayed with her longer than usual. Sahih al-Bukhari 5216 https://sunnah.com/bukhari/67/149

He (SAS) has never hit a servant or a woman and always show utmost care and respect. With this action, he (SAS) has been modern in his dealings by respecting all human rights of his wives and servants. This is really high level of character, which is amazing, particularly, in his era. How kind and merciful he has been with others, particularly, the closest people to him (SAS). This is clear in the following narration:

عَنْ عَائِشَةَ، قَالَتْ: مَا ضَرَبَ رَسُولُ اللهِ ﷺ، بِيَدِهِ شَيْئًا قَطُّ، إِلَّا أَنْ يُجَاهِدَ فِي سَبِيلِ اللهِ، وَلَا ضَرَبَ خَادِمًا وَلَا امْرَأَةً. مشكاة المصابيح.

'Aayeshah, may Allah be pleased with her, reported: "The Prophet, peace be upon him, did not hit anything with his hands, besides the time when he made jihaad in the Path of Allah. He did not hit a servant nor a woman (wife, slave girl, etc.)". Sahih Isnād (Zubair `Aliza'i), Ash-Shama'il Al-Muhammadiyah 347. https://sunnah.com/shamail/48/6

He (SAS) has been a good listener to the problems of his wives with full dedication to find a better solution for them even with naïve matters. He has always been like a pressure relief for their issues in order to make them always happy. He (SAS), like every other husbands, has liked to help his wives pass through difficulties with ease and without any consequences as shown the following narrations:

عَنْ عَائِشَةَ ـ رضى الله عنها ـ أَنَّ النَّبِيَّ ﷺ دَخَلَ عَلَيْهَا وَحَاضَتْ بِسَرِفَ، قَبْلَ أَنْ تَدْخُلَ مَكَّةَ وَهْىَ تَبْكِي فَقَالَ " مَا لَكِ أَنَفِسْتِ ". قَالَتْ نَعَمْ. قَالَ " إِنَّ هَذَا أَمْرٌ كَتَبَهُ اللَّهُ عَلَى بَنَاتِ آدَمَ، فَاقْضِي مَا يَقْضِي الْحَاجُّ غَيْرَ أَنْ لاَ تَطُوفِي بِالْبَيْتِ...... ". البخارى

Narrated `Aisha: that the Prophet (ﷺ) entered upon her when she had her menses at Sarif before entering Mecca, and she was weeping (because she was afraid that she would not be able to perform the Hajj). The Prophet (ﷺ) said, "What is wrong with you? Have you got your period?" She said, "Yes." He said, "This is a matter Allah has decreed for all the daughters of Adam, so perform all the ceremonies of Hajj like the others, but do not perform the Tawaf around the Ka`ba."……" Sahih al-Bukhari 5548. https://sunnah.com/bukhari/73/4

عَنْ أَنَسٍ، قَالَ بَلَغَ صَفِيَّةَ أَنَّ حَفْصَةَ، قَالَتْ بِنْتُ يَهُودِيٍّ . فَبَكَتْ فَدَخَلَ عَلَيْهَا النَّبِيُّ ﷺ وَهِيَ تَبْكِي فَقَالَ " مَا يُبْكِيكِ " . فَقَالَتْ قَالَتْ لِي حَفْصَةُ إِنِّي بِنْتُ يَهُودِيٍّ . فَقَالَ النَّبِيُّ ﷺ " إِنَّكِ لاَبْنَةُ نَبِيٍّ وَإِنَّ عَمَّكِ لَنَبِيٌّ وَإِنَّكِ لَتَحْتَ نَبِيٍّ فَفِيمَ تَفْخَرُ عَلَيْكِ " . ثُمَّ قَالَ " اتَّقِي اللَّهَ يَا حَفْصَةُ " . قَالَ أَبُو عِيسَى هَذَا حَدِيثٌ حَسَنٌ صَحِيحٌ غَرِيبٌ مِنْ هَذَا الْوَجْهِ . الترمذى

Narrated Anas: said: "It reached Safiyyah that Hafsah said: 'The daughter of a Jew' so she wept. Then the Prophet (ﷺ) entered upon her while she was crying, so he said: 'What makes you cry?' She said: 'Hafsah said to me that I am the daughter of a Jew.' So the Prophet (ﷺ) said: 'And you are the daughter of a Prophet, and your uncle is a Prophet, and you are married to a Prophet, so what is she boasting to you about?' Then he said: 'Fear Allah, O Hafsah.'" Sahih Jami` at-Tirmidhi https://sunnah.com/urn/737820

The Prophet (SAS) has also found the time to play with his wives and let them enjoy their time with him. The following two narrations are examples of such actions with them:

عَنْ عَائِشَةَ، رضى الله عنها قَالَتْ قَدِمَ رَسُولُ اللَّهِ ﷺ مِنْ غَزْوَةِ تَبُوكَ أَوْ خَيْبَرَ وَفِي سَهْوَتِهَا سِتْرٌ فَهَبَّتْ رِيحٌ فَكَشَفَتْ نَاحِيَةَ السِّتْرِ عَنْ بَنَاتٍ لِعَائِشَةَ لُعَبٍ فَقَالَ " مَا هَذَا يَا عَائِشَةُ " . قَالَتْ بَنَاتِي . وَرَأَى بَيْنَهُنَّ فَرَسًا لَهُ جَنَاحَانِ مِنْ رِقَاعٍ فَقَالَ " مَا هَذَا الَّذِي أَرَى وَسْطَهُنَّ " . قَالَتْ فَرَسٌ . قَالَ " وَمَا هَذَا الَّذِي عَلَيْهِ " . قَالَتْ جَنَاحَانِ . قَالَ " فَرَسٌ لَهُ جَنَاحَانِ " . قَالَتْ أَمَا سَمِعْتَ أَنَّ لِسُلَيْمَانَ خَيْلاً لَهَا أَجْنِحَةٌ قَالَتْ فَضَحِكَ حَتَّى رَأَيْتُ نَوَاجِذَهُ . صحيح (الألباني)

Narrated Aisha, Ummul Mu'minin: When the Messenger of Allah (ﷺ) arrived after the expedition to Tabuk or Khaybar (the narrator is doubtful), the wind raised an end of a curtain which was hung in front of her store-room, revealing some dolls which belonged to her. He asked: What is this? She replied: My dolls. Among them he saw a horse with wings made of rags, and asked: What is this I see among them? She replied: A horse. He asked: What is this that it has on it? She replied: Two wings. He asked: A horse with two wings? She replied: Have you not heard that Solomon had horses with wings? She said: Thereupon the Messenger of Allah (ﷺ) laughed so heartily that I could see his molar teeth. Sahih (Al-Albani), Sunan Abi Dawud 4932. https://sunnah.com/abudawud/43/160

وَعَنْهَا قَالَتْ: وَاللَّهِ لَقَدْ رَأَيْتُ النَّبِيَّ ﷺ يَقُومُ عَلَى بَابِ حُجْرَتِي وَالْحَبَشَةُ يَلْعَبُونَ بِالْحِرَابِ فِي الْمَسْجِدِ وَرَسُولُ اللَّهِ ﷺ يَسْتُرُنِي بِرِدَائِهِ لِأَنْظُرَ إِلَى لَعِبِهِمْ بَيْنَ أُذُنِهِ وَعَاتِقِهِ ثُمَّ يَقُومُ مِنْ أَجْلِي حَتَّى أَكُونَ أَنَا الَّتِي أَنْصَرِفُ فَاقْدُرُوا قَدْرَ الْجَارِيَةِ الْحَدِيثَةِ السِّنِّ الْحَرِيصَةِ عَلَى اللَّهْوِ. مُتَّفَقٌ عَلَيْهِ

She said: I swear by God that I have seen the Prophet standing at the door of my room when the Abyssinians were playing with spears in the mosque and God's Messenger was covering me with his cloak in order that I might look over his shoulder* at their sport. He would then stand for my sake till I was the one who departed; so estimate the time a young girl eager for amusement would wait." * Literally "between his ear and his shoulder." (Bukhari and Muslim.) https://sunnah.com/mishkat/13/162

He (SAS) has also been so nice and kind to his wives showing all kinds of love, care, and compassion. The following two narrations show these kind of actions:

وَعَنْهَا قَالَتْ: كُنْتُ أَشْرَبُ وَأَنَا حَائِضٌ ثُمَّ أُنَاوِلُهُ النَّبِيَّ ﷺ فَيَضَعُ فَاهُ عَلَى مَوْضِعِ فِيَّ فَيَشْرَبُ وَأَتَعَرَّقُ الْعَرْقَ وَأَنَا حَائِضٌ ثُمَّ أُنَاوِلُهُ النَّبِيَّ ﷺ فَيَضَعُ فَاهُ عَلَى مَوْضِعِ فِي. رَوَاهُ مُسْلِم. صَحِيح (الألباني)

She also said, "I would drink when I was menstruating, then hand it to the Prophet, and he would put his mouth where mine had been and drink; and I would eat flesh from a bone when I was menstruating, then hand it to the Prophet, and he would put his mouth where mine had been." Muslim transmitted it. Mishkat al-Masabih 547. https://sunnah.com/mishkat/3/243

عَنْ عَائِشَةَ، أَنَّهَا قَالَتْ كَانَ نَبِيُّ اللَّهِ ﷺ يَسْتَاكُ فَيُعْطِينِي السِّوَاكَ لِأَغْسِلَهُ فَأَبْدَأُ بِهِ فَأَسْتَاكُ ثُمَّ أَغْسِلُهُ وَأَدْفَعُهُ إِلَيْهِ. حسن (الألباني)

'Aishah narrated: "The Prophet of Allah (ﷺ) would clean his teeth with the Siwak, then he would give me the Siwak in order to wash it. So I would first use it myself, then wash it and return it. Hasan (Al-Albani), Sunan Abi Dawud 52. https://sunnah.com/abudawud/1/52

The following narration shows how the Prophet (SAS) has been smart and sensitive in his dealings with his wives:

وَعَنْهَا قَالَتْ: قَالَ لِي رَسُولُ اللَّهِ ﷺ: «إِنِّي لَأَعْلَمُ إِذَا كُنْتِ عَنِّي رَاضِيَةً وَإِذَا كُنْتِ عَنِّي غَضْبَى» فَقُلْتُ: مِنْ أَيْنَ تَعْرِفُ ذَلِكَ؟ فَقَالَ: "إِذَا كُنْتِ عَنِّي رَاضِيَةً فَإِنَّكِ تَقُولِينَ: لَا وَرَبِّ مُحَمَّدٍ وَإِذَا كُنْتِ عَلَيَّ غَضْبَى قُلْتِ: لَا وَرَبِّ إِبْرَاهِيمَ". قَالَتْ: أَجَلْ وَاللَّهِ يَا رَسُولَ اللَّهِ مَا أَهْجُرُ إِلَّا اسْمَكَ. مُتَّفَقٌ عَلَيْهِ (الألباني)

She told that God's Messenger said to her, "I know when you are pleased with me and when you are angry with me." She asked how he knew that and he replied that when she was pleased with him she said, "No, by Muhammad's Lord," but when she was angry with him she said, "No, by Abraham's Lord." She then said, "I swear by God, Messenger of God, that that is so; it is only your name that I omit." (Bukhari and Muslim.), Mishkat al-Masabih 3245. https://sunnah.com/mishkat/13/163

Working at Home
He (SAS) is the most modest person when it comes to his home. Although he is the Prophet of Allah, the leader of the Muslim community, and the busiest person in his generation with many activities, he has not neglected serving his family like everyone else. He has mended sandals as well as patched and sewed garments as indicated in the

following narrations:

وعن الأسود بن يزيد قال: سئلت عائشة رضي الله عنها: ما كان النبي ﷺ يصنع في بيته؟ قالت: كان يكون في مهنة أهله ـ يعنى: خدمة أهله ـ فإذا حضرت الصلاة، خرج إلى الصلاة" (رواه البخاري).

Al-Aswad bin Yazid (May Allah be pleased with him) reported: 'Aishah (May Allah be pleased with her) was asked: "What did Messenger of Allah (ﷺ) used to do inside his house?" She answered: "He used to keep himself busy helping members of his family, and when it was the time for Salat (the prayer), he would get up for prayer." [Al-Bukhari]. https://sunnah.com/riyadussalihin/introduction/605

عَنْ أَبِيهِ قَالَ: سَأَلْتُ عَائِشَةَ: مَا كَانَ النَّبِيُّ ﷺ يَصْنَعُ فِي بَيْتِهِ؟ قَالَتْ: مَا يَصْنَعُ أَحَدُكُمْ فِي بَيْتِهِ؟ قَالَتْ: مَا يَصْنَعُ أَحَدُكُمْ فِي بَيْتِهِ، يَخْصِفُ النَّعْلَ، وَيَرْقَعُ الثَّوْبَ، وَيَخِيطُ. صحيح الألباني

Hisham said, "I asked 'A'isha, 'What did the Prophet, may Allah bless him and grant him peace, do in his house?' She replied, 'He did what one of you would do in his house. He mended sandals and patched garments and sewed." Sahih (Al-Albani), https://sunnah.com/adab/30/3

Doing his Personal Staff

He (SAS) has also taken care of his personal staff at home. He has been cleaning his clothes, preparing his food, and serving himself like any other man at his home. This is also clear in the following narration:

عَنْ عَمْرَةَ، قَالَتْ: قِيلَ لِعَائِشَةَ: مَاذَا كَانَ يَعْمَلُ رَسُولُ اللهِ ﷺ فِي بَيْتِهِ؟ قَالَتْ: كَانَ بَشَرًا مِنَ الْبَشَرِ، يَفْلِي ثَوْبَهُ، وَيَحْلُبُ شَاتَهُ، وَيَخْدُمُ نَفْسَهُ. مشكات المصابيح.

'Amrah, may Allah be pleased with her, reported that someone asked 'Aayeshah, may Allah be pleased with her, "What was the usual practice of the Prophet (SAS) at home?" She replied: "He was a human from among other humans. He himself removed the lice from his clothing, milked his goats, and did all his work himself". Hasan Isnād (Zubair `Aliza'i), Ash-Shama'il Al-Muhammadiyah 341. https://sunnah.com/shamail/47/13

Fair among his Wives

Fairness is not an easy task, particularly, with wives. It needs lots of effort and sensitivity to be really fair with no complaints from them. This fairness does not only consider the rights of each one but includes their closeness to his heart and love as well. Consequently, fairness in feelings, smiles, kindness, emotions, and others are necessary parts of the global fairness that he (SAS) has practiced. It is almost impossible to achieve such fairness because it needs a full time job and high level of sensitivity to deal with wives of different personalities and attitudes. To make matters worse, it is extremely impossible for a busy man with all the Prophet's activities to achieve such fairness not because he does want but because he might not have time, mind, and effort to do so. However, he (SAS) has been able to do it by nature and also has recommended his companions to perform fairness with their wives, family members, and others. He (SAS) has also been keen to accomplish such fairness even at the time of his death. A few examples of this fairness are shown in the following narrations:

وَعَنْ عُرْوَةَ قَالَ : { قَالَتْ عَائِشَةُ : يَا ابْنَ أُخْتِي ! كَانَ رَسُولُ اَللَّهِ ﷺ -لَا يُفَضِّلُ بَعْضَنَا عَلَى بَعْضٍ فِي اَلْقَسْمِ مِنْ مُكْثِهِ عِنْدَنَا , وَكَانَ قَلَّ يَوْمٌ إِلَّا وَهُوَ يَطُوفُ عَلَيْنَا جَمِيعًا , فَيَدْنُو مِنْ كُلِّ اِمْرَأَةٍ مِنْ غَيْرِ مَسِيسٍ , حَتَّى يَبْلُغَ اَلَّتِي هُوَ يَوْمُهَا , فَيَبِيتُ عِنْدَهَا } رَوَاهُ أَحْمَدُ , وَأَبُو دَاوُدَ وَاللَّفْظُ لَهُ , وَصَحَّحَهُ اَلْحَاكِمُ ;

Narrated 'Urwah (RA): 'Aishah (RA) said: "O my nephew, Allah's Messenger (ﷺ) would not prefer some of us over others regarding the division of the time he would spend with us. It was very rare that he would not visit us all, and come near each of his wives without having intercourse with her, till he reached the one whose day it was, and spent the night with her." [Reported by Ahmad and Abu Dawud, the wording is Abu Dawud's. al-Hakim graded it Sahih (authentic)]. https://sunnah.com/bulugh/8/109

عَنْ أَبِي هُرَيْرَةَ، عَنِ النَّبِيِّ ﷺ قَالَ "مَنْ كَانَتْ لَهُ امْرَأَتَانِ فَمَالَ إِلَى إِحْدَاهُمَا جَاءَ يَوْمَ الْقِيَامَةِ وَشِقُّهُ مَائِلٌ" . صحيح (الألباني)
Narrated AbuHurayrah: The Prophet (ﷺ) said: When a man has two wives and he is inclined to one of them, he will come on the Day of resurrection with a side hanging down. Sahih (Al-Albani) https://sunnah.com/abudawud/12/88

وَعَنْهَا أَنَّ رَسُولَ اللَّهِ ﷺ كَانَ يَسْأَلُ فِي مَرَضِهِ الَّذِي مَاتَ فِيهِ: «أَيْنَ أَنَا غَدًا؟» يُرِيدُ يَوْمَ عَائِشَةَ فَأَذِنَ لَهُ أَزْوَاجُهُ يَكُونُ حَيْثُ شَاءَ فَكَانَ فِي بَيْتِ عَائِشَةَ حَتَّى مَاتَ عِنْدَهَا. رَوَاهُ الْبُخَارِيُّ. صَحِيحٌ (الألباني)
She said that during the illness of which God's Messenger died he was asking, "Where do I go tomorrow? Where do I go tomorrow?" That was on 'A'isha's day. His wives therefore permitted him to go where he wished, and he stayed in 'A'isha's house till he died there. Bukhari transmitted it. https://sunnah.com/mishkat/13/149

Looking at his actions (SAS) towards his wives makes us feel ashamed. Although we do not have his responsibilities (SAS), we are not able to achieve much of the above with only a single wife. I am wondering how he (SAS) has been able to make it happen, i.e., be kind, be available when needed, play, do house and personal affairs, and be fair with his wives. Guidance of Allah (SWT) might be the only reason that has assisted him (SAS) to perform well as a husband. He (SAS) has made effort with full sincerity to be a good husband, hence, Allah (SWT) has supported his actions and has given him the best guidance and results. Similarly, we can do better than our status que if we follow the above two conditions, i.e., make effort with full sincerity. Let us start today to follow his guidance (SAS) of being a good husband and bring joy and prosperity to our families.

Recommendations:
It is recommended to follow the guidance of the Prophet (SAS) at home whether you are the husband or the wife. Let us walk through the following narration and keep that always in mind:

وعن ابن عمر رضي الله عنهما عن النبي ﷺ قال: "كلكم راع، وكلكم مسئول عن رعيته، والأمير راع، والرجل راع على أهل بيته؛ والمرأة راعية على بيت زوجها وولده، فكلكم راع، وكلكم مسؤول عن رعيته" (متفق عليه).

Ibn 'Umar (May Allah be pleased with them) reported: The Prophet (ﷺ) said, "All of you are guardians and are responsible for your subjects. The ruler is a guardian of his subjects, the man is a guardian of his family, the woman is a guardian and is responsible for her husband's house and his offspring; and so all of you are guardians and are responsible for your subjects." [Al-Bukhari and Muslim]. https://sunnah.com/riyadussalihin/introduction/283

The responsibility of a husband or a wife is huge because they together constitute the seed for a family that is the core pillar of a society. This needs from us to carefully look at how to build such family on a strong foundation. Both husband and wife should sincerely look at their responsibilities, plan to gradually complete their shortcomings, and exert all the utmost effort to implement the planned activities. They also should forgive any unaccomplished activities if they are not intentionally missed. The plan should be continuously improved by adding more activities and using innovative ideas. Finally, the husband and the wife should acknowledge the fact that achieving their responsibilities in building the family is an act of worship towards Allah (SWT). You will be rewarded the most for such acts of worship in the Day of Judgement. Let us study and implement the following narrations:

قَالَ: قَالَ رَسُولُ اللَّهِ ﷺ: «أَكْمَلُ الْمُؤْمِنِينَ إِيمَانًا أَحْسَنُهُمْ خُلُقًا وَخِيَارُكُمْ خِيَارُكُمْ لِنِسَائِهِمْ» . رَوَاهُ التِّرْمِذِيُّ وَقَالَ: هَذَا حَدِيثٌ حَسَنٌ صَحِيحٌ وَرَوَاهُ أَبُو دَاوُدَ إِلَى قَوْلِهِ «خلقا» مشكاة المصابيح

Abu Huraira reported God's Messenger as saying, "The believers who show the most perfect faith are those who have the best disposition and the best of you are those who are best to their wives." Tirmidhi transmitted it, saying this is a *hasan sahih* tradition, and Abu Dawud transmitted it up to "disposition." Mishkat al-Masabih 3264. https://sunnah.com/mishkat/13/181

وعن معاوية بن حيدة رضي الله عنه قال : قلت يا رسول الله ﷺ ما حق زوجة أحدنا عليه؟ قال: "أن تطعمها إذا طعمت ، وتكسوها إذا اكتسيت ولا تضرب الوجه، ولا تقبح، ولا تهجر إلا في البيت " حديث حسن رواه أبو داود وقال: معنى "لاتقبح" أي : لا تقل قبحك الله. ابو داود

Mu'awiyah bin Haidah (May Allah be pleased with him) reported: I asked Messenger of Allah (ﷺ): "What right can any wife demand of her husband?" He replied, "You should give her food when you eat, clothe her when you clothe yourself, not strike her on the face, and do not revile her or separate from her except in the house". [Abu Dawud, who categorized it as Hasan]. https://sunnah.com/riyadussalihin/introduction/277

وَعَنْ سَعْدِ بْنِ أَبِي وَقَّاصٍ قَالَ: مَرِضْتُ عَامَ الْفَتْحِ مَرَضًا أَشْفَيْتُ عَلَى الْمَوْتِ فَأَتَانِي رَسُولُ اللَّهِ ﷺ يَعُودُنِي فَقُلْتُ: يَا رَسُولَ اللَّهِ: إِنَّ لِي مَالًا كَثِيرًا وَلَيْسَ يَرِثُنِي إِلَّا ابْنَتِي أَفَأُوصِي بِمَالِي كُلِّهِ؟ قَالَ: «لَا» قُلْتُ: فَثُلُثَيْ مَالِي؟ قَالَ: «لَا» قُلْتُ: فَالشَّطْرُ؟ قَالَ: «لَا» قُلْتُ: فَالثُّلُثُ؟ قَالَ: «الثُّلُثُ وَالثُّلُثُ كَثِيرٌ إِنَّكَ إِنْ تَذَرْ وَرَثَتَكَ أَغْنِيَاءَ خَيْرٌ مِنْ أَنْ تَذَرَهُمْ عَالَةً يَتَكَفَّفُونَ النَّاسَ وَإِنَّكَ لَنْ تُنْفِقَ نَفَقَةً تَبْتَغِي بِهَا وَجْهَ اللَّهِ إِلَّا أُجِرْتَ بِهَا حَتَّى اللُّقْمَةَ تَرْفَعُهَا إِلَى فِي امْرَأَتِكَ» مُتَّفَقٌ عَلَيْهِ (الألباني)

Sa'd b. Abu Waqqas said: During an illness which brought me near to death in the year of the Conquest God's Messenger came to visit me and I said, "Messenger of God, I have a large amount of property and my daughter is my only heir. Shall I will away all my property?" He replied, 'No' I suggested two-thirds, but he objected, then a half, but he still objected. When I suggested a third he replied, "You may will away a third, but that is a lot*. To leave your heirs rich is better than to leave them poor and begging from people. You will not spend anything, seeking thereby to please God, without being rewarded for it, even the mouthful you give your wife." *While this tradition tells that the Prophet gave permission for a man to will away a third of his estate to some person or purpose other than the heirs, it indicates that be thought it would be better not to will away so much. (Bukhari and Muslim.). https://sunnah.com/mishkat/12/30

وَعَنْهُ قَالَ: قَالَ رَسُولُ اللَّهِ ﷺ: «لَا يَفْرُكْ مُؤْمِنٌ مُؤْمِنَةً إِنْ كَرِهَ مِنْهَا خُلُقًا رَضِيَ مِنْهَا آخَرَ» . رَوَاهُ مُسْلِمٌ. صَحِيحٌ الألباني

He reported God's Messenger as saying, "A believer must not hate a believing woman; if he dislikes one of her characteristics he will be pleased with another." Muslim transmitted it. https://sunnah.com/mishkat/13/158

عَنْ جَابِرٍ، قَالَ نَهَى رَسُولُ اللَّهِ ﷺ أَنْ يَطْرُقَ الرَّجُلُ أَهْلَهُ لَيْلاً يَتَخَوَّنُهُمْ أَوْ يَلْتَمِسُ عَثَرَاتِهِمْ . مسلم

It has been narrated (through a different chain of narrations) on the authority of Jabir who said: The Messenger of Allah (ﷺ) forbade that a man should come to his family like (an unexpected) night visitor doubting their fidelity and spying into their lapses. Sahih Muslim 715 ab. https://sunnah.com/muslim/33/264

Chapter IV

The Prophet as a Role Model for Fathers

Overview

The Prophet (SAS) has been a great father to his children and grandchildren. He has also been very kind to the children of his companions, teenage, and youth. We will walk through his dealings (SAS) with children, teenage, and youth. It has clearly shown his kind and merciful fatherhood to his children and the children of others. He (SAS) has also been a great motivator and supporter to teenage and youth as described in the following sections. One of the companions, Anas Ibn Malik, May Allah be pleased with him, reported a general statement about the dealings of the Prophet (SAS) with children and how kind he has been with them as shown in the following narration:

عَنْ أَنَسِ بْنِ مَالِكٍ، قَالَ مَا رَأَيْتُ أَحَدًا كَانَ أَرْحَمَ بِالْعِيَالِ مِنْ رَسُولِ اللَّهِ ﷺ - ..... " . رواه مسلم

Anas Ibn Malik reported: I have never seen anyone kinder to one's family than Allah's Messenger (ﷺ), ... Sahih Muslim 2316, https://sunnah.com/muslim/43/84

The Prophet's (SAS) Dealings with his Children and Grandchildren

He (SAS) has been very kind and merciful with his children. When Fatimah, his daughter, has been approaching the Prophet (SAS), he has welcomed her very much, stood up for her, kissed her and has had her sit in his place. Similarly, she has been doing the same to him. You can conclude such actions from the following narrations:

عَنْ عَائِشَةَ رَضِيَ اللهُ عَنْهَا قَالَتْ: أَقْبَلَتْ فَاطِمَةُ تَمْشِي كَأَنَّ مِشْيَتَهَا مَشْيُ النَّبِيِّ ﷺ، فَقَالَ: مَرْحَبًا بِابْنَتِي، ثُمَّ أَجْلَسَهَا عَنْ يَمِينِهِ، أَوْ عَنْ شِمَالِهِ. صحيح (الألباني)

'A'isha said, "Fatima walked in the same manner that the Prophet, may Allah bless him and grant him peace, walked. He used to say to her, 'Welcome, my daughter!' Then he would have her sit down on his right or his left." Sahih (Al-Albani). https://sunnah.com/adab/42/67

عَنْ عَائِشَةَ أُمِّ الْمُؤْمِنِينَ قَالَتْ: مَا رَأَيْتُ أَحَدًا كَانَ أَشْبَهَ حَدِيثًا وَكَلَامًا بِرَسُولِ اللهِ ﷺ مِنْ فَاطِمَةَ، وَكَانَتْ إِذَا دَخَلَتْ عَلَيْهِ قَامَ إِلَيْهَا، فَرَحَّبَ بِهَا وَقَبَّلَهَا، وَأَجْلَسَهَا فِي مَجْلِسِهِ، وَكَانَ إِذَا دَخَلَ عَلَيْهَا قَامَتْ إِلَيْهِ فَأَخَذَتْ بِيَدِهِ، فَرَحَّبَتْ بِهِ وَقَبَّلَتْهُ، وَأَجْلَسَتْهُ فِي مَجْلِسِهَا، فَدَخَلَتْ عَلَيْهِ فِي مَرَضِهِ الَّذِي تُوُفِّيَ، فَرَحَّبَ بِهَا وَقَبَّلَهَا. صحيح (الألباني)

`A'isha, the Umm al-Mu'minin, said, "I did not see anyone who more resembled the Messenger of Allah, may Allah bless him and grant him peace, in manner of speaking than Fatima. When she came to him, he stood up for her, made her welcome, kissed her and had her sit in his place. When the Prophet came to her, she stood up for him, took his hand, made him welcome, kissed him, and made him sit in her place. She came to him during his final illness and he greeted her and kissed her." Sahih (Al-Albani). https://sunnah.com/adab/42/7

The Prophet (SAS) has exceptionally liked his grandchildren, Al-Hasan and Al-Hussein. He has clearly expressed his love to them, has asked Allah (SWT) to love them, and has loved all who loves them as shown in the following narration:

عَنْ أَبِي هُرَيْرَةَ ـ رضى الله عنه ـ قَالَ كُنْتُ مَعَ رَسُولِ اللَّهِ ﷺ ..... فَقَالَ الْحَسَنُ بِيَدِهِ، هَكَذَا فَالْتَزَمَهُ فَقَالَ " اللَّهُمَّ إِنِّي أُحِبُّهُ، فَأَحِبَّهُ، وَأَحِبَّ مَنْ يُحِبُّهُ ". قَالَ أَبُو هُرَيْرَةَ فَمَا كَانَ أَحَدٌ أَحَبَّ إِلَىَّ مِنَ الْحَسَنِ بْنِ عَلِيٍّ بَعْدَ مَا قَالَ رَسُولُ اللَّهِ ﷺ مَا قَالَ. رواه البخارى

Narrated Abu Huraira: I was with Allah's Messenger (ﷺ) ...... The Prophet (ﷺ) stretched his hand out like this, and Al-Hasan did the same. The Prophet (ﷺ) embraced him and said, "O Allah! I love him, so please love him and love those who love him." Since Allah's Messenger (ﷺ) said that nothing has been dearer to me than Al-Hasan. Sahih al-Bukhari 5884, https://sunnah.com/bukhari/77/101

In several times, he (SAS) has carried his grandchildren while praying in congregation. In one of the prayers, he has made a lengthy prostration because the grandchild has ridden his back and he did not want to disturb the kid. How merciful to kids he (SAS) has been. He (SAS) has made the prostration long for all people who have been praying behind him in order not to interrupt the kid's play. What type of heart is this to even think about such an action? How patient were the companions not to aggressively reflect on the kid's action? If this occurs in any mosque nowadays, you can imagine the response of people towards the Imam and the kid. Can we even allow this to happen at home when our kids play around us during prayer? I think we have to change our attitude towards kids in our homes, mosques, and community centers. Let us look at the Prophet's reaction in the following narration:

عَنْ عَبْدِ اللَّهِ بْنِ شَدَّادٍ، عَنْ أَبِيهِ، قَالَ خَرَجَ عَلَيْنَا رَسُولُ اللَّهِ ﷺ فِي إِحْدَى صَلاَتَىِ الْعِشَاءِ وَهُوَ حَامِلٌ حَسَنًا أَوْ حُسَيْنًا فَتَقَدَّمَ رَسُولُ اللَّهِ ﷺ فَوَضَعَهُ ثُمَّ كَبَّرَ لِلصَّلاَةِ فَصَلَّى فَسَجَدَ بَيْنَ ظَهْرَانَىْ صَلاَتِهِ سَجْدَةً أَطَالَهَا . قَالَ أَبِي فَرَفَعْتُ رَأْسِي وَإِذَا الصَّبِيُّ عَلَى ظَهْرِ رَسُولِ اللَّهِ ﷺ وَهُوَ سَاجِدٌ فَرَجَعْتُ إِلَى سُجُودِي فَلَمَّا قَضَى رَسُولُ اللَّهِ ﷺ الصَّلاَةَ قَالَ النَّاسُ يَا رَسُولَ اللَّهِ إِنَّكَ سَجَدْتَ بَيْنَ ظَهْرَانَىْ صَلاَتِكَ سَجْدَةً أَطَلْتَهَا حَتَّى ظَنَنَّا أَنَّهُ قَدْ حَدَثَ أَمْرٌ أَوْ أَنَّهُ يُوحَى إِلَيْكَ . قَالَ " كُلُّ ذَلِكَ لَمْ يَكُنْ وَلَكِنَّ ابْنِي ارْتَحَلَنِي فَكَرِهْتُ أَنْ أُعَجِّلَهُ حَتَّى يَقْضِيَ حَاجَتَهُ " . سنن النسائى

It was narrated from 'Abdullah bin Shaddad that his father said: "The Messenger of Allah (ﷺ) came out to us for one of the nighttime prayers, and he was carrying Hasan or Husain. The Messenger of Allah (ﷺ) came forward and put him down, then he said the Takbir and started to pray. He prostrated during his prayer, and made the prostration lengthy." My father said: "I raised my head and saw the child on the back of the Messenger of Allah (ﷺ) while he was prostrating so I went back to my prostration. When the Messenger of Allah (ﷺ) finished praying, the people said: "O Messenger of Allah (ﷺ), you prostrated during the prayer for so long that we thought that something had happened or that you were receiving a revelation.' He said: 'No such thing happened. But my son was riding on my back and I did not like to disturb him until he had enough.'" Sahih, Sunan an-Nasa'i 1141. https://sunnah.com/nasai/12/113

Let us look at the practices of the Prophet (SAS) during prayer and how he has dealt with kids during prayer. Nowadays, we lack such practices in our daily life activities. He (SAS) has been carrying his granddaughter while standing during prayer and put her during prostration. This is contrary to the practice of many people who are forbidding kids from entering the mosques. Some others are fighting with parents who are bringing their kids to the mosques. I think we have to change our attitude towards the existence of kids in the mosques. This clear in the following narrations:

عَنْ عَمْرِو بْنِ سُلَيْمٍ الزُّرَقِيِّ، أَنَّهُ سَمِعَ أَبَا قَتَادَةَ، يَقُولُ بَيْنَا نَحْنُ جُلُوسٌ فِي الْمَسْجِدِ إِذْ خَرَجَ عَلَيْنَا رَسُولُ اللَّهِ ﷺ يَحْمِلُ أُمَامَةَ بِنْتَ أَبِي الْعَاصِ بْنِ الرَّبِيعِ وَأُمُّهَا زَيْنَبُ بِنْتُ رَسُولِ اللَّهِ ﷺ وَهِيَ صَبِيَّةٌ يَحْمِلُهَا فَصَلَّى رَسُولُ اللَّهِ ﷺ وَهِيَ عَلَى عَاتِقِهِ يَضَعُهَا إِذَا رَكَعَ وَيُعِيدُهَا إِذَا قَامَ حَتَّى قَضَى صَلاَتَهُ يَفْعَلُ ذَلِكَ بِهَا . سنن النسائى

It was narrated from 'Amr bin Sulaim Az-Zuraqi that he heard Abu Qatadah say: "While we were sitting in the Masjid. The Messenger of Allah (ﷺ) came out to us carrying Umamah bint Abi Al-'As bin Ar-Rabi', whose mother was Zainab, the daughter of the

Messenger of Allah (ﷺ). She was a little girl and he was carrying her. The Messenger of Allah (ﷺ) prayed with her on his shoulder, putting her down when he bowed and picking her up again when he stood up, until he completed his prayer." Sunan an-Nasa'i 711
https://sunnah.com/nasai/8/24

وَعَنْ أَبِي قَتَادَةَ ـ رضى الله عنه ـ قَالَ : { كَانَ رَسُولُ اَللَّهِ ـ ﷺ ـ يُصَلِّي وَهُوَ حَامِلٌ أُمَامَةَ بِنْتِ زَيْنَبَ , فَإِذَا سَجَدَ وَضَعَهَا , وَإِذَا قَامَ حَمَلَهَا } مُتَّفَقٌ عَلَيْهِ.

Narrated Abu Qatada (RA): Allah's Messenger (ﷺ) was (one time) offering prayer while he was carrying Umama, daughter of Zainab, when he prostrated he put her down and when he stood up he lifted her up. [Agreed upon]. https://sunnah.com/bulugh/2/91

The Prophet (SAS) has taught us how to raise our kids in the kindest and most merciful way. When Al-Hassan, his grandchild, has tried to eat from the charitable dates, he (SAS) has gently showed Al-Hassan that his action is not allowed. He (SAS) has gently taught the kid why he should not eat from such food as shown in the following narration:

عن أبي هريرة رضي الله عنه قال: أخذ الحسن بن علي رضي الله عنهما تمرة الصدقة فجعلها في فيه فقال رسول الله ﷺ: "كخ كخ، ارم بها، أما علمت أنَّا لا نأكل الصدقة؟!" وفي رواية: "أنَّا لا تحل لنا الصدقة" (متفق عليه). وقوله: "كِخْ كِخْ" يقال بإسكان الخاء، ويقال بكسرها مع التنوين، وهي كلمة زجر للصبي عن المستقذرات. وكان الحسن رضي الله عنه صبيًا. متفق عليه.

Abu Hurairah (May Allah be pleased with him) reported: Al-Hasan bin 'Ali (May Allah be pleased with them) took one of the dates of the Sadaqah (charity) and put it in his mouth, whereupon Messenger of Allah (ﷺ) said, "Leave it, leave it, throw it away. Do you not know that we do not eat the Sadaqah (charity)?" [Al-Bukhari and Muslim]. https://sunnah.com/riyadussalihin/introduction/298

The Prophet's (SAS) Dealings with the Children of his Companions
It is also clear from his dealings (SAS) with the children of the companions how kind he has been. In the following narration, he (SAS) has shown kindness to one of the companions' new born. Such actions have attracted the hearts of the companions to him (SAS). He (SAS) has given his companions and their families much emphases as shown in the following narration:

عَنْ أَبِي مُوسَى، قَالَ وُلِدَ لِي غُلاَمٌ، فَأَتَيْتُ بِهِ النَّبِيَّ ﷺ فَسَمَّاهُ إِبْرَاهِيمَ، فَحَنَّكَهُ بِتَمْرَةٍ، وَدَعَا لَهُ بِالْبَرَكَةِ، وَدَفَعَهُ إِلَيَّ، وَكَانَ أَكْبَرَ وَلَدِ أَبِي مُوسَى. رواه البخارى

Narrated Abu Musa: I got a son and I took him to the Prophet (ﷺ) who named him Ibrahim, and put in his mouth the juice of a date fruit (which be himself had chewed?, and invoked for Allah's blessing upon him, and then gave him back to me. He was the eldest son of Abii Musa. Sahih al-Bukhari 6198, https://sunnah.com/bukhari/78/222

He (SAS) has also been close to the companions children with his great humbleness and mercy. He has been able to lower his communication to reach the kid's mind and heart, to speak his language, to share his feelings, and to show a lot of support to the kid. This is really an amazing communication style, which necessitates psychological support to the needy even if he is a kid. Look at the following narration:

عَنْ أَنَسِ بْنِ مَالِكٍ، قَالَ كَانَ رَسُولُ اللَّهِ ﷺ يَدْخُلُ عَلَيْنَا وَلِي أَخٌ صَغِيرٌ يُكْنَى أَبَا عُمَيْرٍ وَكَانَ لَهُ نُغَرٌ يَلْعَبُ بِهِ فَمَاتَ فَدَخَلَ عَلَيْهِ النَّبِيُّ ﷺ ذَاتَ يَوْمٍ فَرَآهُ حَزِينًا فَقَالَ " مَا شَأْنُهُ " . قَالُوا مَاتَ نُغَرُهُ فَقَالَ " يَا أَبَا عُمَيْرٍ مَا فَعَلَ النُّغَيْرُ " . صحيح الألباني

Anas b. Malik said: The Messenger of Allah (May peace be upon him) used to come to visit us. I had a younger brother who was called Abu 'Umair by Kunyah (surname). He had a sparrow with which he played, but it died. So one day the prophet (May peace be upon him) came to see him and saw him grieved. He asked: What is the matter with him? The people replied: His sparrow has died. He then said: Abu 'Umair! What has happened to the little sparrow? Sahih (Al-Albani), https://sunnah.com/abudawud/43/197

Looking at prayer as one of the main pillars of Islam, you might think it is more important than all other life activities. However, the Prophet (SAS) has shortened the congregation prayer in the mosque due to the cry of a kid. He has felt that his mother might not feel well about the kid's cry. Therefore, he has ended the prayer faster than usual to sympathize with the mother. Such mercy and kindness position him (SAS) high in the hearts of people whether they are believers or disbelievers. This is clear in the following narration:

أَنَّ أَنَسَ بْنَ مَالِكٍ، حَدَّثَهُ أَنَّ النَّبِيَّ ﷺ قَالَ "إِنِّي لأَدْخُلُ فِي الصَّلاَةِ وَأَنَا أُرِيدُ إِطَالَتَهَا، فَأَسْمَعُ بُكَاءَ الصَّبِيِّ، فَأَتَجَوَّزُ فِي صَلاَتِي مِمَّا أَعْلَمُ مِنْ شِدَّةِ وَجْدِ أُمِّهِ مِنْ بُكَائِهِ ". رواه البخارى

Narrated Anas bin Malik: The Prophet (ﷺ) said, "When I start the prayer I intend to prolong it, but on hearing the cries of a child, I cut short the prayer because I know that the cries of the child will incite its mother's passions." Sahih al-Bukhari 709, https://sunnah.com/bukhari/10/104

The Prophet's (SAS) Dealings with Teenage
There are many narrations that show the kindness of the Prophet (SAS) in dealing with teenage and his recommendation to the companions to take good care of their teenage. He (SAS) has emphasized the importance and necessity of being kind to children and respectful to elders as shown in the following narration:

قَالَ ابْنُ السَّرْحِ - عَنِ النَّبِيِّ ﷺ قَالَ "مَنْ لَمْ يَرْحَمْ صَغِيرَنَا وَيَعْرِفْ حَقَّ كَبِيرِنَا فَلَيْسَ مِنَّا". صحيح الألباني

Narrated Abdullah ibn Amr ibn al-'As: The Prophet (ﷺ) said: Those who do not show mercy to our young ones and do not realize the right of our elders are not from us. Sunan Abi Dawud 4943, Sahih (Al-Albani) https://sunnah.com/abudawud/43/171

He (SAS) has been astonished when he has known that one of the companions has not kissed any of his ten children at all. Such action has shown rigidity in the heart of this man and other similar people. He (SAS) did not like such hearts and actions because they will reflect negatively on the society. Such hearts disunite people instead of uniting them. Look at the Prophet's (SAS) response to the companion's comment in the following narration:

عَنْ أَبِي هُرَيْرَةَ، أَنَّ الأَقْرَعَ بْنَ حَابِسٍ، أَبْصَرَ النَّبِيَّ ﷺ يُقَبِّلُ الْحَسَنَ فَقَالَ إِنَّ لِي عَشَرَةً مِنَ الْوَلَدِ مَا قَبَّلْتُ وَاحِدًا مِنْهُمْ فَقَالَ رَسُولُ اللَّهِ ﷺ " إِنَّهُ مَنْ لاَ يَرْحَمْ لاَ يُرْحَمْ ". رواه مسلم

Abu Huraira reported that al-Aqra' b. Habis saw Allah's Apostle (ﷺ) kissing Hasan. He said: I have ten children, but I have never kissed any one of them, whereupon Allah's Messenger (ﷺ) said: He who does not show mercy (towards his children), no mercy would be shown to him. Sahih Muslim 2318 a, https://sunnah.com/muslim/43/86

He (SAS) has shown utmost respect to the teenage who has preferred to drink from the hands of the Prophet (SAS) first before the elders. He (SAS) asked for the permission of teenage to give the drink first to elders but he rejected. The Prophet (SAS) has accepted the opinion of the teenage as shown in the following narration:

عَنْ سَهْلِ بْنِ سَعْدٍ ـ رضى الله عنه ـ قَالَ أُتِيَ رَسُولُ اللَّهِ ﷺ بِقَدَحٍ فَشَرِبَ وَعَنْ يَمِينِهِ غُلاَمٌ، هُوَ أَحْدَثُ الْقَوْمِ، وَالأَشْيَاخُ عَنْ يَسَارِهِ قَالَ " يَا غُلاَمُ أَتَأْذَنُ لِي أَنْ أُعْطِيَ الأَشْيَاخَ ". فَقَالَ مَا كُنْتُ لأُوثِرَ بِنَصِيبِي مِنْكَ أَحَدًا يَا رَسُولَ اللَّهِ. فَأَعْطَاهُ إِيَّاهُ. رواه البخارى

Narrated Sahl bin Sa`d: Once a tumbler (full of milk or water) was brought to Allah's Messenger (ﷺ) who drank from it, while on his right side there was sitting a boy who was the youngest of those who were present, and on his left side there were old men. The Prophet (ﷺ) asked, "O boy ! Do you allow me to give (the drink) to the elder people (first)?" The boy said, "I will not prefer anybody to have my share from you, O Allah's Apostle!" So, he gave it to the boy. Sahih al-Bukhari 2366, https://sunnah.com/bukhari/42/14

The Prophet (SAS) has recommended the companion not to lie to their children because this action might cause much damage to the children as shown in the following narration:

عَنْ عَبْدِ اللَّهِ بْنِ عَامِرٍ، أَنَّهُ قَالَ دَعَتْنِي أُمِّي يَوْمًا وَرَسُولُ اللَّهِ ﷺ قَاعِدٌ فِي بَيْتِنَا فَقَالَتْ هَا تَعَالَ أُعْطِيكَ. فَقَالَ لَهَا رَسُولُ اللَّهِ ﷺ " وَمَا أَرَدْتِ أَنْ تُعْطِيهِ ". قَالَتْ أُعْطِيهِ تَمْرًا. فَقَالَ لَهَا رَسُولُ اللَّهِ ﷺ " أَمَا إِنَّكِ لَوْ لَمْ تُعْطِيهِ شَيْئًا كُتِبَتْ عَلَيْكِ كِذْبَةٌ ". حسن الألباني

Narrated Abdullah ibn Amir: My mother called me one day when the Messenger of Allah (ﷺ) was sitting in our house. She said: Come here and I shall give you something. The Messenger of Allah (ﷺ) asked her: What did you intend to give him? She replied: I intended to give him some dates. The Messenger of Allah (ﷺ) said: If you were not to give him anything, a lie would be recorded against you. (Al-Albani), https://sunnah.com/abudawud/43/219

Fairness is recommended among your children. If you give one of them something, you should give the others something similar in order not to generate issues among them. This is clear in the following narration:

وَفِي لَفْظٍ : { فَانْطَلَقَ أَبِي إلَى اَلنَّبِيِّ - ﷺ - لِيُشْهِدَهُ عَلَى صَدَقَتِي. فَقَالَ : " أَفَعَلْتَ هَذَا بِوَلَدِكَ كُلِّهِمْ"؟. قَالَ : لَا. قَالَ : " اِتَّقُوا اَللَّهَ , وَاعْدِلُوا بَيْنَ أَوْلَادِكُمْ " فَرَجَعَ أَبِي, فَرَدَّ تِلْكَ اَلصَّدَقَةَ } مُتَّفَقٌ عَلَيْهِ. هذه الرواية للبخاري (2587) ، ومسلم (1623) (13) والسياق لمسلم.

A narration has: My father went then to the Prophet (ﷺ) to call him as a witness to my Sadaqah (i.e. gift) and he asked, "Have you done the same with all your children?" He replied, "No." He said, "Fear Allah and treat your children equally." My father then returned and took back that gift. [Agreed upon]. https://sunnah.com/bulugh/7/184

The Prophet (SAS) has gained the love of teenage for being kind and merciful to them as shown in the following narrations:

عَنْ جَابِرِ بْنِ سَمُرَةَ، قَالَ صَلَّيْتُ مَعَ رَسُولِ اللَّهِ ﷺ صَلاَةَ الأُولَى ثُمَّ خَرَجَ إِلَى أَهْلِهِ وَخَرَجْتُ مَعَهُ فَاسْتَقْبَلَهُ وِلْدَانٌ فَجَعَلَ يَمْسَحُ خَدَّىْ أَحَدِهِمْ وَاحِدًا وَاحِدًا - قَالَ - وَأَمَّا أَنَا فَمَسَحَ خَدِّي - قَالَ - فَوَجَدْتُ لِيَدِهِ بَرْدًا أَوْ رِيحًا كَأَنَّمَا أَخْرَجَهَا مِنْ جُؤْنَةِ عَطَّارٍ. رواه مسلم.

Jabir b. Samura reported: I prayed along with Allah's Messenger (ﷺ) the first prayer. He then went to his family and I also went along with him when he met some children (on the way). He began to pat the cheeks of each one of them. He also patted my cheek and I experienced a coolness or a fragrance of his hand as if it had been brought out from the scent bag of a perfumer. Sahih Muslim 2329, https://sunnah.com/muslim/43/110

عَنِ ابْنِ عَبَّاسٍ،، قَالَ ضَمَّنِي النَّبِيُّ ﷺ إِلَى صَدْرِهِ وَقَالَ " اللَّهُمَّ عَلِّمْهُ الْحِكْمَةَ ".

Narrated Ibn `Abbas: Once the Prophet (ﷺ) embraced me (pressed me to his chest) and said, "O Allah, teach him wisdom (i.e. the understanding of the knowledge of Qur'an). Sahih al-Bukhari 3756, https://sunnah.com/bukhari/62/102

One of the most important narrations that teaches faith is the one narrated by a teenage, i.e., Abdullah Ibn Abbas. The Prophet (SAS) has treated the teenage as an adult and has given him a recommendation for life. It becomes the most popular narration that emphasizes destiny to people as shown in the following narration:

عَنْ عَبْدِ اللَّهِ بْنِ عَبَّاسٍ رَضِيَ اللَّهُ عَنْهُمَا قَالَ: "كُنْتُ خَلْفَ رَسُولِ اللَّهِ ﷺ يَوْمًا، فَقَالَ: يَا غُلَامُ! إِنِّي أُعَلِّمُكَ كَلِمَاتٍ: احْفَظِ اللَّهَ يَحْفَظْكَ، احْفَظِ اللَّهَ تَجِدْهُ تُجَاهَكَ، إِذَا سَأَلْتَ فَاسْأَلِ اللَّهَ، وَإِذَا اسْتَعَنْتَ فَاسْتَعِنْ بِاللَّهِ، وَاعْلَمْ أَنَّ الْأُمَّةَ لَوِ اجْتَمَعَتْ عَلَى أَنْ يَنْفَعُوكَ بِشَيْءٍ لَمْ يَنْفَعُوكَ إِلَّا بِشَيْءٍ قَدْ كَتَبَهُ اللَّهُ لَكَ، وَإِنِ اجْتَمَعُوا عَلَى أَنْ يَضُرُّوكَ بِشَيْءٍ لَمْ يَضُرُّوكَ إِلَّا بِشَيْءٍ قَدْ كَتَبَهُ اللَّهُ عَلَيْكَ، رُفِعَتِ الْأَقْلَامُ، وَجَفَّتِ الصُّحُفُ" . رَوَاهُ التِّرْمِذِيُّ [رقم:2516] وَقَالَ: حَدِيثٌ حَسَنٌ صَحِيحٌ .

وَفِي رِوَايَةِ غَيْرِ التِّرْمِذِيِّ: "احْفَظِ اللَّهَ تَجِدْهُ أَمَامَكَ، تَعَرَّفْ إِلَى اللَّهِ فِي الرَّخَاءِ يَعْرِفْكَ فِي الشِّدَّةِ، وَاعْلَمْ أَنَّ مَا أَخْطَأَكَ لَمْ يَكُنْ لِيُصِيبَكَ، وَمَا أَصَابَكَ لَمْ يَكُنْ لِيُخْطِئَكَ، وَاعْلَمْ أَنَّ النَّصْرَ مَعَ الصَّبْرِ، وَأَنَّ الْفَرَجَ مَعَ الْكَرْبِ، وَأَنَّ الْعُسْرَ يُسْرًا."

On the authority of Abdullah bin Abbas (may Allah be pleased with him) who said: One day I was behind the Prophet (peace and blessings of Allah be upon him) [riding on the same mount] and he said, "O young man, I shall teach you some words [of advice]: Be mindful of Allah and Allah will protect you. Be mindful of Allah and you will find Him in front of you. If you ask, then ask Allah [alone]; and if you seek help, then seek help from Allah [alone]. And know that if the nation were to gather together to benefit you with anything, they would not benefit you except with what Allah had already prescribed for you. And if they were to gather together to harm you with anything, they would not harm you except with what Allah had already prescribed against you. The pens have been lifted and the pages have dried." It was related by at-Tirmidhi, who said it was a good and sound hadeeth. Another narration, other than that of Tirmidhi, reads: Be mindful of Allah, and you will find Him in front of you. Recognize and acknowledge Allah in times of ease and prosperity, and He will remember you in times of adversity. And know that what has passed you by [and you have failed to attain] was not going to befall you, and what has befallen you was not going to pass you by. And know that victory comes with patience, relief with affliction, and hardship with ease. 40 Hadith Nawawi 19, https://sunnah.com/nawawi40/19

He (SAS) has been a good teacher by example to teenage in many occasions as shown in the following narrations:

عَنِ ابْنِ عَبَّاسٍ، قَالَ بِتُّ عِنْدَ خَالَتِي فَقَامَ النَّبِيُّ ﷺ يُصَلِّي مِنَ اللَّيْلِ، فَقُمْتُ أُصَلِّي مَعَهُ فَقُمْتُ عَنْ يَسَارِهِ، فَأَخَذَ بِرَأْسِي فَأَقَامَنِي عَنْ يَمِينِهِ. رواه البخاري

Narrated Ibn `Abbas: Once I passed the night in the house of my aunt Maimuna. The Prophet (ﷺ) stood for the night prayer and I joined him and stood on his left side but he drew me to his right by holding me by the head. Sahih al-Bukhari 699, https://sunnah.com/bukhari/10/94

أَنَّهُ سَمِعَ عُمَرَ بْنَ أَبِي سَلَمَةَ، يَقُولُ كُنْتُ غُلَامًا فِي حَجْرِ رَسُولِ اللَّهِ ﷺ وَكَانَتْ يَدِي تَطِيشُ فِي الصَّحْفَةِ فَقَالَ لِي رَسُولُ اللَّهِ ﷺ " يَا غُلَامُ سَمِّ اللَّهَ، وَكُلْ بِيَمِينِكَ وَكُلْ مِمَّا يَلِيكَ ". فَمَا زَالَتْ تِلْكَ طِعْمَتِي بَعْدُ. رواه البخاري

Narrated `Umar bin Abi Salama: I was a boy under the care of Allah's Messenger (ﷺ) and my hand used to go around the dish while I was eating. So Allah's Messenger (ﷺ) said to me, 'O boy! Mention the Name of Allah and eat with your right hand, and eat of the dish what is nearer to you." Since then I have applied those instructions when eating. Sahih al-Bukhari 5376, https://sunnah.com/bukhari/70/4

If you want to be close to the Prophet (SAS) in the Day of Judgement, ask Allah (SWT) to provide you with two or three daughters. Then, do your best to raise them well in order to be rewarded with Paradise and with the company of the Prophet (SAS) in the Day of Judgement. It is hard but achievable. This is clear in the following narration:

عَنْ أَنَسِ بْنِ مَالِكٍ، قَالَ قَالَ رَسُولُ اللَّهِ ﷺ " مَنْ عَالَ جَارِيَتَيْنِ حَتَّى تَبْلُغَا جَاءَ يَوْمَ الْقِيَامَةِ أَنَا وَهُوَ " . وَضَمَّ أَصَابِعَهُ . رواه مسلم.
Malik reported Allah's Messenger (ﷺ) as saying: He, who brought up two girls properly till they grew up, he and I would come (together) (very closely) on the Day of Resurrection, and he interlaced his fingers (for explaining the point of nearness between him and that person). Sahih Muslim 2631, https://sunnah.com/muslim/45/192

He (SAS) has been very helpful to believers and disbelievers as well. The following story is evident of his kindness and mercy (SAS) even with kids of the disbelievers. He (SAS) has never lost a chance to save people with his kindness as shown in the following narration:

عَنْ أَنَسٍ، أَنَّ غُلاَمًا، مِنَ الْيَهُودِ كَانَ مَرِضَ فَأَتَاهُ النَّبِيُّ ﷺ يَعُودُهُ فَقَعَدَ عِنْدَ رَأْسِهِ فَقَالَ لَهُ " أَسْلِمْ " . فَنَظَرَ إِلَى أَبِيهِ وَهُوَ عِنْدَ رَأْسِهِ فَقَالَ لَهُ أَبُوهُ أَطِعْ أَبَا الْقَاسِمِ . فَأَسْلَمَ فَقَامَ النَّبِيُّ ﷺ وَهُوَ يَقُولُ " الْحَمْدُ لِلَّهِ الَّذِي أَنْقَذَهُ بِي مِنَ النَّارِ " . صحيح الألباني

Narrated Anas: A young Jew became ill. The Prophet (ﷺ) went to visit him. He sat down by his head and said to him: Accept Islam. He looked at his father who was beside him near his head, and he said: Obey Abu al-Qasim. So he accepted Islam, and the Prophet (ﷺ) stood up saying: Praise be to Allah Who has saved him through me from Hell. Sahih (Al-Albani), https://sunnah.com/abudawud/21/7

The Prophet's (SAS) Dealings with Youth
The Prophet (SAS) has a great impact on youth of his era. He has been a great motivator, mentor, and role model for youth. He (SAS) dealt with youth in full respect accommodating their personal differences, capabilities, and skills. He (SAS) has put emphases on raising youth using different means of education. One of these means include camps in which youth would have done education activities away from families and attractions. He (SAS) has been a kind educator and advisor to the youth. He has sensed that the youth campers have missed their families, hence, he has advised them to quickly return home and to practice the religious activities they learn during the camp. This is clear in the following narration:

عَنْ أَبِي سُلَيْمَانَ، مَالِكِ بْنِ الْحُوَيْرِثِ قَالَ أَتَيْنَا النَّبِيَّ ﷺ وَنَحْنُ شَبَبَةٌ مُتَقَارِبُونَ، فَأَقَمْنَا عِنْدَهُ عِشْرِينَ لَيْلَةً، فَظَنَّ أَنَّا اشْتَقْنَا أَهْلَنَا، وَسَأَلَنَا عَمَّنْ تَرَكْنَا فِي أَهْلِنَا، فَأَخْبَرْنَاهُ، وَكَانَ رَفِيقًا رَحِيمًا فَقَالَ " ارْجِعُوا إِلَى أَهْلِيكُمْ فَعَلِّمُوهُمْ وَمُرُوهُمْ، وَصَلُّوا كَمَا رَأَيْتُمُونِي أُصَلِّي، وَإِذَا حَضَرَتِ الصَّلاَةُ فَلْيُؤَذِّنْ لَكُمْ أَحَدُكُمْ، ثُمَّ لِيَؤُمَّكُمْ أَكْبَرُكُمْ". رواه البخاري

Narrated Abu Sulaiman and Malik bin Huwairith: We came to the Prophet (ﷺ) and we were (a few) young men of approximately equal age and stayed with him for twenty nights. Then he thought that we were anxious for our families, and he asked us whom we had left behind to look after our families, and we told him. He was kindhearted and merciful, so he said, "Return to your families and teach them (religious knowledge) and order them (to do good deeds) and offer your prayers in the way you saw me offering my prayers, and when the stated time for the prayer becomes due, then one of you should pronounce its call (i.e. the Adhan), and the eldest of you should lead you in prayer. Sahih al-Bukhari 6008, https://sunnah.com/bukhari/78/39

The Prophet (SAS) has been rationalized and balanced in his dealing with youth. He (SAS) has talked to the youth's minds and hearts in a very quiet and respectful way. He has taught them how to practice their religion in a moderate and balanced way. He has taught them to balance between emotion and rationale; needs of spirit or soul and that of their bodies; as well as good knowledge and its implementation practices as shown in the following narration:

عَنْ أَنَسِ بْنِ مَالِكٍ رَضِيَ اللَّهُ عَنْهُ يَقُولُ جَاءَ ثَلَاثَةُ رَهْطٍ إِلَى بُيُوتِ أَزْوَاجِ النَّبِيِّ ﷺ يَسْأَلُونَ عَنْ عِبَادَةِ النَّبِيِّ ﷺ فَلَمَّا أُخْبِرُوا كَأَنَّهُمْ تَقَالُّوهَا فَقَالُوا وَأَيْنَ نَحْنُ مِنَ النَّبِيِّ ﷺ قَدْ غُفِرَ لَهُ مَا تَقَدَّمَ مِنْ ذَنْبِهِ وَمَا تَأَخَّرَ قَالَ أَحَدُهُمْ أَمَّا أَنَا فَإِنِّي أُصَلِّي اللَّيْلَ أَبَدًا وَقَالَ آخَرُ أَنَا أَصُومُ الدَّهْرَ وَلَا أُفْطِرُ وَقَالَ آخَرُ أَنَا أَعْتَزِلُ النِّسَاءَ فَلَا أَتَزَوَّجُ أَبَدًا فَجَاءَ رَسُولُ اللَّهِ ﷺ إِلَيْهِمْ فَقَالَ: «أَنْتُمُ الَّذِينَ قُلْتُمْ كَذَا وَكَذَا أَمَا وَاللَّهِ إِنِّي لَأَخْشَاكُمْ لِلَّهِ وَأَتْقَاكُمْ لَهُ لَكِنِّي أَصُومُ وَأُفْطِرُ وَأُصَلِّي وَأَرْقُدُ وَأَتَزَوَّجُ النِّسَاءَ فَمَنْ رَغِبَ عَنْ سُنَّتِي فَلَيْسَ مِنِّي» مُتَّفَقٌ عَلَيْهِ

Anas said: Three people came to the Prophet's wives and asked how the Prophet conducted his worship. When they were told about it they seemed to consider it little and said, "What a difference there is between us and the Prophet whose former and latter sins have been forgiven him by God!" One of them said, "As for me, I will always pray during the night." Another said, "I will fast during the daytime and not break my fast." The other said, "I will have nothing to do with women and will never marry." Then the Prophet came to them and said, "Are you the people who said such and such? By God, I am the one of you who fears and reverences God most, yet I fast and I break my fast; I pray and I sleep; and I marry women. He who is displeased with my sunna has nothing to do with me." (Bukhari and Muslim.), Mishkat al-Masabih 145 https://sunnah.com/mishkat/1/138

He (SAS) has recognized the personal differences among youth and has given each of them a task based on his/her strengths. The following narration has shown his recognition (SAS) to the skills of Zaid Ibn Thabit:

عَنْ خَارِجَةَ بْنِ زَيْدِ بْنِ ثَابِتٍ، عَنْ أَبِيهِ، زَيْدِ بْنِ ثَابِتٍ قَالَ أَمَرَنِي رَسُولُ اللَّهِ ﷺ أَنْ أَتَعَلَّمَ لَهُ كَلِمَاتٍ مِنْ كِتَابِ يَهُودَ . قَالَ " إِنِّي وَاللَّهِ مَا آمَنُ يَهُودَ عَلَى كِتَابٍ " . قَالَ فَمَا مَرَّ بِي نِصْفُ شَهْرٍ حَتَّى تَعَلَّمْتُهُ لَهُ قَالَ فَلَمَّا تَعَلَّمْتُهُ كَانَ إِذَا كَتَبَ إِلَى يَهُودَ كَتَبْتُ إِلَيْهِمْ وَإِذَا كَتَبُوا إِلَيْهِ قَرَأْتُ لَهُ كِتَابَهُمْ . قَالَ أَبُو عِيسَى هَذَا حَدِيثٌ حَسَنٌ صَحِيحٌ . وَقَدْ رُوِيَ مِنْ غَيْرِ هَذَا الْوَجْهِ عَنْ زَيْدِ بْنِ ثَابِتٍ رَوَاهُ الأَعْمَشُ عَنْ ثَابِتِ بْنِ عُبَيْدٍ الأَنْصَارِيِّ عَنْ زَيْدِ بْنِ ثَابِتٍ قَالَ أَمَرَنِي رَسُولُ اللَّهِ ﷺ أَنْ أَتَعَلَّمَ السُّرْيَانِيَّةَ . جامع الترمذي

Narrated Zaid bin Thabit: "The Messenger of Allah (ﷺ) ordered me to learn some statements from writings of the Jews for him, and he said: 'For indeed by Allah! I do no trust the Jews with my letters.'" He said: "Half a month did not pass before I learned it, when he (ﷺ) wanted to write to the Jews I would write it to them, and when they wrote to him I would read their letters to him." Jami` at-Tirmidhi 2715, https://sunnah.com/tirmidhi/42/28

The Prophet (SAS) has been very kind with people, particularly, youth. Whenever, he (SAS) has an activity with youth, he has always taken care of them and has been sensitive to their physiological and psychological needs. The following narrations emphasize how lovely and kind the Prophet (SAS) has been with youth:

قَالَ أَتَيْتُ جَابِرَ بْنَ عَبْدِ اللَّهِ الأَنْصَارِيَّ، فَقُلْتُ لَهُ حَدِّثْنِي بِمَا، سَمِعْتَ مِنْ، رَسُولِ اللَّهِ ﷺ قَالَ سَافَرْتُ مَعَهُ فِي بَعْضِ أَسْفَارِهِ ـ قَالَ أَبُو عَقِيلٍ لاَ أَدْرِي غَزْوَةً أَوْ عُمْرَةً ـ فَلَمَّا أَنْ أَقْبَلْنَا قَالَ النَّبِيُّ ﷺ " مَنْ أَحَبَّ أَنْ يَتَعَجَّلَ إِلَى أَهْلِهِ فَلْيُعَجِّلْ ". .... رواه البخاري

Narrated Muslim from Abu `Aqil from Abu Al-Mutawakkil An-Naji: I called on Jabir bin `Abdullah Al-Ansari and said to him, "Relate to me what you have heard from Allah's Messenger (ﷺ)." He said, "I accompanied him on one of the journeys." (Abu `Aqil said, "I do not know whether that journey was for the purpose of Jihad or `Umra.") "When we were returning," Jabir continued, "the Prophet (ﷺ) said, 'Whoever wants to return earlier to his family, should hurry up.' .... " Sahih al-Bukhari 2861 https://sunnah.com/bukhari/56/77

عَنْ جَابِرِ بْنِ عَبْدِ اللَّهِ، قَالَ كُنَّا مَعَ النَّبِيِّ ﷺ فِي غَزْوَةٍ، فَلَمَّا قَفَلْنَا كُنَّا قَرِيبًا مِنَ الْمَدِينَةِ تَعَجَّلْتُ عَلَى بَعِيرٍ لِي قَطُوفٍ، فَلَحِقَنِي رَاكِبٌ مِنْ خَلْفِي فَنَخَسَ بَعِيرِي بِعَنَزَةٍ كَانَتْ مَعَهُ، فَسَارَ بَعِيرِي كَأَحْسَنِ مَا أَنْتَ رَاءٍ مِنَ الإِبِلِ، فَالْتَفَتُّ فَإِذَا أَنَا بِرَسُولِ اللَّهِ ﷺ فَقُلْتُ يَا رَسُولَ اللَّهِ إِنِّي حَدِيثُ عَهْدٍ بِعُرْسٍ. قَالَ " أَتَزَوَّجْتَ ". قُلْتُ نَعَمْ. قَالَ " أَبِكْرًا أَمْ ثَيِّبًا ". قَالَ قُلْتُ بَلْ ثَيِّبًا. قَالَ " فَهَلاَّ بِكْرًا تُلاَعِبُهَا وَتُلاَعِبُكَ

". قَالَ فَلَمَّا قَدِمْنَا ذَهَبْنَا لِنَدْخُلَ، فَقَالَ " أَمْهِلُوا حَتَّى تَدْخُلُوا لَيْلاً ـ أَىْ عِشَاءً ـ لِكَىْ تَمْتَشِطَ الشَّعِثَةُ، وَتَسْتَحِدَّ الْمُغِيبَةُ ". رواه البخارى.

Narrated Jabir bin `Abdullah: We were with the Prophet (ﷺ) in Ghazwa, and when we returned and approached Medina, I wanted to hurry while riding a slow camel. A rider overtook me and pricked my camel with a spear which he had, whereupon my camel started running as fast as any other fast camel you may see. I looked back, and behold, the rider was Allah's Messenger (ﷺ) . I said, "O Allah's Messenger (ﷺ)! I am newly married " He asked, "Have you got married?" I replied, "Yes." He said, "A virgin or a matron?" I replied, "(Not a virgin) but a matron" He said, "Why didn't you marry a young girl so that you could play with her and she with you?" When we reached (near Medina) and were going to enter it, the Prophet (ﷺ) said, "Wait till you enter your home early in the night so that the lady whose hair is unkempt may comb her hair and that the lady whose husband has been away may shave her pubic hair." Sahih al-Bukhari 5247
https://sunnah.com/bukhari/67/180

أَخْبَرَنِي أَبُو السَّائِبِ، مَوْلَى هِشَامِ بْنِ زُهْرَةَ أَنَّهُ دَخَلَ عَلَى أَبِي سَعِيدٍ الْخُدْرِيِّ فِي بَيْتِهِ قَالَ فَوَجَدْتُهُ يُصَلِّي فَجَلَسْتُ أَنْتَظِرُهُ حَتَّى يَقْضِيَ صَلاَتَهُ .... قَالَ كَانَ فِيهِ فَتًى مِنَّا حَدِيثُ عَهْدٍ بِعُرْسٍ ـ قَالَ ـ فَخَرَجْنَا مَعَ رَسُولِ اللَّهِ ﷺ إِلَى الْخَنْدَقِ فَكَانَ ذَلِكَ الْفَتَى يَسْتَأْذِنُ رَسُولَ اللَّهِ ﷺ بِأَنْصَافِ النَّهَارِ فَيَرْجِعُ إِلَى أَهْلِهِ فَاسْتَأْذَنَهُ يَوْمًا فَقَالَ لَهُ رَسُولُ اللَّهِ ﷺ " خُذْ عَلَيْكَ سِلاَحَكَ فَإِنِّي أَخْشَى عَلَيْكَ قُرَيْظَةَ " . فَأَخَذَ الرَّجُلُ سِلاَحَهُ ثُمَّ رَجَعَ فَإِذَا امْرَأَتُهُ بَيْنَ الْبَابَيْنِ قَائِمَةً فَأَهْوَى إِلَيْهَا الرُّمْحَ لِيَطْعُنَهَا بِهِ وَأَصَابَتْهُ غَيْرَةٌ فَقَالَتْ لَهُ اكْفُفْ عَلَيْكَ رُمْحَكَ وَادْخُلِ الْبَيْتَ حَتَّى تَنْظُرَ مَا الَّذِي أَخْرَجَنِي . فَدَخَلَ فَإِذَا بِحَيَّةٍ عَظِيمَةٍ مُنْطَوِيَةٍ عَلَى الْفِرَاشِ فَأَهْوَى إِلَيْهَا بِالرُّمْحِ فَانْتَظَمَهَا بِهِ ثُمَّ خَرَجَ فَرَكَزَهُ فِي الدَّارِ فَاضْطَرَبَتْ عَلَيْهِ فَمَا يُدْرَى أَيُّهُمَا كَانَ أَسْرَعَ مَوْتًا الْحَيَّةُ أَمِ الْفَتَى قَالَ فَجِئْنَا إِلَى رَسُولِ اللَّهِ ﷺ فَذَكَرْنَا ذَلِكَ لَهُ وَقُلْنَا ادْعُ اللَّهَ يُحْيِيهِ لَنَا . فَقَالَ " اسْتَغْفِرُوا لِصَاحِبِكُمْ " .... " . رواه مسلم.

Abu as-Sa'ib, the freed slaved of Hisham b. Zuhra, said that he visited Abu Sa'id Khudri in his house, (and he further) said: I found him saying his prayer, so I sat down waiting for him to finish his prayer ……. So I sat down and as he finished (the prayer) he pointed to a room in the house and said: Do you see this room? I said: Yes. He said: There was a young man amongst us who had been newly wedded. We went with Allah's Messenger (ﷺ) (to participate in the Battle) of Trench when a young man in the midday used to seek permission from Allah's Messenger (ﷺ) to return to his family. One day he sought permission from him and Allah's Messenger (ﷺ) (after granting him the permission) said to him: Carry your weapons with you for I fear the tribe of Quraiza (may harm you). The man carried the weapons and then came back and found his wife standing between the two doors. He bent towards her smitten by jealousy and made a dash towards her with a spear in order to stab her. She said: Keep your spear away and enter the house until you see that which has made me come out. He entered and found a big snake coiled on the bedding. He darted with the spear and pierced it and then went out having fixed it in the house, but the snake quivered and attacked him and no one knew which of them died first, the snake or the young man. We came to Allah's Apostle (ﷺ) and made a mention to him and said: Supplicate to Allah that that (man) may be brought back to life. Thereupon he said: Ask forgiveness for your companion ……. Sahih Muslim 2236 a,
https://sunnah.com/muslim/39/190

One of the major characters, which strengthen youth's personality, is confidence. The Prophet (SAS) has therefore been busy building self- confidence in the minds of youth, which has not been an easy task. He (SAS) has been working hard to build potential leaders of the community and make youth trust their abilities in shaping the future of the entire society. He has been always motivational by giving youth large and sensitive functions, which have inspired them for better achievements, for building their self-confidence, and for alleviating their level of zeal and perseverance. History is full of these examples, such as the first messenger of Islam, i.e., Musab Ibn Umair, who has been sent to Madinah to represent Islam, to teach people, and to invite others to Islam. He has then been in his age of youth. He has accomplished a great success where, in one year, Islam has spread in most of the Madinah houses. Another example of youth is Attab bin Usayd who has been assigned the ruler of Makkah after opening the city by the Prophet (SAS). He has been in youth age then as well. The third example of youth leadership is Usama Ibn Zaid when he has been assigned as the leader of the Muslim army against Roman in his youth age. This has been a tradition of the Prophet's dealings with youth as shown in the following narrations:

عَنِ ابْنِ عُمَرَ ـ رضى الله عنهما ـ قَالَ أَمَّرَ رَسُولُ اللَّهِ ﷺ أُسَامَةَ عَلَى قَوْمٍ، فَطَعَنُوا فِي إِمَارَتِهِ، فَقَالَ "إِنْ تَطْعَنُوا فِي إِمَارَتِهِ، فَقَدْ طَعَنْتُمْ فِي إِمَارَةِ أَبِيهِ مِنْ قَبْلِهِ، وَايْمُ اللَّهِ لَقَدْ كَانَ خَلِيقًا لِلإِمَارَةِ، وَإِنْ كَانَ مِنْ أَحَبِّ النَّاسِ إِلَىَّ، وَإِنَّ هَذَا لَمِنْ أَحَبِّ النَّاسِ إِلَىَّ بَعْدَهُ ".
رواه البخارى

Narrated Ibn `Umar: Allah's Messenger (ﷺ) appointed Usama bin Zaid as the commander of some people. Those people criticized his leadership. The Prophet (ﷺ) said, "If you speak ill of his leadership, you have already spoken ill of his father's leadership before. By Allah, he deserved to be a Commander, and he was one of the most beloved persons to me and now this (i.e. Usama) is one of the most beloved persons to me after him. Sahih al-Bukhari 4250, https://sunnah.com/bukhari/64/285

The Prophet (SAS) has selected the youth leaders according to very strict criteria including, competency, efficiency, ability, knowledge, faith, characters, and wisdom. The application of these criteria have been obvious in all youth examples that are discussed above, i.e., Hassan Ibn Thabit, Usama Ibn Zaid, Musab Ibn Umair, and Attab Ibn Usaid. This is how we benefit from his tradition (SAS) in dealing with youth at all times. We should work hard to teach and guide youth to be leaders of the future. Then, give youth the opportunity to lead and develop at different levels of management in the community and the society at large. This needs patience and perseverance because we will find mistakes from youth that require patience and also laziness of youth that needs perseverance.

Recommendations:
It is quite clear that youth age is very important in building the good personality. Therefore, we should put a lot of emphases on this age with high level of interest and focus. If we are able to build a faithful youth, we will be following the Prophet's recommendation in the following narration:

وعنه قال: قال رسول الله ، ﷺ : "سبعة يظلهم الله في ظله يوم لا ظل إلا ظله: إمام عادل، وشاب نشأ في عبادة الله ، ورجل قلبه معلق في المساجد، ورجلان تحابا في الله، اجتمعا عليه، وتفرقا عليه، ورجل دعته امرأة ذات منصب وجمال، فقال: إنى أخاف الله، ورجل تصدق بصدقة فأخفاها حتى لا تعلم شماله ما تنفق يمينه، ورجل ذكر الله خالياً ففاضت عيناه" (متفق عليه) .

Abu Hurairah (May Allah be pleased with him) reported: Messenger of Allah (ﷺ) said, "Seven people Allah will give them His Shade on the Day when there would be no shade but the Shade of His Throne (i.e., on the Day of Resurrection): And they are: a just ruler; a youth who grew up with the worship of Allah; a person whose heart is attached to the mosques, two men who love and meet each other and depart from each other for the sake of Allah; a man whom an extremely beautiful woman seduces (for illicit relation), but he (rejects this offer and) says: 'I fear Allah'; a man who gives in charity and conceals it

(to such an extent) that the left hand does not know what the right has given; and a man who remembers Allah in solitude and his eyes become tearful". [Al-Bukhari and Muslim].
https://sunnah.com/riyadussalihin/introduction/449

In order to achieve such objective, we should accommodate few principles, such as:
1- Train and discuss with youth the moderate and rationalized concepts of Islam in all life activities. This knowledge is the immunization for youth against any extreme ideologies.
2- Use the rationalized discussion style when dealing with youth or your children.
3- Give youth responsibilities and train them to carry out their functions in a good way since their young ages. Be patient and ask them to have perseverance.

Chapter V

The Prophet as a Role Model for Teachers

Overview

As a teacher for his and future generations, the Prophet (SAS) has shown great skills. He has been very talented and has taught his companions the religion using modern techniques in teaching and learning. This includes teaching by example, using questions and discussion techniques, considering the individual differences, using attractive visual aids and styles, etc. In the coming sections, we will walk through his teaching styles (SAS) that have been implemented more than fourteen hundred years ago. It has clearly shown his patience in teaching the companions and the other sectors of the society. One of the companions, Mu'awiyah bin Al-Hakam As-Sulami, May Allah be pleased with him, reported a general statement about the teaching style of the Prophet (SAS) and how kind he has been as shown in the following narration:

وعن معاوية بن الحكم السلمي رضي الله عنه قال: "..... فلما صلى رسول الله ﷺ ، فبأبي هو وأمي، **ما رأيت معلما قبله ولا بعده أحسن تعليماً منه** ......" (رواه مسلم).

Mu'awiyah bin Al-Hakam As-Sulami (May Allah be pleased with him) reported: .... "When Messenger of Allah (ﷺ) concluded his Salat. **I have never before seen an instructor who gave better instruction than he**, may my father and mother be sacrificed for him……" (Muslim). https://sunnah.com/riyadussalihin:700

The contemporary teaching mechanisms evaluate teachers based on the understanding level of his/her students. If we apply such concept on the Prophet (SAS) as a teacher, we will find out that he is the best teacher ever. The companions of the Prophet (SAS) have carried the message all over the globe to teach others Islam. They have been able to reach almost everywhere in the world. The population of Muslims nowadays is about a quarter of the world's population. This indicates the great success of the companions, i.e., students of the Prophet (SAS). It also shows the greatness of their teacher, i.e., the Prophet (SAS). The best description of the Prophet's (SAS) students, i.e., companions, is what is shown in the Quran in the following verse:

كُنتُمْ خَيْرَ أُمَّةٍ أُخْرِجَتْ لِلنَّاسِ [آل عمران:110].

Chapter Al-Imran **(110) You are the best nation produced [as an example] for mankind**.

In the coming sections, we will describe the innovative Prophet's styles of teaching:

The Use of Questions / Discussion Styles to Attract the Attention of his Followers: This teaching style has been regularly utilized by the Prophet (SAS). He has always been asking questions and waiting for an answer from his followers. The questions have attracted the companions' attention to several facts and open their minds to think about what he (SAS) has been planning to explain afterwards. An example of this style is shown in the following narration where the Prophet (SAS) has asked about "the bankrupt?" The companions have answered based on their knowledge. Then, he started to explain to them the correct definition of bankrupt after stimulating their minds to think and attract their attention to fully listen to his explanation (SAS). I can imagine the status of the companions who have been eagerly and fully focused waiting for the answer from the Prophet (SAS). This is one of the most effective teaching techniques that facilitates learning of his followers.

وعن أبي هريرة رضي الله عنه، أن رسول الله ﷺ قال: "أتدرون من المفلس؟" قالوا : المفلس فينا من لا درهم له ولا متاع فقال: "إن المفلس من أمتي يأتي يوم القيامة بصلاة وصيام وزكاة، ويأتي قد شتم هذا، وقذف هذا وأكل مال هذا، وسفك دم هذا، وضرب هذا، فيعطى هذا من حسناته، وهذا من حسناته، فإن فنيت حسناته قبل أن يقضي ما عليه، أخذ من خطاياهم فطرحت عليه، ثم طرح في النار" (رواه مسلم).

Abu Hurairah (May Allah be pleased with him) reported: Messenger of Allah (ﷺ) said, "Do you know who is the bankrupt?" They said: "The bankrupt among us is one who has neither money with him nor any property". He said, "The real bankrupt of my Ummah would be he who would come on the Day of Resurrection with Salat, Saum and Sadaqah (charity), (but he will find himself bankrupt on that day as he will have exhausted the good deeds) because he reviled others, brought calumny against others, unlawfully devoured the wealth of others, shed the blood of others and beat others; so his good deeds would be credited to the account of those (who suffered at his hand). If his good deeds fall short to clear the account, their sins would be entered in his account and he would be thrown in the (Hell) Fire". [Muslim]. https://sunnah.com/riyadussalihin/introduction/218

The Prophet (SAS) has utilized the same style, i.e., questions, to attract the full attention of the companions when he has asked them about backbiting as shown in the following narration:

وَعَنْ أَبِي هُرَيْرَةَ - رضى الله عنه - أَنَّ رَسُولَ اَللَّهِ ﷺ قَالَ: { أَتَدْرُونَ مَا اَلْغِيبَةُ؟ } قَالُوا: اَللَّهُ وَرَسُولُهُ أَعْلَمُ. قَالَ: ذِكْرُكَ أَخَاكَ بِمَا يَكْرَهُ. قِيلَ: أَرَأَيْتَ إِنْ كَانَ فِي أَخِي مَا أَقُولُ؟ قَالَ: إِنْ كَانَ فِيهِ مَا تَقُولُ فَقَدِ اغْتَبْتَهُ, وَإِنْ لَمْ يَكُنْ فَقَدْ بَهَتَّهُ } أَخْرَجَهُ مُسْلِمٌ.

Abu Hurairah (RAA) narrated, 'The Messenger of Allah (ﷺ) asked, "**Do you know what backbiting is**?" They replied, `Allah and His Messenger (ﷺ) know best.' He said, "It is saying something about your brother which he dislikes." Someone asked, 'Supposing that what I said about my brother was true?' and the Messenger of Allah (ﷺ) said: "If what you say about him is true you have backbitten him and if it is not true you have slandered him." Related by Muslim. https://sunnah.com/urn/2118050

In the following narration, he (SAS) has given the companions the news from Allah (SWT) regarding the Kauthar. However, the companions knew nothing about the Kauthar with clear questions in their eyes. In such positive learning environment, he (SAS) has raised the key question, which he has seen in the eyes and felt in the minds of his companions. When he (SAS) has asked such question, he has attracted the full companions' attention as shown below:

عَنْ أَنَسٍ، قَالَ بَيْنَا رَسُولُ اللَّهِ ﷺ ذَاتَ يَوْمٍ بَيْنَ أَظْهُرِنَا إِذْ أَغْفَى إِغْفَاءَةً ثُمَّ رَفَعَ رَأْسَهُ مُتَبَسِّمًا فَقُلْنَا مَا أَضْحَكَكَ يَا رَسُولَ اللَّهِ قَالَ " أُنْزِلَتْ عَلَىَّ آنِفًا سُورَةٌ " . فَقَرَأَ " بِسْمِ اللَّهِ الرَّحْمَنِ الرَّحِيمِ { إِنَّا أَعْطَيْنَاكَ الْكَوْثَرَ * فَصَلِّ لِرَبِّكَ وَانْحَرْ * إِنَّ شَانِئَكَ هُوَ الأَبْتَرُ} " . ثُمَّ قَالَ " **أَتَدْرُونَ مَا الْكَوْثَرُ** " . فَقُلْنَا اللَّهُ وَرَسُولُهُ أَعْلَمُ . قَالَ " فَإِنَّهُ نَهْرٌ وَعَدَنِيهِ رَبِّي عَزَّ وَجَلَّ عَلَيْهِ خَيْرٌ كَثِيرٌ هُوَ حَوْضٌ تَرِدُ عَلَيْهِ أُمَّتِي يَوْمَ الْقِيَامَةِ آنِيَتُهُ عَدَدَ النُّجُومِ فَيُخْتَلَجُ الْعَبْدُ مِنْهُمْ فَأَقُولُ رَبِّ إِنَّهُ مِنْ أُمَّتِي . فَيَقُولُ مَا تَدْرِي مَا أَحْدَثَتْ بَعْدَكَ " . زَادَ ابْنُ حُجْرٍ فِي حَدِيثِهِ بَيْنَ أَظْهُرِنَا فِي الْمَسْجِدِ . وَقَالَ " مَا أَحْدَثَ بَعْدَكَ " .

Anas reported: One day the Messenger of Allah (ﷺ) was sitting amongst us that he dozed off. He then raised his head smilingly. We said: What makes you smile. Messenger of Allah? He said: A Sura has just been revealed to me, and then recited: In the name of Allah, the Compassionate, the Merciful. Verily, We have given thee Kauthar (fount of abundance). Therefore turn to thy Lord for prayer and offer sacrifice, and surely thy enemy is cut off (from the good). Then he (the Holy Prophet) said: **Do you know what Kauthar is**? We said: Allah and His Messenger know best. The Prophet (ﷺ) said: It (Kauthar) is a canal which my Lord, the Exalted and Glorious has promised me, and there is an abundance of good in it. It is a cistern and my people would come to it on the Day of Resurrection, and tumblers there would be equal to the number of stars. A servant would be turned away from (among the people gathered there). Upon this I would say: My Lord, he is one of my people, and He (the Lord) would say: You do not know that he innovated new things (in Islam) after you. Ibn Hujr made this addition in the hadith:" He (the Holy Prophet) was sitting amongst us in the mosque, and He (Allah) said: (You don't know) what he innovated after you" Sahih Muslim 400a, https://sunnah.com/muslim:400a

Similarly, he (SAS) has used the same question style to explain the interpretation of a verse from the Quran as shown in the following narration:

وعن أبي هريرة، رضي الله عنه ، قال: قرأ رسول الله ﷺ {يومئذ تحدث أخبارها} ثم قال: "أتدرون ما أخبارها؟" قالوا الله ورسوله أعلم. قال: "فإن أخبارها أن تشهد كل عبد أو أمة بما عمل على ظهرها تقول: عملت كذا وكذا في يوم كذا وكذا، فهذه أخبارها" ((رواه الترمذي وقال : حديث حسن صحيح)).

Abu Hurairah (May Allah be pleased with him) reported: Messenger of Allah (ﷺ) recited, "That Day it (the earth) will reveal its news (about all that happened over it of good or evil)." (99:4). Then he (ﷺ) inquired, "**Do you know what its news are**?" He was told: "Allah and His Messenger know better". He said, "Its news is that it shall bear witness against every slave man and woman they did on its back. It will say: 'You did this and this on such and such day.' Those will be its news." [At-Tirmidhi, who classified it as Hadith Hasan Sahih]. https://sunnah.com/riyadussalihin:408

The Prophet (SAS) has also used the question style with the companions in congregation and with individuals as shown in the following narration:

عَنْ مُعَاذِ بْنِ جَبَلٍ، قَالَ قَالَ النَّبِيُّ ﷺ " يَا مُعَاذُ أَتَدْرِي مَا حَقُّ اللَّهِ عَلَى الْعِبَادِ ". قَالَ اللَّهُ وَرَسُولُهُ أَعْلَمُ. قَالَ " أَنْ يَعْبُدُوهُ وَلاَ يُشْرِكُوا بِهِ شَيْئًا، أَتَدْرِي مَا حَقُّهُمْ عَلَيْهِ ". قَالَ اللَّهُ وَرَسُولُهُ أَعْلَمُ. قَالَ " أَنْ لاَ يُعَذِّبَهُمْ ".

Narrated Mu`adh bin Jabal: The Prophet (ﷺ) said, "O Mu`adh! **Do you know what Allah's Right upon His slaves is**?" I said, "Allah and His Apostle know best." The Prophet (ﷺ) said, "To worship Him (Allah) Alone and to join none in worship with Him (Allah). Do you know what their right upon Him is?" I replied, "Allah and His Apostle know best." The Prophet (ﷺ) said, "Not to punish them (if they do so). Sahih al-Bukhari 7373. https://sunnah.com/bukhari:7373

Discussion is the second style, which has mainly been utilized by the Prophet (SAS) in teaching his companions. It has been an effective style in explaining the rationale behind questionable matters in the minds of his followers. Rationalized discussion is always a good approach to reach the minds of discussers. As an example of such style, he (SAS) has explained the rationale of telling all his wives the opinion of Aisha, may Allah (SWT) be pleased with her, as shown in the following narration:

عَنْ جَابِرِ بْنِ عَبْدِ اللَّهِ، قَالَ دَخَلَ أَبُو بَكْرٍ يَسْتَأْذِنُ عَلَى رَسُولِ اللَّهِ ﷺ فَوَجَدَ النَّاسَ جُلُوسًا بِبَابِهِ لَمْ يُؤْذَنْ لأَحَدٍ مِنْهُمْ ـ قَالَ ـ فَأُذِنَ لأَبِي بَكْرٍ فَدَخَلَ ثُمَّ أَقْبَلَ عُمَرُ فَاسْتَأْذَنَ فَأُذِنَ لَهُ فَوَجَدَ النَّبِيَّ ﷺ جَالِسًا حَوْلَهُ نِسَاؤُهُ وَاجِمًا سَاكِتًا ـ قَالَ ـ فَقَالَ لأَقُولَنَّ شَيْئًا أُضْحِكُ النَّبِيَّ ﷺ فَقَالَ يَا رَسُولَ اللَّهِ لَوْ رَأَيْتَ بِنْتَ خَارِجَةَ سَأَلَتْنِي النَّفَقَةَ فَقُمْتُ إِلَيْهَا فَوَجَأْتُ عُنُقَهَا. فَضَحِكَ رَسُولُ اللَّهِ ﷺ وَقَالَ " هُنَّ حَوْلِي كَمَا تَرَى يَسْأَلْنَنِي النَّفَقَةَ ". فَقَامَ أَبُو بَكْرٍ إِلَى عَائِشَةَ يَجَأُ عُنُقَهَا فَقَامَ عُمَرُ إِلَى حَفْصَةَ يَجَأُ عُنُقَهَا كِلاَهُمَا يَقُولُ تَسْأَلْنَ رَسُولَ

اللَّهِ ﷺ مَا لَيْسَ عِنْدَهُ . فَقُلْنَ وَاللَّهِ لاَ نَسْأَلُ رَسُولَ اللَّهِ ﷺ شَيْئًا أَبَدًا لَيْسَ عِنْدَهُ ثُمَّ اعْتَزَلَهُنَّ شَهْرًا أَوْ تِسْعًا وَعِشْرِينَ ثُمَّ نَزَلَتْ عَلَيْهِ هَذِهِ الآيَةُ { يَا أَيُّهَا النَّبِيُّ قُلْ لأَزْوَاجِكَ } حَتَّى بَلَغَ {لِلْمُحْسِنَاتِ مِنْكُنَّ أَجْرًا عَظِيمًا} قَالَ فَبَدَأَ بِعَائِشَةَ فَقَالَ " يَا عَائِشَةُ إِنِّي أُرِيدُ أَنْ أَعْرِضَ عَلَيْكِ أَمْرًا أُحِبُّ أَنْ لاَ تَعْجَلِي فِيهِ حَتَّى تَسْتَشِيرِي أَبَوَيْكِ " . قَالَتْ وَمَا هُوَ يَا رَسُولَ اللَّهِ فَتَلاَ عَلَيْهَا الآيَةَ قَالَتْ أَفِيكَ يَا رَسُولَ اللَّهِ أَسْتَشِيرُ أَبَوَىَّ بَلْ أَخْتَارُ اللَّهَ وَرَسُولَهُ وَالدَّارَ الآخِرَةَ وَأَسْأَلُكَ أَنْ لاَ تُخْبِرَ امْرَأَةً مِنْ نِسَائِكَ بِالَّذِي قُلْتُ . قَالَ " لاَ تَسْأَلُنِي امْرَأَةٌ مِنْهُنَّ إِلاَّ أَخْبَرْتُهَا إِنَّ اللَّهَ لَمْ يَبْعَثْنِي مُعَنِّتًا وَلاَ مُتَعَنِّتًا وَلَكِنْ بَعَثَنِي مُعَلِّمًا مُيَسِّرًا " .

Jabir b. 'Abdullah (Allah be pleased with them) reported: Abu Bakr (Allah be pleased with him) came and sought permission to see Allah's Messenger (ﷺ). He found people sitting at his door and none amongst them had been granted permission, but it was granted to Abu Bakr and he went in. Then came 'Umar and he sought permission and it was granted to him, and he found Allah's Apostle (ﷺ) sitting sad and silent with his wives around him. He (Hadrat 'Umar) said: I would say something which would make the Prophet (ﷺ) laugh, so he said: Messenger of Allah, I wish you had seen (the treatment meted out to) the daughter of Khadija when you asked me some money, and I got up and slapped her on her neck. Allah's Messenger (may peace be upon him) laughed and said: They are around me as you see, asking for extra money. Abu Bakr (Allah be pleased with him) then got up went to 'A'isha (Allah be pleased with her) and slapped her on the neck, and 'Umar stood up before Hafsa and slapped her saying: You ask Allah's Messenger (ﷺ) which he does not possess. They said: By Allah, we do not ask Allah's Messenger (ﷺ) for anything he does not possess. Then he withdrew from them for a month or for twenty-nine days. Then this verse was revealed to him:" Prophet: Say to thy wives... for a mighty reward" (xxxiii. 28). He then went first to 'A'isha (Allah be pleased with her) and said: I want to propound something to you, 'A'isha, but wish no hasty reply before you consult your parents. She said: Messenger of Allah, what is that? He (the Holy Prophet) recited to her the verse, whereupon she said: Is it about you that I should consult my parents, Messenger of Allah? Nay, I choose Allah, His Messenger, and the Last Abode; but I ask you not to tell any of your wives what I have said He replied: Not one of them will ask me without my informing her. God did not send me to be harsh, or cause harm, but He has sent me to teach and make things easy. Sahih Muslim 1478 https://sunnah.com/muslim/18/39

Teachers should be convincing and make sense in the discussion approach because it increases the learning of the discusser(s). This style has been an effective approach in teaching as clearly stated in the following narration:

وعن معاوية بن الحكم السلمي رضي الله عنه قال: "بينا أنا أصلي مع رسول الله ﷺ ، إذا عطس رجل من القوم فقلت: يرحمك الله، فرماني القوم بأبصارهم ! فقلت: واثكل أمياه ! ما شأنكم تنظرون إلىّ؟ فجعلوا يضربون بأيديهم على أفخاذهم ! فلما رأيتهم يصمتونني لكني سكت. فلما صلى رسول الله ﷺ، فبأبي هو وأمي، ما رأيت معلما قبله ولا بعده أحسن تعليماً منه، فوالله ما كهرني ولا ضربني ولا شتمني، قال: "إن هذه الصلاة لا يصلح فيها شئ من كلام الناس، إنما هى التسبيح والتكبير، وقراءة القرآن" أو كما قال رسول الله ﷺ قلت: يا رسول الله، إنى حديث عهد بجاهلية، وقد جاء الله بالإسلام، وإن منا رجالً يأتون الكهان؟ قال: "فلا تأتهم، قلت: ومنا رجال يتطيرون؟ قال: ذاك شئ يجدونه في صدورهم، فلا يصدهم" (رواه مسلم).

Mu'awiyah bin Al-Hakam As-Sulami (May Allah be pleased with him) reported: While I was in Salat with Messenger of Allah (ﷺ), a man in the congregation sneezed and I responded with: 'Yarhamuk-Allah (Allah have mercy on you).' The people stared at me with disapproving looks. So I said: "May my mother lose me. Why are you staring at me?" Thereupon, they began to strike their thighs with their hands. When I saw them urging to me to remain silent, I became angry but restrained myself. When Messenger of Allah (ﷺ) concluded his Salat. **I have never before seen an instructor who gave better instruction than he,** may my father and mother be sacrificed for him. He neither

remonstrated me, nor beat me, nor abused me. He simply said,"It is not permissible to talk during Salat because it consists of glorifying Allah, declaring His Greatness as well as recitation of the Qur'an," or he said words to that effect." I said: "O Allah's Messenger, I have but recently accepted Islam, and Allah has favoured us with Islam. There are still some people among us who go to consult soothsayers." He said, "Do not consult them." Then I said: "There are some of us who are guided by omens." He said, "These things which come to their minds. They should not be influenced by them." (Muslim).
https://sunnah.com/riyadussalihin/1/21

The following incident has been the best example of discussion style when a believer has asked the Prophet (SAS) to give him a permission to commit adultery. This is a big sin in Islam that is strictly prohibited. The Prophet's companions have been irritated with such a request. However, the Prophet (SAS) has been totally different and dealt with such incident with full wisdom, patience, and kindness. Such teaching style has made the person who asked the question fully satisfied and disliked what he has asked for as shown in the following narration:

وَعَنْ أَبِي أُمَامَةَ، قَالَ: إِنَّ فَتًى شَابًّا أَتَى النَّبِيَّ ﷺ فَقَالَ: يَا رَسُولَ اللَّهِ، ائْذَنْ لِي بِالزِّنَا، فَأَقْبَلَ الْقَوْمُ عَلَيْهِ، فَزَجَرُوهُ، قَالُوا: مَهْ مَهْ، فَقَالَ: " ادْنُهْ "، فَدَنَا مِنْهُ قَرِيبًا، قَالَ: فَجَلَسَ، قَالَ: " أَتُحِبُّهُ لِأُمِّكَ؟ "، قَالَ: لَا وَاللَّهِ، جَعَلَنِي اللَّهُ فِدَاءَكَ، قَالَ: " وَلَا النَّاسُ يُحِبُّونَهُ لِأُمَّهَاتِهِمْ "، قَالَ: " أَفَتُحِبُّهُ لِابْنَتِكَ؟ "، قَالَ: لَا وَاللَّهِ يَا رَسُولَ اللَّهِ، جَعَلَنِي اللَّهُ فِدَاءَكَ، قَالَ: " وَلَا النَّاسُ يُحِبُّونَهُ لِبَنَاتِهِمْ، قَالَ: أَفَتُحِبُّهُ لِأُخْتِكَ؟ "، قَالَ: لَا وَاللَّهِ، جَعَلَنِي اللَّهُ فِدَاءَكَ، قَالَ: " وَلَا النَّاسُ يُحِبُّونَهُ لِأَخَوَاتِهِمْ، قَالَ: أَفَتُحِبُّهُ لِعَمَّتِكَ؟ "، قَالَ: لَا وَاللَّهِ، جَعَلَنِي اللَّهُ فِدَاءَكَ، قَالَ: " وَلَا النَّاسُ يُحِبُّونَهُ لِعَمَّاتِهِمْ، قَالَ: أَفَتُحِبُّهُ لِخَالَتِكَ؟ "، قَالَ: لَا وَاللَّهِ، جَعَلَنِي اللَّهُ فِدَاءَكَ، قَالَ: " وَلَا النَّاسُ يُحِبُّونَهُ لِخَالَاتِهِمْ، قَالَ: فَوَضَعَ يَدَهُ عَلَيْهِ، وَقَالَ: " اللَّهُمَّ اغْفِرْ ذَنْبَهُ، وَطَهِّرْ قَلْبَهُ، وَحَصِّنْ فَرْجَهُ "، فَلَمْ يَكُنْ بَعْدُ ذَلِكَ الْفَتَى يَلْتَفِتُ إِلَى شَيْءٍ. (رواه الإمام أحمد [21708] ورواته ثقات).

Abi Umamah narrated that a young man came to the Prophet, may Allah's prayers and peace be upon him, and said: O Prophet of Allah, do you permit me to commit adultery? The people shouted at him, then the Prophet, may Allah bless him and grant him peace, said, "Get him closer to me until the man sat before the Prophet." So the Prophet, may peace and blessings be upon him, said: Do you like your mother to commit adultery? The man said: No, may Allah made me redeem you, he said: Likewise people do not like it for their mothers. He said: do you like it for your daughter? The man said No, may Allah made me redeem you, he said: Likewise people do not like it for their daughters. Do you like it for your sister? The man said No, may Allah made me redeem you, he said: Likewise people do not like it for their sisters. Do you like it for your aunt? The man said No, may Allah made me redeem you, he said: Likewise people do not like it for their aunts. Then, the Prophet (SAS) put his hands on the man's chest and said: O Allah, forgive his sin, purify his heart, and protect his private organs, so nothing was more hateful to this young man than adultery. Narrated by Ahmed. https://dorar.net/hadith/sharh/112427

It is obvious that the question and discussion styles have been very effective in stimulating the learning process in the minds of the Prophet's companions. They have completely focused in and been fully aware of his words (SAS). While being in such state of learning, they have memorized his golden words (SAS). Therefore, he (SAS) has opened the minds and hearts of his companions using the question and discussion styles.

Always Change the Topic to Combat Boring Approach:
The Prophet (SAS) has frequently changed his style of teaching. He (SAS) has used the

question style in several occasions and has employed the discussion style in others. However, in different occasions, he (SAS) has also applied the lecturing style during sermons to transfer knowledge to his companions. This variety of styles has made it more attractive for the companions to fully listen to his guidance and to record his golden words. This has been quite clear as reported in the following narration:

عَنِ ابْنِ مَسْعُودٍ، قَالَ كَانَ النَّبِيُّ ﷺ يَتَخَوَّلُنَا بِالْمَوْعِظَةِ فِي الأَيَّامِ، كَرَاهَةَ السَّآمَةِ عَلَيْنَا.

Narrated Ibn Mas`ud: The Prophet (ﷺ) used to take care of us in preaching by selecting a suitable time, so that we might not get bored. (He abstained from pestering us with sermons and knowledge all the time). Sahih al-Bukhari 68. https://sunnah.com/bukhari/3/10

Despite being passionate, he (SAS) has always been easy in matters related to people and their implementation of the religious matters. This style also has made it simple to his companions and has positioned him (SAS) high in their hearts. It is one of the great characters of successful teachers as shown in the following narration:

عن عائشة رضي الله عنها قالت: ما خير رسول الله ﷺ بين أمرين قط إلا أخذ أيسرهما، ما لم يكن إثماً، فإن كان إثماً، كان أبعد الناس منه، وما انتقم رسول الله ﷺ لنفسه في شئ قط، إلا أن تنتهك حرمة الله، فينتقم الله تعالى. (متفق عليه)

Aishah (May Allah be pleased with her) reported: Whenever the Prophet (ﷺ) was given a choice between two matters, he would (always) choose the easier as long as it was not sinful to do so; but if it was sinful he was most strict in avoiding it. He never took revenge upon anybody for his own sake; but when Allah's Legal Bindings were outraged, he would take revenge for Allah's sake. [Al-Bukhari and Muslim]. https://sunnah.com/riyadussalihin/introduction/640

Changing the teaching style is an effective approach to increase the learning efficiency of the companions. This will also combat being bored of only using one style. You feel incredulous when you hear about these styles that have been exploited more than fourteen hundred years ago. Who has taught the Prophet (SAS) all these effective styles in teaching his companions? He (SAS) has been illiterate and has never been exposed to experiences to teach him all these styles. It is a miracle to find him effectively mastering such styles at the right time and location. It is only Allah (SWT) who has taught him (SAS) all these techniques to reach the hearts and minds of his companions.

Consider the Individual Differences among the Companions:
The successful teacher always pays attention to the individual differences among students. Otherwise, he/she will not be able to touch their minds and hearts with the delivered knowledge. This has amazed me when I have seen the Prophet (SAS) and his responses to different people with diverse answers for similar questions. It has been quite obvious when he (SAS) has been asked for advice from different companions. His responses have been totally different to each one of them. One day, he (SAS) has been asked for advice, he has responded do not get angry as shown below:

وَعَنْهُ أَنَّ رَجُلاً قَالَ: { يَا رَسُولَ اَللَّهِ! أَوْصِنِي. فَقَالَ: لَا تَغْضَبْ, فَرَدَّدَ مِرَارًا. قَالَ: لَا تَغْضَبْ } أَخْرَجَهُ اَلْبُخَارِيُّ. (6116) .

Abu Hurairah (RAA) narrated, 'A man said, "O Messenger of Allah, advise me." The Messenger of Allah (ﷺ) said: "Do not get angry." The man repeated that several times and he replied, "Do not get angry." Related by Al-Bukhari. https://sunnah.com/urn/2118020

In another day, he (SAS) has been asked the same question from a different companion where he advised him to have piety as shown below:

عَنْ سُلَيْمِ بْنِ جَابِرٍ الْهُجَيْمِيِّ قَالَ: أَتَيْتُ النَّبِيَّ ﷺ وَهُوَ مُحْتَبٍ فِي بُرْدَةٍ، وَإِنَّ هُدَّابَهَا لَعَلَى قَدَمَيْهِ، فَقُلْتُ: يَا رَسُولَ اللهِ، أَوْصِنِي، قَالَ: عَلَيْكَ بِاتِّقَاءِ اللهِ، وَلاَ تَحْقِرَنَّ مِنَ الْمَعْرُوفِ شَيْئًا، وَلَوْ أَنْ تُفْرِغَ لِلْمُسْتَسْقِي مِنْ دَلْوِكَ فِي إِنَائِهِ، أَوْ تُكَلِّمَ أَخَاكَ وَوَجْهُكَ مُنْبَسِطٌ، وَإِيَّاكَ وَإِسْبَالَ الْإِزَارِ، فَإِنَّهَا مِنَ الْمَخِيلَةِ، وَلاَ يُحِبُّهَا اللهُ، وَإِنِ امْرُؤٌ عَيَّرَكَ بِشَيْءٍ يَعْلَمُهُ مِنْكَ فَلاَ تُعَيِّرْهُ بِشَيْءٍ تَعْلَمُهُ مِنْهُ، دَعْهُ يَكُونُ وَبَالُهُ عَلَيْهِ، وَأَجْرُهُ لَكَ، وَلاَ تَسُبَّنَّ شَيْئًا. قَالَ: فما سببت بعد دابة ولا إنساناً. صحيح (الألباني)

Salim ibn Jabir al-Hujaymi said, "I came up to the Prophet, may Allah bless him and grant him peace, when he was wrapped up in a cloak whose edges were cover his feet. I said, 'Messenger of Allah, advise me.' He said, 'You must have fearful awareness of Allah. Do not scorn anything correct, even pouring water from your bucket into the bucket of someone else who asks you for water or talking to your brother with a happy face. Beware of dragging your waist-wrapper - it is part of arrogance and Allah does not like it. If a man blames you for something he knows about you, do not blame him for anything you know of him. Leave him to his own evil. You will have your reward. Do not abuse anything.'"
Sahih (Al-Albani), https://sunnah.com/adab/48/8

Similarly, he (SAS) responded to another companion by talking less and to another one by feeding people as described in the following narrations:

وعن عقبة بن عامر رضي الله عنه قال: قلت يا رسول الله ما النجاة؟ قال: "أمسك عليك لسانك، وليسعك بيتك، وابكِ على خطيئتك" (رواه الترمذي، وقال: حديث حسن).

'Uqbah bin 'Amir (May Allah be pleased with him) said: I asked the Messenger of Allah (ﷺ), "How can salvation be achieved?" He replied, "Control your tongue, keep to your house, and weep over your sins." [At-Tirmidhi]. https://sunnah.com/riyadussalihin/17/10

عَنْ عَبْدِ اللَّهِ بْنِ عَمْرٍو، أَنَّ رَجُلاً، سَأَلَ النَّبِيَّ ﷺ أَيُّ الإِسْلاَمِ خَيْرٌ قَالَ " تُطْعِمُ الطَّعَامَ، وَتَقْرَأُ السَّلاَمَ عَلَى مَنْ عَرَفْتَ، وَعَلَى مَنْ لَمْ تَعْرِفْ ".

Narrated 'Abdullah bin 'Amr: A man asked the Prophet, "What Islamic traits are the best?" The Prophet said, "Feed the people, and greet those whom you know and those whom you do not know." Sahih al-Bukhari 6236. https://sunnah.com/bukhari/79/10

When looking at the above answers for similar questions, you conclude that he (SAS) has well understood his companions and realized their individual difference in characters. Therefore, he answered them all differently based on their shortcomings or things they have liked the most. For the companion who is easily getting angry, his response (SAS) has been "do not get angry". For the other one who has needed to have piety and to be humble, he (SAS) has advised him accordingly. Similarly, he has responded to others with replies that have suited their situation based on his prior knowledge to their personalities. This urges teachers to understand the behavior and personal characters of their students in order to be able to touch their minds and hearts. This also enables teachers to select the most effective teaching and learning approaches for their students to maximize their learning of the required knowledge.

Explanation and Teaching using Visual Aids and Illustrative Examples:
One of the basic teaching skills of the Prophet (SAS) has been using visual aids and illustrative examples to increase the learning of his companions. This has been a practical teaching style that enriches the learning experience and prepares the audience using

positive learning environment. Using such a style, **the Prophet (SAS) has described to his companions the example of a human being in life using visual aids as shown in the following narration and Figure 1:**

وعن ابن مسعود رضي الله عنه قال: خط النبي ﷺ خطا مربعا، وخط خطاً فى الوسط خارجاً منه، وخط خططاً صغاراً إلى هذا الذى فى الوسط من جانبه الذى فى الوسط، فقال: "هذا الإنسان، وهذا أجله محيطا به ـأو قد أحاط به ـ وهذا هو خارج أمله، وهذه الخطط الصغار الأعراض فإن أخطأه هذا ، نهشه هذا ، وإن أخطأه هذا نهشه هذا "(رواه البخاري) وهذه صورته:

Ibn Mas'ud (May Allah be pleased with him) reported: The Prophet (PBUH) drew up a square and in the middle of it he drew a line, the end of which jutted out beyond the square. Further across the middle line, he drew a number of smaller lines. Then he (PBUH) said, "The figure represents man and the encircling square is the death or lifespan, which is encompassing him. The middle line represents his desires and the smaller lines are sicknesses and problems of life. If one of those misses him, another distresses him, and if that one misses him, he falls a victim to another." [Al-Bukhari]. Here is its image as shown in Figure 1: https://sunnah.com/riyadussalihin/introduction/576

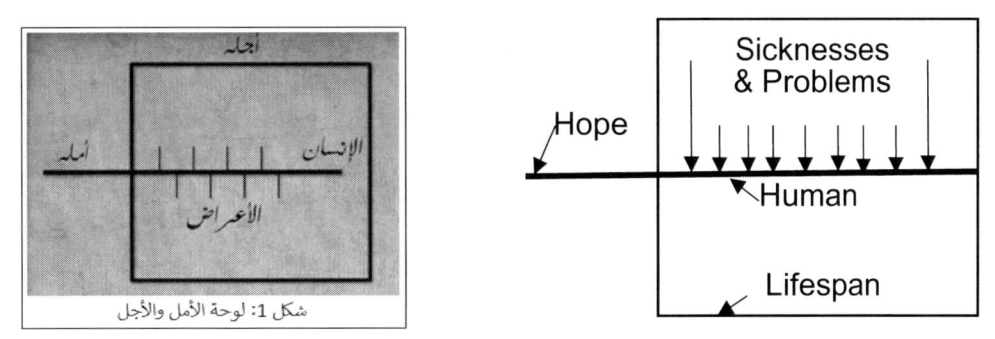

Figure 1: The Example of Human Being in the Mind of the Prophet (SAS).

This drawing is a good representation of reality, which well explains the taught topic by the Prophet (SAS). The visual aid has made it easier for the companions to understand the concept of life. In another narration, he (SAS) has also explained the path of Allah and the paths of Shaytan using a drawing similar to that of Figure 2 as follows:

وَعَنْ عَبْدِ اللَّهِ بْنِ مَسْعُودٍ قَالَ خَطَّ لَنَا رَسُولُ اللَّهِ ﷺ خَطًّا ثُمَّ قَالَ: «هَذَا سَبِيلُ اللَّهِ ثُمَّ خَطَّ خُطُوطًا عَنْ يَمِينِهِ وَعَنْ شِمَالِهِ وَقَالَ هَذِهِ سُبُلٌ عَلَى كُلِّ سَبِيلٍ مِنْهَا شَيْطَانٌ يَدْعُو إِلَيْهِ» ثُمَّ قَرَأَ (إِنَّ هَذَا صِرَاطِي مُسْتَقِيمًا فَاتَّبِعُوهُ) الْآيَة. رَوَاهُ أَحْمد وَالنَّسَائِيّ والدارمي. إسناده حسن   (زبير على زئى)

'Abdallah b. Mas'ud told how God's messenger drew a line for them and then said, "This is God's path." Thereafter he drew several lines on his right and left and said, "These are paths on each of which there is a devil who invites people to follow it." And he recited, "And that this is my path, straight; follow it..." Ahmad, Nasa'i and Darimi transmitted it. Isnād Hasan (Zubair `Aliza'i), Mishkat al-Masabih 166. https://sunnah.com/mishkat:166

The narrative of using of illustrative examples, which refer to the environment around the learner, is one of the most effective styles in teaching. It enables the learner to realize and visualize the taught subject. The illustrative example approach has also been utilized by the Prophet (SAS) in many occasions to facilitate the understanding of and improve the learning experience in the discussed topic. Here are few cases of such style in the following narrations:

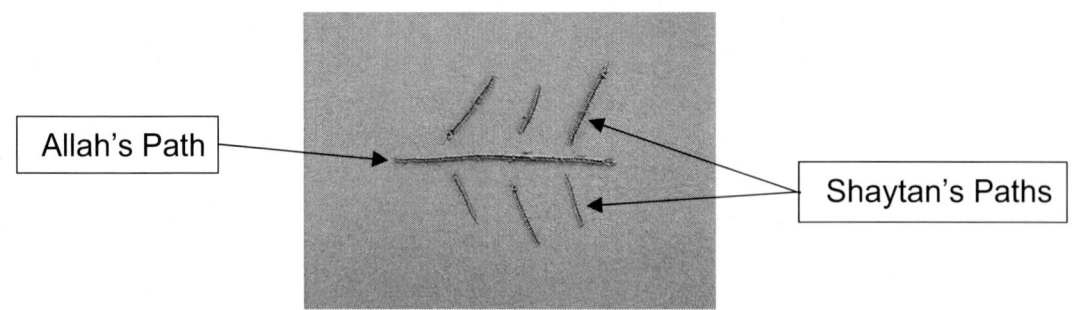

Figure 2: The Example of Allah's Path and that of Shaytan

قَالَ سَمِعْتُ ابْنَ عُمَرَ، يَقُولُ قَالَ النَّبِيُّ ﷺ " **مَثَلُ الْمُؤْمِنِ كَمَثَلِ شَجَرَةٍ خَضْرَاءَ، لاَ يَسْقُطُ وَرَقُهَا، وَلاَ يَتَحَاتُّ** ". فَقَالَ الْقَوْمُ هِيَ شَجَرَةُ كَذَا. هِيَ شَجَرَةُ كَذَا، فَأَرَدْتُ أَنْ أَقُولَ هِيَ النَّخْلَةُ. وَأَنَا غُلاَمٌ شَابٌّ فَاسْتَحْيَيْتُ، فَقَالَ " **هِيَ النَّخْلَةُ** ". وَعَنْ شُعْبَةَ حَدَّثَنَا خُبَيْبُ بْنُ عَبْدِ الرَّحْمَنِ عَنْ حَفْصِ بْنِ عَاصِمٍ عَنِ ابْنِ عُمَرَ مِثْلَهُ وَزَادَ فَحَدَّثْتُ بِهِ عُمَرَ فَقَالَ لَوْ كُنْتَ قُلْتَهَا لَكَانَ أَحَبَّ إِلَىَّ مِنْ كَذَا وَكَذَا.

Narrated Ibn `Umar: The Prophet (ﷺ) said, "**The example of a believer is like a green tree, the leaves of which do not fall.**" The people said. "It is such-and-such tree: It is such-and-such tree." I intended to say that it was the datepalm tree, but I was a young boy and felt shy (to answer). The Prophet (ﷺ) said, "It is the date-palm tree." Ibn `Umar added, " I told that to `Umar who said, 'Had you said it, I would have preferred it to such-and such a thing." Sahih al-Bukhari 6122. https://sunnah.com/bukhari:6122

وعن أبي موسى الأشعري رضي الله عنه أن النبي ﷺ قال: "**إنما مثل الجليس الصالح وجليس السوء، كحامل المسك، ونافخ الكير**، فحامل المسك، إما أن يحذيك، وإما أن تبتاع منه، وإما أن تجد منه ريحًا طيبة، ونافخ الكير، إما أن يحرق ثيابك ، وإما أن تجد منه ريحًا منتنة" ((متفق عليه)) .

Abu Musa Al-Ash'ari (May Allah be pleased with him) reported: I heard the Prophet (ﷺ) saying, "**The similitude of good company and that of bad company is that of the owner of musk and of the one blowing the bellows.** The owner of musk would either offer you some free of charge, or you would buy it from him, or you smell its pleasant fragrance; and as for the one who blows the bellows (i.e., the blacksmith), he either burns your clothes or you smell a repugnant smell". [Al- Bukhari and Muslim]. https://sunnah.com/riyadussalihin:363

It is concluded that visual aids and illustrative examples are powerful tools that enrich student's learning experience. The Prophet (SAS) has mastered these tools in many occasions as listed above.

Learning by Motivation
The Prophet (SAS) has always been motivating the companions by the great reward of their actions. He (SAS) has utilized this style in his explanation to open the minds and the hearts of his companions. It has been a great style, which attracts the attention of the companions to compete and develop self-motivation. The great reward has also inspired the companions to excel and exert their utmost effort to please Allah (SWT). For example, the reward of a house in Paradise to the one who gives up arguing, abandons lying, and has good characters. It is very motivational to carefully listen and practice the teachings of the Prophet (SAS) because the reward is amazing, i.e., own a house in Paradise. Once listening, the companions would pay their attention to know how to achieve such a reward. It is an amazing style, which has a great impact on the audience, as shown in the following narration:

وعن أبى أمامه الباهلى رضي الله عنه قال: قال رسول الله ﷺ: "أنا زعيم ببيت في ربض الجنة لمن ترك المراء، وإن كان محقاً، وببيت في وسط الجنة لمن ترك الكذب، وإن كان مازحاً، وببيت في أعلى الجنة لمن حسن خلقه" (حديث صحيح رواه أبو داود).

Abu Umamah Al-Bahili (May Allah be pleased with him) reported: Messenger of Allah (ﷺ) said, "I guarantee a house in Jannah for one who gives up arguing, even if he is in the right; and I guarantee a home in the middle of Jannah for one who abandons lying even for the sake of fun; and I guarantee a house in the highest part of Jannah for one who has good manners." [Abu Dawud]. https://sunnah.com/riyadussalihin/introduction/629

In other examples, he (SAS) has identified the reward, i.e., gaining the love of the Prophet and being close to him in the Day of Judgement, to those who have attained good characters and vice versa. Once the companions listen to the reward, they have given him (SAS) all their ears, minds, and hearts to know how this could be accomplished. The motivation style of the Prophet (SAS) has been clear in the following narrations:

وعن جابر رضي الله عنه أن رسول الله ﷺ قال: "إن من أحبكم إلي، وأقربكم مني مجلساً يوم القيامة أحاسنكم أخلاقاً، وإن أبغضكم إلي وأبعدكم مني يوم القيامة، الثرثارون والمتشدقون والمتفيهقون" قالوا: يا رسول الله قد علمنا "الثرثارون والمتشدقون" فما المتفيهقون؟ قال: "المتكبرون" (رواه الترمذي وقال: حديث حسن). "الثرثار": هو كثير الكلام تكلفاً. "والمتشدق": المتطاول على الناس بكلامه، ويتكلم بملء فيه تصافحاً وتعظيماً لكلامه؛ "والمتفيهق": أصله من الفهق، وهو الامتلاء، وهو الذى يملأ فمه بالكلام، ويتوسع فيه ويغرب به تكبراً وارتفاعاً، وإظهاراً للفضيلة على غيره. وروى الترمذي عن عبد الله بن المبارك رحمه الله في تفسير حسن الخلق قال: هو طلاقة الوجه، وبذل المعروف، وكف الأذى.

Jabir (May Allah be pleased with him) reported: The Messenger of Allah (ﷺ) said, "The dearest and nearest among you to me on the Day of Resurrection will be one who is the best of you in manners; and the most abhorrent among you to me and the farthest of you from me will be the pompous, the garrulous, and Al-Mutafaihiqun." The Companions asked him: "O Messenger of Allah! We know about the pompous and the garrulous, but we do not know who Al-Mutafaihiqun are." He replied: "The arrogant people." [At-Tirmidhi, who classified it as Hadith Hasan]. https://sunnah.com/riyadussalihin/introduction/630

وعن أبي هريرة رضي الله عنه قال: قال رسول الله ﷺ "أكمل المؤمنين إيمانا أحسنهم خُلقا، وخياركم خياركم لنسائهم" (رواه الترمذي وقال: حديث حسن صحيح).

Abu Hurairah (May Allah be pleased with him) reported: Messenger of Allah (ﷺ) said, "The believers who show the most perfect Faith are those who have the best behavior, and the best of you are those who are the best to their wives". [At-Tirmidhi, Hasan Sahih]. https://sunnah.com/riyadussalihin/introduction/278

وعن عبد الله بن عمرو بن العاص رضي الله عنهما قال: لم يكن رسول الله ﷺ فاحشاً ولا متفحشاً. وكان يقول: "إن من خياركم أحسنكم أخلاقاً" (متفق عليه).

'Abdullah bin 'Amr bin Al-'as (May Allah be pleased with them) reported: Messenger of Allah (ﷺ) did not indulge in loose talk nor did he like to listen to it. He used to say, "The best of you is the best among you in conduct." [Al-Bukhari and Muslim]. https://sunnah.com/riyadussalihin/introduction/624

- وعن أبي محمد فضاله بن عبيد الأنصاري رضي الله عنه ، أنه سمع رسول الله ﷺ يقول : "طوبى لمن هدي إلى الإسلام ، وكان عيشه كفافا ،وقنع " ((رواه الترمذي وقال :حديث حسن صحيح))

Fadalah bin 'Ubaid Al-Ansari (May Allah be pleased with him) reported: I heard Messenger of Allah (ﷺ) say: "Happiness is due to him who is guided to Islam and possesses provision that suffices him for his day and remains content." [At- Tirmidhi, who classified it as Hadith Hasan Sahih]. https://sunnah.com/riyadussalihin:512

The Prophet (SAS) has also utilized the demotivation style to discourage people from doing evil actions or attaining evil characters. Further to motivation / demotivation style is the repetition of reward / punishment at the beginning of his narration or talk. Such a technique is very powerful in attracting the attention of audience to the speaker. Both styles are clear in the following narration:

وَعَنْهُ قَالَ: قَالَ رَسُولُ اللَّهِ ﷺ: «رَغِمَ أَنْفُ رَجُلٍ ذُكِرْتُ عِنْدَهُ فَلَمْ يُصَلِّ عَلَيَّ وَرَغِمَ أَنْفُ رَجُلٍ دَخَلَ عَلَيْهِ رَمَضَانُ ثُمَّ انْسَلَخَ قَبْلَ أَنْ يُغْفَرَ لَهُ وَرَغِمَ أَنْفُ رَجُلٍ أَدْرَكَ عِنْدَهُ أَبَوَاهُ الْكِبَرَ أَوْ أَحَدُهُمَا فَلَمْ يُدْخِلَاهُ الْجَنَّةَ» . رَوَاهُ التِّرْمِذِيُّ .صَحِيحٌ (الألباني)

He reported God's Messenger as saying, "May he be abased who does not invoke a blessing on me when I am mentioned in his presence. May he be abased who passes through the whole of Ramadan before his sins are forgiven him. May he be abased one or both of whose parents have reached old age without causing him to enter paradise. This means that he has shown them no kindness. Tirmidhi transmitted it. Mishkat al-Masabih 927. https://sunnah.com/mishkat:927

In conclusion, it is evident that the Prophet (SAS) has been a great role model for teachers in practicing most of the contemporary teaching / learning styles. He (SAS) has mastered the different styles, such as questions, discussion, changing topics, visual aids, illustrative examples, motivation, and demotivation. He has also accommodated and respected the individual differences when dealing with the companions. He (SAS) implemented his great characters, i.e., patience, kindness, mercy, and respect, in teaching. These characters have proved to be effective in transferring the message during teaching.

This chapter is just a message for teachers to carefully study the teaching styles and characters of the Prophet (SAS) to serve several purposes. First, it clarifies the miracles in the Prophet's (SAS) practices fourteen hundred years ago, which have been recently discovered. There might be other styles, which are not discovered until today. They need someone to dig and study more his life (SAS) to discover, clarify, and explain such unknown styles. This will serve humanity with new teaching approaches and techniques. Second, we should implement his styles (SAS) to benefit our pedagogical curriculum in all taught subjects, particularly the ones dealing with religion. These styles can also be used in all our activities, such as lectures, seminars, discussion groups, meetings, etc.

Recommendations:
We should follow the teachings of our beloved teacher and Prophet (SAS) in the following three recommendations (motivation / demotivation style): (1) always ask for forgiveness; (2) supplicate for the Prophet (SAS); and (3) be kind to your parents and ask them to supplicate for you.

سَمِعْتُ عَبْدَ اللَّهِ بْنَ بُسْرٍ، يَقُولُ قَالَ النَّبِيُّ ـ ﷺ ـ " طُوبَى لِمَنْ وَجَدَ فِي صَحِيفَتِهِ اسْتِغْفَارًا كَثِيرًا " .

1- 'Abdullah bin Busr said that: the Prophet (SAS) said: "Glad tidings to those who find a lot of seeking forgiveness in the record of their deeds." Sunan Ibn Majah 3818. https://sunnah.com/ibnmajah:3818

وعن أبي هريرة رضي الله عنه قال: قال رسول الله ﷺ : "رغم أنف رجل ذكرت عنده فلم يصلِ عليَّ" رواه الترمذي وقال حديث حسن.

2- Abu Hurairah (May Allah be pleased with him) reported: The Messenger of Allah (ﷺ) said, "May his nose soil with dust in whose presence mention is made of me and he does not supplicate for me." [At-Tirmidhi]. https://sunnah.com/riyadussalihin:1400

وعنه عن النبي ﷺ قال: " رغم أنف، ثم رغم أنف، ثم رغم أنف من أدرك أبويه عند الكبر، أحدهما أو كليهما، فلم يدخل

الجنة" (رواه مسلم).

3- Abu Hurairah (May Allah be pleased with him) reported: The Prophet (ﷺ) said, "May he be disgraced! May he be disgraced! May he be disgraced, whose parents, one or both, attain old age during his life time, and he does not enter Jannah (by rendering being dutiful to them)". [Muslim]. https://sunnah.com/riyadussalihin:317

Chapter VI

The Prophet as a Role Model for Leaders

Overview

Role models are always the best motivators for others to build good behavior and attitudes because they show the practices of interpreting and materializing concepts into actions in life. The Prophet (SAS) has been the role model for human beings in all aspects of life, particularly, leadership. He has attained great characters and ethics, which are materialized in his (SAS) life actions. The companions have been greatly attached to him (SAS) because his actions perfectly coincide with his talks in a transparent manner. They have seen the great principles implemented in real life. They have learned, recorded, and reported / narrated a lot from him (SAS). They reported all his (SAS) talks, actions, emotions, silence, anger, happiness, etc. His life (SAS) has been an open book with high level of transparency and details in all aspects of life. In particular, his leadership (SAS) style has been divine in a perfect way with no mistakes. If he (SAS) errs due to human nature, he has always regretted and returned the rights to their owners. Malek Ibn Dinar said that "the scholar, who is not practicing his knowledge, his talks would not reach the hearts of his audience." This explains the complete submission and love of the companions to the Prophet (SAS) due to the perfect match of talks and actions. Abdullah Ibn Almubarak said that "Hamdoon Ibn Ahmed was asked: why were the words of the generation followed the companions (i.e., Salaf) better than us? He replied, "They talked with sincerity to please Allah (SWT), to achieve dignity to Islam, and to save their souls from Hellfire. However, we talked to please people, to achieve self-dignity, and to accomplish status in life." The mismatch between talks and actions has never been the practice of true believers or scholars who always implement what they say. These true believers and scholars always approach people to teach and advise them with high level of patience for the reasons described in the following narration:

عَنِ ابْنِ عُمَرَ، عَنِ النَّبِيِّ ﷺ قَالَ: الْمُؤْمِنُ الَّذِي يُخَالِطُ النَّاسَ، وَيَصْبِرُ عَلَى أَذَاهُمْ، خَيْرٌ مِنَ الَّذِي لاَ يُخَالِطُ النَّاسَ، وَلاَ يَصْبِرُ عَلَى أَذَاهُمْ. صحيح (الألباني)

Ibn 'Umar reported that the Prophet, may Allah bless him and grant him peace, said, "The believer who mixes with people and endures their wrong doing is better than the person who does not mix with people nor endure their wrong actions." Sahih (Al-Albani). Al-Adab Al-Mufrad 388. https://sunnah.com/adab:388

The Prophet (SAS) has attained many characters of being the best leader, which include: (1) mercy, forgiveness, humbleness, and tolerance, (2) blending the hearts of his companions, (3) seek advice and opinion of his companions, (4) appoint the appropriate person in the right place, and (5) being a brave person. In the following sections, I will walk you through details of these leadership characters.

Mercy, Forgiveness, Humbleness, and Tolerance

The Prophet (SAS) has been a role model for the companions in all life matters. He has been merciful, soft, lenient, and humble with them. He has been following the orders of Allah (SWT) in the following verse:

وَاخْفِضْ جَنَاحَكَ لِلْمُؤْمِنِينَ(88) الحجر

Chapter Al-Hijr (88) …... **And lower your wing to the believers**. https://quran.com/15/88

If he (SAS) has been harsh on his companions, they would have been disobeying and rejecting him as explained in the following verse:

فَبِمَا رَحْمَةٍ مِنَ اللَّهِ لِنْتَ لَهُمْ ۖ وَلَوْ كُنْتَ فَظًّا غَلِيظَ الْقَلْبِ لَانْفَضُّوا مِنْ حَوْلِكَ ۖ فَاعْفُ عَنْهُمْ وَاسْتَغْفِرْ لَهُمْ وَشَاوِرْهُمْ فِي الْأَمْرِ ۖ فَإِذَا عَزَمْتَ فَتَوَكَّلْ عَلَى اللَّهِ ۚ إِنَّ اللَّهَ يُحِبُّ الْمُتَوَكِّلِينَ(159) آل عمران

Chapter Al-Imran (159) **So by mercy from Allah, [O Muhammad], you were lenient with them. And if you had been rude [in speech] and harsh in heart, they would have disbanded from about you. So pardon them and ask forgiveness for them and consult them in the matter. And when you have decided, then rely upon Allah. Indeed, Allah loves those who rely [upon Him]**. https://quran.com/3/159/

However, the companions have loved him (SAS) to the extent; they have preferred him to their children, family, and souls. This has been part of their belief and religion as shown in the following narrations:

عَبْدَ اللَّهِ بْنَ هِشَامٍ، قَالَ كُنَّا مَعَ النَّبِيِّ ﷺ وَهُوَ آخِذٌ بِيَدِ عُمَرَ بْنِ الْخَطَّابِ فَقَالَ لَهُ عُمَرُ يَا رَسُولَ اللَّهِ لأَنْتَ أَحَبُّ إِلَىَّ مِنْ كُلِّ شَىْءٍ إِلاَّ مِنْ نَفْسِي. فَقَالَ النَّبِيُّ ﷺ " لاَ وَالَّذِي نَفْسِي بِيَدِهِ حَتَّى أَكُونَ أَحَبَّ إِلَيْكَ مِنْ نَفْسِكَ ". فَقَالَ لَهُ عُمَرُ فَإِنَّهُ الآنَ وَاللَّهِ لأَنْتَ أَحَبُّ إِلَىَّ مِنْ نَفْسِي. فَقَالَ النَّبِيُّ ﷺ " الآنَ يَا عُمَرُ ". البخاري

Narrated `Abdullah bin Hisham: We were with the Prophet (ﷺ) and he was holding the hand of `Umar bin Al-Khattab. `Umar said to Him, "O Allah's Messenger (ﷺ)! You are dearer to me than everything except my own self." The Prophet (ﷺ) said, "No, by Him in Whose Hand my soul is, (you will not have complete faith) till I am dearer to you than your own self." Then `Umar said to him, "However, now, by Allah, you are dearer to me than my own self." The Prophet (ﷺ) said, "Now, O `Umar, (now you are a believer). Sahih al-Bukhari 6632. https://sunnah.com/bukhari:6632

عَنِ الأَعْرَجِ، عَنْ أَبِي هُرَيْرَةَ ـ رضى الله عنه ـ أَنَّ رَسُولَ اللَّهِ ﷺ قَالَ " فَوَالَّذِي نَفْسِي بِيَدِهِ لاَ يُؤْمِنُ أَحَدُكُمْ حَتَّى أَكُونَ أَحَبَّ إِلَيْهِ مِنْ وَالِدِهِ وَوَلَدِهِ ". البخاري

Narrated Abu Huraira: "Allah's Messenger (ﷺ) said, "By Him in Whose Hands my life is, none of you will have faith till he loves me more than his father and his children." Sahih al-Bukhari 14. https://sunnah.com/bukhari:14

The above characters are central for those who would like to be good leaders. Forgiveness and tolerance are also key leadership characters. The Prophet (SAS) has mastered these characters along his life with believers and disbelievers. The following narration highlights such characters with one of the companions who attended the Battle of Badr:

عُبَيْدُ اللَّهِ بْنُ أَبِي رَافِعٍ، ـ وَهُوَ كَاتِبُ عَلِيٍّ ـ قَالَ سَمِعْتُ عَلِيًّا، رضى الله عنه وَهُوَ يَقُولُ بَعَثَنَا رَسُولُ اللَّهِ ﷺ أَنَا وَالزُّبَيْرَ وَالْمِقْدَادَ فَقَالَ " انْطَلِقُوا حَتَّى تَأْتُوا رَوْضَةَ خَاخٍ فَإِنَّ بِهَا ظَعِينَةً مَعَهَا كِتَابٌ فَخُذُوهُ مِنْهَا ". فَانْطَلَقْنَا تَعَادَى بِنَا خَيْلُنَا فَإِذَا نَحْنُ بِالْمَرْأَةِ فَقُلْنَا أَخْرِجِي الْكِتَابَ. فَقَالَتْ مَا مَعِي كِتَابٌ. فَقُلْنَا لَتُخْرِجِنَّ الْكِتَابَ أَوْ لَتُلْقِيَنَّ الثِّيَابَ. فَأَخْرَجَتْهُ مِنْ عِقَاصِهَا فَأَتَيْنَا بِهِ رَسُولَ اللَّهِ ﷺ فَإِذَا فِيهِ مِنْ حَاطِبِ بْنِ أَبِي بَلْتَعَةَ إِلَى نَاسٍ مِنَ الْمُشْرِكِينَ مِنْ أَهْلِ مَكَّةَ يُخْبِرُهُمْ بِبَعْضِ أَمْرِ رَسُولِ اللَّهِ ﷺ فَقَالَ رَسُولُ اللَّهِ ﷺ " يَا حَاطِبُ مَا هَذَا ". قَالَ لاَ تَعْجَلْ عَلَىَّ يَا رَسُولَ اللَّهِ إِنِّي كُنْتُ امْرَأً مُلْصَقًا فِي قُرَيْشٍ ـ قَالَ سُفْيَانُ كَانَ حَلِيفًا لَهُمْ وَلَمْ يَكُنْ مِنْ أَنْفُسِهَا ـ وَكَانَ مِمَّنْ كَانَ مَعَكَ مِنَ الْمُهَاجِرِينَ لَهُمْ قَرَابَاتٌ يَحْمُونَ بِهَا أَهْلِيهِمْ فَأَحْبَبْتُ إِذْ فَاتَنِي ذَلِكَ مِنَ النَّسَبِ فِيهِمْ أَنْ أَتَّخِذَ فِيهِمْ يَدًا يَحْمُونَ بِهَا قَرَابَتِي وَلَمْ أَفْعَلْهُ كُفْرًا وَلاَ ارْتِدَادًا عَنْ دِينِي وَلاَ رِضًا بِالْكُفْرِ بَعْدَ الإِسْلاَمِ. فَقَالَ النَّبِيُّ ﷺ " صَدَقَ ". فَقَالَ عُمَرُ دَعْنِي يَا رَسُولَ اللَّهِ أَضْرِبْ عُنُقَ هَذَا الْمُنَافِقِ. فَقَالَ " إِنَّهُ قَدْ شَهِدَ بَدْرًا وَمَا يُدْرِيكَ لَعَلَّ اللَّهَ اطَّلَعَ عَلَى أَهْلِ بَدْرٍ فَقَالَ اعْمَلُوا مَا شِئْتُمْ فَقَدْ غَفَرْتُ لَكُمْ ". فَأَنْزَلَ اللَّهُ عَزَّ وَجَلَّ { يَا أَيُّهَا الَّذِينَ آمَنُوا لاَ تَتَّخِذُوا عَدُوِّي وَعَدُوَّكُمْ أَوْلِيَاءَ} وَلَيْسَ فِي حَدِيثِ أَبِي بَكْرٍ وَزُهَيْرٍ ذِكْرُ الآيَةِ وَجَعَلَهَا إِسْحَاقُ فِي رِوَايَتِهِ مِنْ

تِلاَوَةِ سُفْيَانَ . مسلم

Ubaidullah b. Rafi', who was the scribe of 'Ali, reported: I heard 'Ali (Allah be pleased with him) as saying: Allah's Messenger (ﷺ) sent me and Zubair and Miqdad saying: Go to the garden of, Khakh [it is a place between Medina and Mecca at a distance of twelve miles from Medina] and there you will find a woman riding a camel. She would be in possession of a letter, which you must get from her. So we rushed on horses and when we met that woman, we asked her to deliver that letter to us. She said: There is no letter with me. We said: Either bring out that letter or we would take off your clothes. She brought out that letter from (the plaited hair of) her head. We delivered that letter to Allah's Messenger (ﷺ) in which Hatib b. Abu Balta'a had informed some people amongst the polytheists of Mecca about the affairs of Allah's Messenger (ﷺ). Allah's Messenger (ﷺ) said: Hatib, what is this? He said: Allah's messenger, do not be hasty in judging my intention. I was a person attached to the Quraish. Sufyan said: He was their ally but had no relationship with them. (Hatib further said): Those who are with you amongst the emigrants have blood-relationship with them (the Quraish) and thus they would protect their families. I wished that when I had no blood-relationship with them I should find some supporters from (amongst them) who would help my family. I have not done this because of any unbelief or apostasy and I have no liking for the unbelief after I have (accepted) Islam. Thereupon Allah's Apostle (ﷺ) said: You have told the truth. 'Umar said: Allah's Messenger, permit me to strike the neck of this hypocrite. But he (the Holy Prophet) said: He was a participant in Badr and you little know that Allah revealed about the people of Badr: Do what you like for there is forgiveness for you. And Allah, the Exalted and Glorious, said:" O you who believe, do not take My enemy and your enemy for friends" (lx. 1). And there is no mention of this verse in the hadith transmitted on the authority of Abu Bakr and Zubair and Ishaq has in his narration made a mention of the recitation of this verse by Sufyan. Sahih Muslim 2494 a, https://sunnah.com/muslim/44/232

The aforementioned characters make the Prophet (SAS) the great example and model for the companions to follow. They have liked him (SAS) more than all life ties. After he (SAS) passed away, most companions have been crying when they remembered him and his actions with them. When they missed his (SAS) mercy, forgiveness, tolerance, etc, they couldn't control their emotions and started crying. Even the followers, who didn't see the Prophet (SAS), when they remembered his actions and characters, they cried because they missed, valued, and loved him. Plants have expressed the emotions of love towards the Prophet (SAS) as well. In the following narration, you will see the action of the Palm tree when the Prophet (SAS) relocate the delivery of Friday Sermon to a manufactured pulpit:

وعن جابر رضي الله عنه قال: كان جذع يقوم إليه النبي ﷺ ، يعني في الخطبة. فلما وضع المنبر، سمعنا للجذع مثل صوت العشار حتى نزل النبي، ﷺ ، فوضع يده عليه فسكن". وفي رواية: فلما كان يوم الجمعة قعد النبي، ﷺ على المنبر، فصاحت النخلة التي كان يخطب عندها حتى كادت أن تنشق. وفي رواية : فصاحت صياح الصبي، فنزل النبي ﷺ ، حتى أخذها فضمها إليه، فجعلت تئن أنين الصبي الذي يسكت حتى استقرت ، قال: "بكت على ما كانت تسمع من الذكر" (رواه البخاري).

Jabir (May Allah be pleased with him) said: There was a trunk of a date-palm tree upon which the Prophet (ﷺ) used to recline while delivering Khutbah (sermon). When a pulpit was placed in the mosque, we heard the trunk crying out like a pregnant she-camel. The Prophet (ﷺ) came down from the pulpit and put his hand on the trunk and it became quiet.

Another narration is: The Prophet (ﷺ) used to stand by a tree or a date-palm on Friday (to give the Khutbah). Then, an Ansari woman or man said, "O Messenger of Allah! Shall we make a pulpit for you?" He replied, "If you wish." So, they made a pulpit for him and when it was Friday, the Prophet (ﷺ) sat on the pulpit [to deliver the Khutbah (sermon)] and the trunk of the date- palm on which he used to recline cried out as if it would split asunder.

Another narration is: It cried like a child and the Prophet (ﷺ) descended (from the pulpit) and embraced it while it continued moaning like a child being quietened. The Prophet (ﷺ) said, "It was crying for (missing) what it used to hear of Dhikr near it." [Al-Bukhari]. https://sunnah.com/riyadussalihin:1831

Al-Hassan, one of the scholars, said to his followers when he reported the above narration: The plant cried because it missed the Prophet (SAS). You, i.e., the followers, are supposed to be the ones who should miss him more. This is how the great leader (SAS) has attracted the hearts of his companions and the followers until the Day of Judgement.

Blending the Hearts of his Companions

One of the best skills of good leaders is how to blend the hearts of their followers to construct a strong social structure. This blending process is challenging, particularly, among different ethnics, tribes, and sectors of the society. However, it has been implemented in an innovative and a smart way. The Prophet (SAS) has utilized the brotherhood approach to accomplish such blending. It has been a genius idea that breaks the ice between emigrants from Makkah and supporters in Madinah. The Prophet (SAS) assign individuals from his supporters in Madinah to be brothers of individual emigrants from Makkah. Each pair of brothers has all brotherhood rights similar to that of brothers in blood. Then, later, verses have been revealed to stop inheritance between non-blood brothers. However, all other brotherhood aspects have continued to close the gaps and strengthen their relationships. The above concept is depicted in the following narration:

عَنِ ابْنِ عَبَّاسٍ، فِي قَوْلِهِ { وَالَّذِينَ عَقَدَتْ أَيْمَانُكُمْ فَآتُوهُمْ نَصِيبَهُمْ } قَالَ كَانَ الْمُهَاجِرُونَ حِينَ قَدِمُوا الْمَدِينَةَ تُوَرِّثُ الأَنْصَارَ دُونَ ذَوِي رَحِمِهِ لِلأُخُوَّةِ الَّتِي آخَى رَسُولُ اللَّهِ ﷺ بَيْنَهُمْ فَلَمَّا نَزَلَتْ هَذِهِ الآيَةُ { وَلِكُلٍّ جَعَلْنَا مَوَالِيَ مِمَّا تَرَكَ } قَالَ نَسَخَتْهَا { وَالَّذِينَ عَقَدَتْ أَيْمَانُكُمْ فَآتُوهُمْ نَصِيبَهُمْ } مِنَ النُّصْرَةِ وَالنَّصِيحَةِ وَالرِّفَادَةِ وَيُوصِي لَهُ وَقَدْ ذَهَبَ الْمِيرَاثُ . صحيح (الألباني)

Ibn 'Abbas explained the following Qur'anic verse: "To those also, to whom your right hand was pledged, give your portion." When the Emigrants came to Medina. they inherited from the Helpers without any blood-relationship with them for the brotherhood which the Messenger of Allah (ﷺ) established between them. When the following verse was revealed: "To (benefit) everyone we have appointed shares and heirs to property left by parent and relatives." it abrogated the verse: "To those also, to whom your right hand was pledged, give their due portion." This alliance was made for help, well-wishing and cooperation. Now a legacy can be made for him. (The right to) inheritance was abolished. Sunan Abi Dawud 2922, Sahih (Al-Albani), https://sunnah.com/abudawud/19/38

The developed concept of brotherhood by the Prophet (SAS) has been the first of its kind in history, to the best of my knowledge. It has established a strong relationship among the believers from different backgrounds. This concept builds the foundation of brotherly love that blends all individuals and families to constitute an exceptional society. The enemies of yesterday become brothers today with great ties. They all learn how to sacrifice for the benefit of others in the society without any limits. All great characters, in the individual, family, and community levels, have been practiced with high level of precision and piety. The amazing brotherhood approach has led to all the above benefits. It shows outstanding vision of the Prophet (SAS) as a leader who has planted social principles today for better tomorrow.

Seek Advice and Opinion of his Companions
One of the most important leadership characters is seeking consultation from the followers and companions. The concept of consultation is one of the essential ones in building strong communities and unified societies. Consultation is also a major principle that can be applied in the individual, family, community, and country levels. Therefore, Allah (SWT) ordered the Prophet (SAS) to consult his companions in all matters as shown in the following verse:

فَبِمَا رَحْمَةٍ مِنَ اللَّهِ لِنْتَ لَهُمْ وَلَوْ كُنْتَ فَظًّا غَلِيظَ الْقَلْبِ لَانْفَضُّوا مِنْ حَوْلِكَ فَاعْفُ عَنْهُمْ وَاسْتَغْفِرْ لَهُمْ وَشَاوِرْهُمْ فِي الْأَمْرِ فَإِذَا عَزَمْتَ فَتَوَكَّلْ عَلَى اللَّهِ إِنَّ اللَّهَ يُحِبُّ الْمُتَوَكِّلِينَ [آل عمران: 159].

Chapter Al-Imran (159) **So by mercy from Allah, [O Muhammad], you were lenient with them. And if you had been rude [in speech] and harsh in heart, they would have disbanded from about you. So pardon them and ask forgiveness for them and consult them in the matter. And when you have decided, then rely upon Allah. Indeed, Allah loves those who rely [upon Him].**

Similarly, Allah (SWT) has described the believers as those who consult among themselves in all matters as shown in the following verse:

وَالَّذِينَ اسْتَجَابُوا لِرَبِّهِمْ وَأَقَامُوا الصَّلَاةَ وَأَمْرُهُمْ شُورَىٰ بَيْنَهُمْ وَمِمَّا رَزَقْنَاهُمْ يُنْفِقُونَ(38) الشورى

Chapter Al-Shura (38) **And those who have responded to their lord and established prayer and whose affair is [determined by] consultation among themselves, and from what We have provided them, they spend**.

Imam Al-Hasan has commented on the consultation principle by explaining its benefits in this life and the Hereafter. He said that "mutual consultation among people has always led to the best guidance in life" as shown in the following narration:

عَنِ الْحَسَنِ قَالَ: وَاللَّهِ مَا اسْتَشَارَ قَوْمٌ قَطُّ إِلَّا هُدُوا لِأَفْضَلِ مَا بِحَضْرَتِهِمْ، ثُمَّ تَلَا: {وَأَمْرُهُمْ شُورَى بَيْنَهُمْ}. صحيح (الألباني)

Al-Hasan said, "People never seek advice without being guided to the best possibility available to them." Then he recited, "and manage their affairs by mutual consultation." (42:38), Sahih (Al-Albani). https://sunnah.com/adab:258

Consultation of people has been the common practices of the Prophet (SAS) in all matters. It has been one of the pillars of social and political Islamic systems. The Prophet (SAS) has utilized the consultation principle with his family, friends, political matters, battles, etc, as shown in the following sample of narrations:

يَزِيدُ أَحَدُهُمَا عَلَى صَاحِبِهِ قَالَا خَرَجَ النَّبِيُّ ﷺ عَامَ الْحُدَيْبِيَةِ فِي بِضْعِ عَشْرَةَ مِائَةً مِنْ أَصْحَابِهِ، ...... فَقَالَ " أَشِيرُوا أَيُّهَا النَّاسُ عَلَيَّ، أَتَرَوْنَ أَنْ أَمِيلَ إِلَى عِيَالِهِمْ وَذَرَارِيِّ هَؤُلَاءِ الَّذِينَ يُرِيدُونَ أَنْ يَصُدُّونَا عَنِ الْبَيْتِ، فَإِنْ يَأْتُونَا كَانَ اللَّهُ عَزَّ وَجَلَّ قَدْ قَطَعَ عَيْنًا مِنَ الْمُشْرِكِينَ، وَإِلَّا تَرَكْنَاهُمْ مَحْرُوبِينَ ". قَالَ أَبُو بَكْرٍ يَا رَسُولَ اللَّهِ، خَرَجْتَ عَامِدًا لِهَذَا الْبَيْتِ، لَا تُرِيدُ قَتْلَ أَحَدٍ وَلَا حَرْبَ أَحَدٍ، فَتَوَجَّهْ لَهُ، فَمَنْ صَدَّنَا عَنْهُ قَاتَلْنَاهُ. قَالَ " امْضُوا عَلَى اسْمِ اللَّهِ ". البخارى

Narrated Al-Miswar bin Makhrama and Marwan bin Al-Hakam: (one of them said more than his friend): The Prophet (ﷺ) set out in the company of more than one thousand of his companions in the year of Al-Hudaibiya, ……... The Prophet (ﷺ) said, "**O people! Give me your opinion**. Do you recommend that I should destroy the families and offspring of those who want to stop us from the Ka`ba? If they should come to us (for peace) then Allah will destroy a spy from the pagans, or otherwise we will leave them in a miserable state." On that Abu Bakr said, "O Allah Apostle! You have come with the intention of visiting this House (i.e. Ka`ba) and you do not want to kill or fight anybody. So proceed to it, and whoever should stop us from it, we will fight him." On that the Prophet (ﷺ) said, "Proceed on, in the Name of Allah!" Sahih al-Bukhari 4178, 4179. https://sunnah.com/bukhari:4178

عَنْ عَائِشَةَ، قَالَتْ لَمَّا ذُكِرَ مِنْ شَأْنِي الَّذِي ذُكِرَ وَمَا عَلِمْتُ بِهِ قَامَ رَسُولُ اللَّهِ ﷺ خَطِيبًا فَتَشَهَّدَ فَحَمِدَ اللَّهَ وَأَثْنَى عَلَيْهِ بِمَا هُوَ أَهْلُهُ ثُمَّ قَالَ " أَمَّا بَعْدُ أَشِيرُوا عَلَىَّ فِي أُنَاسٍ أَبَنُوا أَهْلِي وَايْمُ اللَّهِ مَا عَلِمْتُ عَلَى أَهْلِي مِنْ سُوءٍ قَطُّ وَأَبَنُوهُمْ بِمَنْ وَاللَّهِ مَا عَلِمْتُ عَلَيْهِ مِنْ سُوءٍ قَطُّ وَلاَ دَخَلَ بَيْتِي قَطُّ إِلاَّ وَأَنَا حَاضِرٌ وَلاَ غِبْتُ فِي سَفَرٍ إِلاَّ غَابَ مَعِي " . …….. . مسلم

'A'Isha reported: When I came under discussion what the people had to say about me, Allah's Messenger (ﷺ) stood up for delivering an address and he recited tashahhud (I bear witness to the fact that there is no god but Allah) and praised Allah, lauded Him what He rightly deserves and then said: Coming to the point. **Give me your opinion** about them who have brought false charge about my family. ……. Sahih Muslim 2770c. https://sunnah.com/muslim:2770c

عَنْ عَطَاءٍ، قَالَ لَمَّا احْتَرَقَ الْبَيْتُ زَمَنَ يَزِيدَ بْنِ مُعَاوِيَةَ حِينَ غَزَاهَا أَهْلُ الشَّامِ فَكَانَ مِنْ أَمْرِهِ مَا كَانَ تَرَكَهُ ابْنُ الزُّبَيْرِ حَتَّى قَدِمَ النَّاسُ الْمَوْسِمَ يُرِيدُ أَنْ يُجَرِّئَهُمْ - أَوْ يُحَرِّبَهُمْ - عَلَى أَهْلِ الشَّامِ فَلَمَّا صَدَرَ النَّاسُ قَالَ يَا أَيُّهَا النَّاسُ أَشِيرُوا عَلَىَّ فِي الْكَعْبَةِ أَنْقُضُهَا ثُمَّ أَبْنِي بِنَاءَهَا أَوْ أُصْلِحُ مَا وَهَى مِنْهَا …… مسلم

'Ata' reported: The House was burnt during the time of Yazid b. Muawiya when the people of Syria had fought (in Mecca). And it happened with it (the Ka'ba) what was (in store for it). Ibn Zubair (Allah be pleased with him) felt it (in the same state) until the people came in the season (of Hajj). (The idea behind was) that he wanted to exhort them or incite them (to war) against the people of Syria. When the people had arrived he said to them: **O people, advise me about the Ka'ba**. Should I demolish it and then build it from its very foundation, or should I repair whatever has been damaged of it? ………… Sahih Muslim 1333f. https://sunnah.com/muslim:1333f

قَالَ حَدَّثَنِي عُمَرُ بْنُ الْخَطَّابِ قَالَ لَمَّا كَانَ يَوْمُ بَدْرٍ نَظَرَ رَسُولُ اللَّهِ ﷺ إِلَى الْمُشْرِكِينَ وَهُمْ أَلْفٌ وَأَصْحَابُهُ ثَلاَثُمِائَةٍ وَتِسْعَةَ عَشَرَ رَجُلاً فَاسْتَقْبَلَ نَبِيُّ اللَّهِ صلى الله عليه وسلم الْقِبْلَةَ ثُمَّ مَدَّ يَدَيْهِ فَجَعَلَ يَهْتِفُ بِرَبِّهِ " …….. قَالَ أَبُو زُمَيْلٍ قَالَ ابْنُ عَبَّاسٍ فَلَمَّا أَسَرُوا الأُسَارَى قَالَ رَسُولُ اللَّهِ ﷺ لأَبِي بَكْرٍ وَعُمَرَ " مَا تَرَوْنَ فِي هَؤُلاَءِ الأُسَارَى " . ….. . مسلم

It has been narrated on the authority of `Umar b. al-Khattab who said: When it was the day on which the Battle of Badr was fought, ….. …. The Messenger of Allah (ﷺ) said to Abu Bakr and `Umar (Allah be pleased with them): **What is your opinion about these detainees?** ……." Sahih Muslim 1763. https://sunnah.com/muslim:1763

Based upon the Prophet's (SAS) practices in consultation, all guided Caliphates have followed similar practices in ruling the Muslim society. It has become the common practice of Muslim rulers for centuries. Consultation principle is the pillar of justice and the seed of modern and advanced society. This is how the Prophet's (SAS) leadership has been implemented worldwide for centuries. The principle of consultation, which is considered the pillar of any political system, has been the major cause of success in the Islamic country(ies) and vice versa. Therefore, brotherhood and consultation principles have been the adhesive, which cohesively blend and reinforce the hearts of individuals, families, and communities within the social fabrics of the society. Both principles have acted like magic in unifying the society. It is recommended for those who are looking for a better society to sincerely implement these two principles in all their matters. Otherwise, all the wishes become dreams that have no basis in reality.

Appoint the Appropriate Person in the Right Place:
One of the characters, which good leaders should acquire, is carrying out the responsibility and trust. The leader should appoint the appropriate person with the good characters in the right place. The Prophet (SAS) has taught us how to appoint leaders and what are the essential characters for the appointees. He (SAS) has shown that strong personality and trust are the main characters of good leaders as shown in the following narration:

وعنه قال: قلت يا رسول الله ألا تستعملني؟ فضرب بيده على منكبي ثم قال: "يا أبا ذر إنك ضعيف، وإنها أمانة، وإنها يوم القيامة خزي وندامة، إلا من أخذها بحقها، وأدى الذى عليه فيها" (رواه مسلم).

Abu Dharr (May Allah be pleased with him) reported: I said to Messenger of Allah (ﷺ): "Why do you not appoint me to an (official) position?" He (ﷺ) patted me on the shoulder with his hand and said, "O Abu Dharr, you are a weak man and it is a trust and it will be a cause of disgrace and remorse on the Day of Resurrection except for the one who takes it up with a full sense of responsibility and fulfills what is entrusted to him (discharges its obligations efficiently)." [Muslim]. https://sunnah.com/riyadussalihin/introduction/675

He (SAS) has stressed on the fact that trust is part of the faith and one main character of good leaders. He has also shown that trust is a core value of believers as shown in the following narration:

وَعَنْ أَنَسٍ رَضِيَ اللَّهُ عَنْهُ قَالَ: قَلَّمَا خَطَبَنَا رَسُولُ اللَّهِ ﷺ إِلَّا قَالَ: «لَا إِيمَانَ لِمَنْ لَا أَمَانَةَ لَهُ وَلَا دِينَ لِمَنْ لَا عَهْدَ لَهُ». رَوَاهُ الْبَيْهَقِيُّ فِي شُعَبِ الْإِيمَانِ. حسن - الألباني

Anas said: God's messenger seldom addressed us without saying, "He who is not trustworthy has no faith, and he who does not keep his covenant has no religion." Baihaqi transmitted it in Shu'ab al-Iman. Hasan (Zubair `Aliza'i) https://sunnah.com/mishkat:35

Trust, as a core value, has also been commanded by Allah (SWT) to respect your responsibility as shown in the following verse:

﴿إِنَّ اللَّهَ يَأْمُرُكُمْ أَن تُؤَدُّوا الْأَمَانَاتِ إِلَىٰ أَهْلِهَا﴾ [النساء: 58].

Chapter Al-Nisaa **(58) Indeed, Allah commands you to render trusts to whom they are due and when you judge between people to judge with justice. .....** https://quran.com/4/58

It is also described in the Quran that trust is a heavy responsibility to carry out. It has not been undertaken by earth, heaven, and mountains; however, it is carried out by human. This is clearly shown in the following verse:

﴿إِنَّا عَرَضْنَا الْأَمَانَةَ عَلَى السَّمَاوَاتِ وَالْأَرْضِ وَالْجِبَالِ فَأَبَيْنَ أَن يَحْمِلْنَهَا وَأَشْفَقْنَ مِنْهَا وَحَمَلَهَا الْإِنسَانُ إِنَّهُ كَانَ ظَلُومًا جَهُولًا﴾ [الأحزاب:72]

Chapter Al-Ahzab **(72) Indeed, we offered the Trust to the heavens and the earth and the mountains, and they declined to bear it and feared it; but man [undertook to] bear it. Indeed, he was unjust and ignorant.** https://quran.com/33/72

The Prophet (SAS) has considered the responsibility of appointing leaders on battles and rulers for cities and districts as trust. He has taken it serious because it greatly impacts the followers of these leaders and appointees. He has given the responsibility to those who are qualified and appropriate to carry out such trust. He (SAS) has recommended his followers not to ask for appointments because if you have been nominated and assigned by others to carry out such appointment, Allah (SWT) will support you to succeed. However, if you ask for the appointment, you will be left on your own as shown in the following narration:

وعن أبى سعيد عبد الرحمن بن سمرة رضي الله عنه ، قال: قال رسول الله ﷺ ، "يا عبد الرحمن بن سمرة: لا تسأل الإمارة، فإنك إن أعطيتها عن غير مسألة أعنت عليها، وإن أعطيتها عن مسألةٍ وكلت إليها، وإذا حلفت على يمين ، فرأيت غيرها خيراً منها، فأت الذى هو خير ، وكفر عن يمينك" (متفق عليه) .

'Abdur-Rahman bin Samurah (May Allah be pleased with him) reported: The Messenger of Allah (ﷺ) said to me, "Do not ask for position of authority. If you are granted this position without asking for it, you will be helped (by Allah) in discharging its responsibilities; but if you are given it as a result of your request, you will be left alone as its captive. If you take an oath to do something and then find a better alternative, you should adopt the latter and expiate for your oath." [Al-Bukhari and Muslim]. https://sunnah.com/riyadussalihin:673

The Prophet (SAS) has also shown that you will request to be appointed as leaders although it is a heavy trust with large impact on you in the day of Judgement. Being appointed as a leader is attractive to our souls but it is risky to our life and the Hereafter due to the responsibility in front of Allah (SWT). If we do not correctly carry out the responsibility as required, then, it will be hard on us in the day of Judgement as shown in the following narration:

وعن أبى هريرة رضي الله عنه أن رسول الله ﷺ قال: "إنكم ستحرصون على الإمارة، وستكون ندامة يوم القيامة" (رواه البخارى).

Abu Hurairah (May Allah be pleased with him) reported: Messenger of Allah (ﷺ) said, "You will covet for getting a position of authority, but remember that it will be a cause of humiliation and remorse on the Day of Resurrection." [Al- Bukhari]. https://sunnah.com/riyadussalihin:676

The above discussion does not contradict with the interpretation of the request from Prophet Yusuf to be appointed as the minister of economy in Egypt at his time. If we feel the capability and ability to carry out the responsibility of leadership in a specific domain and there is a need, it is acceptable to stand up and request the appointment as shown in the case of Prophet Yusuf in the following verse (criteria of appointment: knowledge and trust):

قَالَ اجْعَلْنِي عَلَىٰ خَزَائِنِ الْأَرْضِ ۖ إِنِّي حَفِيظٌ عَلِيمٌ [يوسف:55]

Chapter Yusuf **(55) [Joseph] said, "Appoint me over the storehouses of the land. Indeed, I will be a knowing guardian."** https://quran.com/12/55

Despite the above permission to stand up and nominate yourself to the appointment, one should have the intention that his/her request of leadership is for the sake of Allah and not for any life or personal purposes. It should be done for the benefits of the society not for personal benefits. Allah (SWT) is the only one who knows such intention and therefore it is going to be hard in the day of judgement if the intention is otherwise.

We have seen how the Prophet (SAS) has given the responsibility to those who deserve with no bias or infamy. He (SAS) has described to the leaders how to select their appointees. He (SAS) has rejected a request for appointment from one of his beloved companions because he has not fulfilled the appropriate characters / criteria, i.e., strong personality, knowledge, trust, etc).

A Brave Person

The great leader should be a brave person otherwise he/she will not be able to attain leadership. Therefore, courage is one of the core characters of such a great leader. This character has been quite clear in the entire life of the Prophet (SAS) from childhood until death. He has been brave in all his actions with no fear in his heart before and after the message. It has become obvious after the message as he has been protected by Allah (SWT). There are many situations in his life (SAS), which have shown such brave actions, I will just mention few of them in the following paragraphs. For example, Anas Ibn Malek reported that the Prophet (SAS) has been the most courageous person ever and has reported an incident when the entire city has heard unusual noise and has gone out to check the source / identity of this noise. They have met the Prophet (SAS) coming back after checking the source of noise. This means that he has been the first to respond to the source of noise and has gone quickly to check without thinking of how hazardous this action to his life. This is the character of the brave person and leader who has undermined all risks for the safety of his followers. This is part of the leader's responsibility and trust that we discussed in the previous section. The story is described in the following narration:

عَنْ أَنَسِ بْنِ مَالِكٍ، قَالَ كَانَ رَسُولُ اللَّهِ ﷺ أَحْسَنَ النَّاسِ وَكَانَ أَجْوَدَ النَّاسِ وَكَانَ أَشْجَعَ النَّاسِ وَلَقَدْ فَزِعَ أَهْلُ الْمَدِينَةِ ذَاتَ لَيْلَةٍ فَانْطَلَقَ نَاسٌ قِبَلَ الصَّوْتِ فَتَلَقَّاهُمْ رَسُولُ اللَّهِ ﷺ رَاجِعًا وَقَدْ سَبَقَهُمْ إِلَى الصَّوْتِ وَهُوَ عَلَى فَرَسٍ لأَبِي طَلْحَةَ عُرْىٍ فِي عُنُقِهِ السَّيْفُ وَهُوَ يَقُولُ " لَمْ تُرَاعُوا لَمْ تُرَاعُوا " . قَالَ " وَجَدْنَاهُ بَحْرًا أَوْ إِنَّهُ لَبَحْرٌ " . قَالَ وَكَانَ فَرَسًا يُبَطَّأُ . مسلم

Anas b. Malik reported that Allah's Messenger (ﷺ) was the sublimest among people (in character) and the most generous amongst them and he was the bravest of men. One night the people of Medina felt disturbed and set forth in the direction of a sound when Allah's Messenger (ﷺ) met them on his way back as he had gone towards that sound ahead of them. He was on the horse of Abu Talha which had no saddle over it, and a sword was slung round his neck, and he was saying: There was nothing to be afraid of, and he also said: We found it (this horse) like a torrent of water (indicating its swift-footedness), whereas the horse had been slow before that time. Sahih Muslim 2307 a, https://sunnah.com/muslim/43/65

Ali Ibn Abi Taleb reported how brave the Prophet (SAS) has been. As a great leader, he (SAS) has been always the closest to the enemy during battles to the contrary of leaders nowadays. The companions have taken the Prophet (SAS) as a shield to protect themselves. This has been a great practice for the leader to be a good role model for his followers as shown in the following narration:

عَنْ عَلِيٍّ، رَضِيَ اللَّهُ عَنْهُ قَالَ كُنَّا إِذَا احْمَرَّ الْبَأْسُ وَلَقِيَ الْقَوْمُ الْقَوْمَ اتَّقَيْنَا بِرَسُولِ اللَّهِ ﷺ فَمَا يَكُونُ مِنَّا أَحَدٌ أَدْنَى مِنَ الْقَوْمِ مِنْهُ. مسند أحمد

It was narrated that 'Ali (رضي الله عنه) said: When the fighting intensified and the two sides met in battle, we sought shelter with the Messenger of Allah (ﷺ) and no one was closer to the enemy than him. Musnad Ahmad 1347, https://sunnah.com/ahmad/5/747

Another great example of the Prophet's (SAS) braveness has been the day of battle of

Hunain. At this time, the Muslim army has been the largest ever with large number of solders, many horses, and large number of weapons. Muslims felt in their hearts that they cannot be defeated with this huge army. However, Allah (SWT) has taught them a tough lesson in this battle. Victory has always been from Allah (SWT) to those who are humble with high level of core values to defend the truth. It has never been for only those who have large armies with advanced tools and weapons. The lesson has been harsh to Muslims where most of them escape from the battle with only tens of them who have returned back to the battle after the call from the Prophet (SAS) who has never left his place. He has called all his companions to come back and be patient against the attack from the enemy. Allah (SWT) has given his Prophet (SAS) victory with few tens of companions who have been brave and steadfast against the enemy. This incident is shown in the following narration:

عَنْ أَبِي، إِسْحَاقَ قَالَ جَاءَ رَجُلٌ إِلَى الْبَرَاءِ فَقَالَ أَكُنْتُمْ وَلَّيْتُمْ يَوْمَ حُنَيْنٍ يَا أَبَا عُمَارَةَ فَقَالَ أَشْهَدُ عَلَى نَبِيِّ اللَّهِ ﷺ مَا وَلَّى وَلَكِنَّهُ انْطَلَقَ أَخِفَّاءُ مِنَ النَّاسِ وَحُسَّرٌ إِلَى هَذَا الْحَيِّ مِنْ هَوَازِنَ وَهُمْ قَوْمٌ رُمَاةٌ فَرَمَوْهُمْ بِرِشْقٍ مِنْ نَبْلٍ كَأَنَّهَا رِجْلٌ مِنْ جَرَادٍ فَانْكَشَفُوا فَأَقْبَلَ الْقَوْمُ إِلَى رَسُولِ اللَّهِ ﷺ وَأَبُو سُفْيَانَ بْنُ الْحَارِثِ يَقُودُ بِهِ بَغْلَتَهُ فَنَزَلَ وَدَعَا وَاسْتَنْصَرَ وَهُوَ يَقُولُ " أَنَا النَّبِيُّ لاَ كَذِبْ أَنَا ابْنُ عَبْدِ الْمُطَّلِبْ اللَّهُمَّ نَزِّلْ نَصْرَكَ " . قَالَ الْبَرَاءُ كُنَّا وَاللَّهِ إِذَا احْمَرَّ الْبَأْسُ نَتَّقِي بِهِ وَإِنَّ الشُّجَاعَ مِنَّا لَلَّذِي يُحَاذِي بِهِ . يَعْنِي النَّبِيَّ ﷺ . مسلم

It has been narrated (through a different chain of transmitters) by Abu Ishiq that a person said to Bara' (b. 'Azib): Abu Umara, did you flee on the Day of Hunain? He replied: The Messenger of Allah (ﷺ) did not retreat. (What actually happened was that some hasty young men who were either inadequately armed or were unarmed met a group of men from Banu Hawazin and Banu Nadir who happened to be (excellent) archers. The latter shot at them a volley of arrows that did not miss. The people turned to the Messenger of Allah (ﷺ). Abu Sufyan b. Harith was leading his mule. So he got down, prayed and invoked God's help. He said: I am the Prophet. This is no untruth. I am the son of Abd al-Muttalib. O God, descend Thy help. Bara' continued: When the battle grew fierce. We, by God, would seek protection by his side, and the bravest among us was he who confronted the onslaught and it was the Prophet (ﷺ). Sahih Muslim 1776 b, https://sunnah.com/muslim/32/98

The above describes how the Prophet (SAS) has been brave and role model leader to his companions. He has been sacrificing his life before his companions' life. He has been ahead of all of them in all risky situations with no fear. These are the characters of the great leaders who significantly impact the society around them. The Prophet (SAS), based upon the above analogy, has been a brave, a strong, a merciful, a lenient, and a humble person at the times when all these characters are needed. For example, he (SAS) has been brave at the battles when braveness is the most wanted character. Despite this braveness, he (SAS) has been merciful and lenient to all his followers where he has never hit a woman, a child, or a servant. These are the times when mercy and lenience are needed. Consequently, Allah (SWT) has described the Prophet (SAS) of great moral character as shown in the following verse:

وَإِنَّكَ لَعَلَى خُلُقٍ عَظِيمٍ (4) القلم

Chapter Al-Qalam **(4) And indeed, you are of a great moral character.**
https://quran.com/68/4/

Recommendations:
It is recommended to recite the following supplication in order for Allah (SWT) to make our children good citizens and leaders as well:

وَالَّذِينَ يَقُولُونَ رَبَّنَا هَبْ لَنَا مِنْ أَزْوَاجِنَا وَذُرِّيَّاتِنَا قُرَّةَ أَعْيُنٍ وَاجْعَلْنَا لِلْمُتَّقِينَ إِمَامًا (74) الفرقان

Chapter Al-Furqan **(74)** And those who say, "Our Lord, grant us from among our wives and offspring comfort to our eyes and make us an example for the righteous." https://quran.com/25/74

Chapter VII

Concluded Remarks and Recommendations

Summary of Concluded Remarks

This book 'Muhammad: The Prophet and Messenger of Allah', covers the misconceptions and facts regarding Prophet Muhammad (SAS). I would like here to summarize the key points of the discussed materials in this book as follows:

The person, whom some ignorant people are trying to insult, i.e., the Prophet (SAS), is an incredible person based on the description of his character by the creator, Allah (SWT), and the Prophet's companions. If the Prophet (SAS) is living in our era, the world would have been totally different. The description of the Prophet (SAS) in this book is too little to what he (SAS) deserves. If we find a person who has only one of the described characters in this book, we position him/her high in our minds and hearts. What about if he has all the discussed characters and more? This is a response to those people who are trying to insult our beloved Prophet (SAS). If you are insulting or undermining the person who has all the discussed characters, you are the devil himself. I supplicate to Allah (SWT) to guide you to the best and to know the Prophet (SAS) more. This might change your life and your place in the Hereafter.

I am really proud of being a follower of such a great man who has been sent as a mercy to mankind. He (SAS) has taught me how to behave and deal with people from all kinds. Whenever I am in a situation with any type of people, I always find guidance from him (SAS) in similar situations. I now deeply sense his feelings (SAS) when dealing with opponents, ignorant, or disbelievers and how much patience this might entail. I sincerely feel his state of mind (SAS) when dealing with employees and co-workers from different cultures with wide spectrum of values and practices. Now, I find the guidance in his teachings and practices with his great companions and followers. The Prophet (SAS) is the great role model to mankind in all aspects of life. One day, those who are trying to insult him (SAS), will know how great he is. I hope it will not be a miserable day for them. This type of people think that such day is far away, however, it is apparently closer than what they have expected.

The Prophet (SAS) has selected the youth leaders according to very strict criteria including, competency, efficiency, ability, knowledge, faith, characters, and wisdom. The application of these criteria have been obvious in all youth examples that are discussed this book, i.e., Hassan Ibn Thabit, Usama Ibn Zaid, Musab Ibn Umair, and Attab Ibn Usaid. This is how we benefit from his tradition (SAS) in dealing with youth at all times. We should work hard to teach and guide youth to be leaders of the future. Then, give youth the opportunity to lead and develop at different levels of management in the community and the society at large. This needs patience and perseverance because we will find mistakes from youth that require patience and also laziness of youth that needs perseverance.

Looking at his actions (SAS) towards his wives makes us feel ashamed. Although we do not have his responsibilities (SAS), we are not able to achieve much of the above with only a single wife. I am wondering how he (SAS) has been able to make it happen, i.e., be kind, be available when needed, play, do house and personal affairs, and be fair with his wives. Guidance of Allah (SWT) might be the only reason that has assisted him (SAS) to perform well as a husband. He (SAS) has made effort with full sincerity to be a good husband, hence, Allah (SWT) has supported his actions and has given him the best guidance and results. Similarly, we can do better than our status que if we follow the above two conditions, i.e., make effort with full sincerity. Let us start today to follow his guidance (SAS) of being a good husband and bring joy and prosperity to our families.

It is evident that the Prophet (SAS) has been a great role model for teachers in practicing most of the contemporary teaching / learning styles. He (SAS) has mastered the different styles, such as questions, discussion, changing topics, visual aids, illustrative examples, motivation, and demotivation. He has also accommodated and respected the individual differences when dealing with the companions. He (SAS) implemented his great characters, i.e., patience, kindness, mercy, and respect, in teaching. These characters have proved to be effective in transferring the message during teaching.

This is just a message for teachers to carefully study the teaching styles and characters of the Prophet (SAS) to serve several purposes. First, it clarifies the miracles in the Prophet's (SAS) practices fourteen hundred years ago, which have been recently discovered. There might be other styles, which are not discovered until today. They need someone to dig and study more his life (SAS) to discover, clarify, and explain such unknown styles. This will serve humanity with new teaching approaches and techniques. Second, we should implement his styles (SAS) to benefit our pedagogical curriculum in all taught subjects, particularly the ones dealing with religion. These styles can also be used in all our activities, such as lectures, seminars, discussion groups, meetings, etc.

The presented material in this book describes how the Prophet (SAS) has been brave and role model leader to his companions. He has been sacrificing his life before his companions' life. He has been ahead of all of them in all risky situations with no fear. These are the characters of the great leaders who significantly impact the society around them. The Prophet (SAS) has been a brave, a strong, a merciful, a lenient, and a humble person at the times when all these characters are needed. For example, he (SAS) has been brave at the battles when braveness is the most wanted character. Despite this braveness, he (SAS) has been merciful and lenient to all his followers where he has never hit a woman, a child, or a servant. These are the times when mercy and lenience are needed. Consequently, Allah (SWT) has described the Prophet (SAS) of great moral character as shown in the following verse:

وَإِنَّكَ لَعَلَىٰ خُلُقٍ عَظِيمٍ(4) القلم

Chapter Al-Qalam **(4) And indeed, you are of a great moral character.**
https://quran.com/68/4/

Summary of Recommendations:
A- Based upon the above discussion, I think the Prophet (SAS) deserve our continuous

remembrance and prayers/supplications. Therefore, I am recommending to pray or supplicate for the Prophet (SAS) many times daily according to his recommendation as shown below:

وعن عبد الله بن عمرو بن العاص، رضي الله عنهما أنه سمع رسول الله ﷺ يقول: "من صلى علي صلاةً، صلى الله عليه بها عشرًا" (رواه مسلم).

1- 'Abdullah bin 'Amr bin Al-'As (May Allah be pleased with them) reported: I heard the Messenger of Allah (ﷺ) saying: "Whoever supplicates Allah to exalt my mention, Allah will exalt his mention ten times." [Muslim]. https://sunnah.com/riyadussalihin/14/1

وعن أبي محمد كعب بن عجرة رضي الله عنه قال: خرج علينا النبي ﷺ فقلنا: يا رسول الله، قد علمنا كيف نسلم عليك، فكيف نصلي عليك؟ قال: "قولوا: اللهم صلِ على محمد، وعلى آل محمد، كما صليت على آل إبراهيم، إنك حميد مجيد. اللهم بارك على محمد وعلى آل محمد، كما باركت على آل إبراهيم، إنك حميد مجيد" (متفق عليه).

2- Abu Muhammad Ka'b bin 'Ujrah (May Allah be pleased with him) reported: The Prophet (ﷺ) came to us and we asked him, "O Messenger of Allah, we already know how to greet you (i.e., say As-salamu 'alaikum), but how should we supplicate for you?" He (ﷺ) said, "Say: [O Allah, exalt the mention of Muhammad and the family of Muhammad as you exalted the family of Ibrahim. You are Praised and Glorious. O Allah, bless Muhammad and the family of Muhammad as You blessed the family of Ibrahim. You are Praised and Glorious.'" [Al-Bukhari and Muslim]. https://sunnah.com/riyadussalihin/14/9

B- I tried my best to be brief in explaining the different personal characters of our beloved Prophet (SAS). I also tried to make every character presented in very few pages in order to make it easy for the readers to share with others and discuss with their children. Therefore, it is recommended that you do the following activities in order to positively defend our beloved Prophet (SAS):

3- Share the individual characters with your groups of friends and followers to benefit from such information and spread the good things about our beloved Prophet who is under attack from a few ignorant individuals.

4- Print each character and discuss with your children in order to immune them against all actions of disbelievers who are trying to dilute his reputation (SAS). This action will give them the appropriate minimum knowledge about him (SAS), which will serve two purposes: (a) increase their knowledge about the Prophet (SAS) and (b) encourage them to practice such great characters in their daily life activities.

5- Make a short and long term plans to practice these characters in the individual and family levels. This is crucial to be role models of good characters in an era that is full of bad characters and behaviors.

C- To defend the Prophet (SAS), first, it is necessary to follow his guidance in all matters. Because we are a little far away from all his teachings in many matters, we should work gradually to learn and apply them. I will start with the essentials, i.e., authentic Sunnah prayers per day, to establish a good base for future practical activities. So, I suggest that we follow his teachings (SAS) in these prayers first, then we can move to other traditions. Try to make a gradual plan to apply the authentic Sunnah for prayers as listed in the following narrations, i.e., 10 per day (two before Fajr & Zuhr prayers and two after Zuhr, Maghrib, and Isha prayers) or 12 per day (four before

Zuhr prayer instead of two):

عَنْ عَائِشَةَ، قَالَتْ قَالَ رَسُولُ اللَّهِ ـ ﷺ ـ " مَنْ ثَابَرَ عَلَى ثِنْتَىْ عَشْرَةَ رَكْعَةً مِنَ السُّنَّةِ بُنِيَ لَهُ بَيْتٌ فِي الْجَنَّةِ أَرْبَعٍ قَبْلَ الظُّهْرِ وَرَكْعَتَيْنِ بَعْدَ الظُّهْرِ وَرَكْعَتَيْنِ بَعْدَ الْمَغْرِبِ وَرَكْعَتَيْنِ بَعْدَ الْعِشَاءِ وَرَكْعَتَيْنِ قَبْلَ الْفَجْرِ " . (رواه ابن ماجه).

It was narrated that 'Aishah said: "The Messenger of Allah (ﷺ) said: 'Whoever persists in performing twelve Rak'ah from the Sunnah, a house will be built for him in Paradise: four before the Zuhr, two Rak'ah after Zuhr, two Rak'ah after Maghrib, two Rak'ah after the 'Isha' and two Rak'ah before Fajr.'" Ibn Majeh, https://sunnah.com/ibnmajah/5/338

وَعَنْ ابْنِ عُمَرَ ـ رَضِيَ اَللَّهُ عَنْهُمَا ـ قَالَ : {حَفِظْتُ مِنْ اَلنَّبِيِّ ـ ﷺ ـ عَشْرَ رَكَعَاتٍ: رَكْعَتَيْنِ قَبْلَ اَلظُّهْرِ , وَرَكْعَتَيْنِ بَعْدَهَا , وَرَكْعَتَيْنِ بَعْدَ اَلْمَغْرِبِ فِي بَيْتِهِ , وَرَكْعَتَيْنِ بَعْدَ اَلْعِشَاءِ فِي بَيْتِهِ , وَرَكْعَتَيْنِ قَبْلَ اَلصُّبْحِ} مُتَّفَقٌ عَلَيْهِ. رواه البخاري (1180) ، ومسلم (729) ، واللفظ للبخاري .

Narrated Ibn 'Umar (RA): I memorized from the Prophet (ﷺ) ten (voluntary) Rak'at - two Rak'at before the Zuhr prayer and two after it; two Rak'at after Magbrib prayer in his house, and two Rak'at after 'Isha' prayer in his house, and two Rak'at before the Fajr prayer. [Agreed upon]. https://sunnah.com/bulugh/2/254

This plan should be realistic in adopting your current situation. If you do not apply any of these Sunnah prayers, then, you can start by a Sunnah of one prayer like after Zuhr prayer, for example. You continue doing it for a week or two, then, add another prayer, for example Maghrib, then, Isha, then, Fajr, then, four before Zuhr prayer. You continue week after week until you train yourself very well on these Sunnah prayers. Once you master all of them, you move to another target, which includes Dhoha and Qiyam prayers. You start with two Rak'ahs and increase gradually to the best of your ability.

In Fasting, you develop a gradual plan of voluntary fasting of one day a month, then, increase it gradually until you reach Mondays and Thursdays of every week. Similarly, you plan for charity and Zakat. You start small and gradually increase to the best of your ability. You start from your position in following the Sunnah of the Prophet (SAS) today and gradually increase until you reach the set targets for yourself. I pray to Allah (SWT) to help us achieve such good targets in a short period of time in order to be called: **Servants of Allah** (SWT).

D- It is quite clear that youth age is very important in building the good personality. Therefore, we should put a lot of emphases on this age with high level of interest and focus. If we are able to build a faithful youth, we will be following the Prophet's recommendation in the following narration:

وعنه قال: قال رسول الله ، ﷺ ، :"سبعة يظلهم الله في ظله يوم لا ظل إلا ظله: إمام عادل، وشاب نشأ في عبادة الله ، ورجل قلبه معلق في المساجد، ورجلان تحابا في الله، اجتمعا عليه، وتفرقا عليه، ورجل دعته امرأة ذات منصب وجمال، فقال: إنى أخاف الله، ورجل تصدق بصدقة فأخفاها حتى لا تعلم شماله ما تنفق يمينه، ورجل ذكر الله خالياً ففاضت عيناه" (متفق عليه).

Abu Hurairah (May Allah be pleased with him) reported: Messenger of Allah (ﷺ) said, "Seven people Allah will give them His Shade on the Day when there would be no shade but the Shade of His Throne (i.e., on the Day of Resurrection): And they are: a just ruler; a youth who grew up with the worship of Allah; a person whose heart is attached to the mosques, two men who love and meet each other and depart from each other for the sake of Allah; a man whom an extremely beautiful woman seduces (for illicit relation), but he (rejects this offer and) says: 'I fear Allah'; a man who gives in charity and conceals it (to such an extent) that the left hand does not know what the right has given; and a man who remembers Allah in solitude and his eyes become tearful". [Al-Bukhari and Muslim]. https://sunnah.com/riyadussalihin/introduction/449

In order to achieve such objective, we should accommodate few principles, such as:

6- Train and discuss with youth the moderate and rationalized concepts of Islam in all life activities. This knowledge is the immunization for youth against any extreme ideologies.
7- Use the rationalized discussion style when dealing with youth or your children.
8- Give youth responsibilities and train them to carry out their functions in a good way since their young ages. Be patient and ask them to have perseverance.

E- It is recommended to follow the guidance of the Prophet (SAS) at home whether you are the husband or the wife. The responsibility of a husband or a wife is huge because they together constitute the seed for a family that is the core pillar of a society. This needs from us to carefully look at how to build such family on a strong foundation. Both husband and wife should sincerely look at their responsibilities, plan to gradually complete their shortcomings, and exert all the utmost effort to implement the planned activities. They also should forgive any unaccomplished activities if they are not intentionally missed. The plan should be continuously improved by adding more activities and using innovative ideas. Finally, the husband and the wife should acknowledge the fact that achieving their responsibilities in building the family is an act of worship towards Allah (SWT). You will be rewarded the most for such acts of worship in the Day of Judgement.

F- We should follow the teachings of our beloved teacher and Prophet (SAS) in the following three recommendations (motivation / demotivation style): (1) always ask for forgiveness; (2) supplicate for the Prophet (SAS); and (3) be kind to your parents and ask them to supplicate for you.

سَمِعْتُ عَبْدَ اللَّهِ بْنَ بُسْرٍ، يَقُولُ قَالَ النَّبِيُّ ﷺ ـ " طُوبَى لِمَنْ وَجَدَ فِي صَحِيفَتِهِ اسْتِغْفَارًا كَثِيرًا " .

9- 'Abdullah bin Busr said that: the Prophet (SAS) said: "Glad tidings to those who find a lot of seeking forgiveness in the record of their deeds." Sunan Ibn Majah 3818. https://sunnah.com/ibnmajah:3818

وعن أبي هريرة رضي الله عنه قال: قال رسول الله ﷺ : "رغم أنف رجل ذكرت عنده فلم يصلِ علي" رواه الترمذي وقال حديث حسن.

10- Abu Hurairah (May Allah be pleased with him) reported: The Messenger of Allah (ﷺ) said, "May his nose soil with dust in whose presence mention is made of me and he does not supplicate for me." [At-Tirmidhi]. https://sunnah.com/riyadussalihin:1400

وعنه عن النبي ﷺ قال: " رغم أنف، ثم رغم أنف، ثم رغم أنف من أدرك أبويه عند الكبر، أحدهما أو كليهما، فلم يدخل الجنة" (رواه مسلم).

11- Abu Hurairah (May Allah be pleased with him) reported: The Prophet (ﷺ) said, "May he be disgraced! May he be disgraced! May he be disgraced, whose parents, one or both, attain old age during his life time, and he does not enter

Jannah (by rendering being dutiful to them)". [Muslim]. https://sunnah.com/riyadussalihin:317

G- It is recommended to recite the following supplication in order for Allah (SWT) to make our children good citizens and leaders as well:

وَالَّذِينَ يَقُولُونَ رَبَّنَا هَبْ لَنَا مِنْ أَزْوَاجِنَا وَذُرِّيَّاتِنَا قُرَّةَ أَعْيُنٍ وَاجْعَلْنَا لِلْمُتَّقِينَ إِمَامًا (74) الفرقان

Chapter Al-Furqan **(74) And those who say, "Our Lord, grant us from among our wives and offspring comfort to our eyes and make us an example for the righteous."** https://quran.com/25/74

Here, I end the book of "Muhammad: The Prophet and Messenger of Allah". I ask Allah (SWT) to grant me sincerity in the written words so that they reach your hearts. I hope you benefit from these words and act upon them. May Allah (SWT) guide us all to the best, shower us with His blessings, and keep us on the right path. Ameen.

.... وَآخِرُ دَعْوَاهُمْ أَنِ الْحَمْدُ لِلَّهِ رَبِّ الْعَالَمِينَ (10) سورة يونس

Chapter Yunus **(10) …. And the last of their call will be, "Praise to Allah, Lord of the worlds!"**

April 2021 (Ramadan 1442)

Abbreviations:

SWT = glorified and exalted be He (سبحانه وتعالى SWT)
SAS = prayers and peace be upon Prophet Muhammad (صَلَّى ٱللَّهُ عَلَيْهِ وَسَلَّمَ SAS)

References:
1- Abd-El-Tawab, Y. (2011). "How the Prophet Has Dealt with Youth," https://www.islamstory.com/ar/artical/405/%D9%87%D8%AF%D9%8A-%D8%A7%D9%84%D8%B1%D8%B3%D9%88%D9%84-%D9%81%D9%8A-%D8%A7%D9%84%D8%AA%D8%B9%D8%A7%D9%85%D9%84-%D9%85%D8%B9-%D8%A7%D9%84%D8%B4%D8%A8%D8%A7%D8%A8
2- Al-Abbasy, M. (2007). "The Prophet and Kids," http://cp.alukah.net/sharia/0/877/
3- Al-Naqeeb, K. (2015). "The Leadership of the Prophet (SAS)," https://www.alukah.net/social/0/96205/#ixzz6dxyI8K8l
4- Alnawawi "The Gardens of the Righteous: Riyad Al-Saliheen," Reprinted in 1992, Islamic Office Publisher.
5- El-Saqqar, M. (2020). "The Prophet (SAS) as a Teacher," http://www.saaid.net/Doat/mongiz/7.htm
6- Hameesah, B. (2020). "The Prophet (SAS) as a Teacher," http://www.saaid.net/Doat/hamesabadr/82.htm
7- https://quran.com/
8- https://sunnah.com/
9- https://ar.islamway.net/article/27283/%D9%85%D9%88%D8%A7%D9%82%D9%81-%D9%86%D8%A8%D9%88%D9%8A%D8%A9-%D9%85%D8%B9-%D8%A7%D9%84%D8%A3%D8%B7%D9%81%D8%A7%D9%84
10- https://www.islamweb.net/ar/article/174047/%D9%85%D9%88%D8%A7%D9%82%D9%81-%D9%86%D8%A8%D9%88%D9%8A%D8%A9-%D9%85%D8%B9-%D8%A7%D9%84%D8%A3%D8%B7%D9%81%D8%A7%D9%84
11- https://www.islamweb.net/ar/fatwa/77964
12- https://kalemtayeb.com/safahat/item/17282
13- https://www.withprophet.com/ar/%D8%B1%D8%B3%D9%88%D9%84-%D8%A7%D9%84%D9%84%D9%87-%D8%B5%D9%84%D9%89-%D8%A7%D9%84%D9%84%D9%87-%D8%B9%D9%84%D9%8A%D9%87-%D9%88%D8%B3%D9%84%D9%85-%D8%A3%D8%A8%D8%A7-%D8%B1%D8%AD%D9%8A%D9%85%D8%A7-%D9%88%D8%AC%D8%AF%D8%A7-%D8%B9%D8%B7%D9%88%D9%81%D8%A7
14- Ibn Qudamah Al-Maqdisi "Mukhtasar Minhaj Al-Qasidin," Translated by Wail Shihah, Revised by Said Faris, Dar Al-Manarah, Publishing & Distribution, 2002.
15- Islamway (2020). "The character of the Prophet with opponents," https://ar.islamway.net/article/23935/%D8%A3%D8%AE%D9%84%D8%A7%D9%82-%D8%A7%D9%84%D8%B1%D8%B3%D9%88%D9%84-%D9%85%D8%B9-%D8%A7%D9%84%D9%85%D8%AE%D8%B7%D8%A6%D9%8A%D9%86-%D9%81%D9%8A-%D8%AD%D9%82%D9%87
16- Islamway (2020). "The character of the Prophet with opponents," https://ar.islamway.net/article/23935/%D8%A3%D8%AE%D9%84%D8%A7%D9%82

17- Islamweb(2020). https://www.islamweb.net/ar/fatwa/6667/%D8%A7%D9%84%D8%A2%D9%8A%D8%A7%D8%AA-%D8%A7%D9%84%D9%83%D8%B1%D9%8A%D9%85%D8%A9-%D8%A7%D9%84%D8%AA%D9%8A-%D8%AA%D8%AA%D8%AD%D8%AF%D8%AB-%D8%B9%D9%86-%D8%A3%D8%AE%D9%84%D8%A7%D9%82-%D9%88%D8%B4%D9%85%D8%A7%D8%A6%D9%84-%D8%A7%D9%84%D8%B1%D8%B3%D9%88%D9%84-%D8%B9%D9%84%D9%8A%D9%87-%D8%A7%D9%84%D8%B5%D9%84%D8%A7%D8%A9-%D9%88%D8%A7%D9%84%D8%B3%D9%84%D8%A7%D9%85

18- Jumah, M. (2017). "Prophet's Characters in the Quran," https://www.alukah.net/sharia/0/122006/.

19- Marwan, M. (2020). "How the Prophet's Characters were," https://mawdoo3.com/%D9%83%D9%8A%D9%81%D9%83%D8%A7%D9%86%D8%AA%D8%A3%D8%AE%D9%84%D8%A7%D9%82%D8%A7%D9%84%D8%B1%D8%B3%D9%88%D9%84#citenote-vzELrtzvzD-36.

20- Meshal, T. (2020). "The Prophet (SAS) as a Leader," https://mawdoo3.com/%D8%B5%D9%81%D8%A7%D8%AA_%D8%A7%D9%84%D8%B1%D8%B3%D9%88%D9%84_%D9%81%D9%8A_%D8%A7%D9%84%D9%82%D9%8A%D8%A7%D8%AF%D8%A9

21- Saaid (2020). "Characters of the Prophet (SAS)," http://www.saaid.net/mohamed/19.htm.

22- Sunjuq, R. (2021). "How the Prophet Has Dealt with Children," https://mawdoo3.com/%D9%83%D9%8A%D9%81_%D9%83%D8%A7%D9%86_%D8%A7%D9%84%D8%B1%D8%B3%D9%88%D9%84_%D9%8A%D8%B9%D8%A7%D9%85%D9%84_%D8%A7%D9%84%D8%A3%D8%B7%D9%81%D8%A7%D9%84

23- Tafseer Al-Quraan: Ibn Kathir, Al-Tabari, Al-Saadi, Al-Baghawi, Al-Qurtubi.

©journeytoparadise.org
journeytoparadise2020@gmail.com

Manufactured by Amazon.ca
Acheson, AB